ARTHUR RIZER

Jefferson's Pen

The Art of Persuasion

AMERICAN BAR ASSOCIATION
Defending Liberty
Pursuing Justice

Cover design by Andrew Alcala/ABA Design

The materials contained herein represent the opinions of the authors and/or the editors, and should not be construed to be the views or opinions of the law firms or companies with whom such persons are in partnership with, associated with, or employed by, nor of the American Bar Association unless adopted pursuant to the bylaws of the Association.

Nothing contained in this book is to be considered as the rendering of legal advice for specific cases, and readers are responsible for obtaining such advice from their own legal counsel. This book is intended for educational and informational purposes only.

Printed in the United States of America.

20 19 18 17   5 4 3 2

ISBN: 978-1-63425-390-1

e-ISBN: 978-1-63425-391-8

Discounts are available for books ordered in bulk. Special consideration is given to state bars, CLE programs, and other bar-related organizations. Inquire at Book Publishing, ABA Publishing, American Bar Association, 321 N. Clark Street, Chicago, Illinois 60654-7598.

www.ShopABA.org

To my Father, Arthur L. Rizer Jr.—you are the greatest man I know. Thank you for being my mentor, my friend, but most importantly, my Dad.

—Arthur Rizer

To my Mother and Father, for everything.

—J. Berkeley Bentley

ACKNOWLEDGMENTS

I thank my research assistant, copy editor, and the coauthor of Chapter 1 and the Conclusion, Berkeley Bentley, for his help in ensuring not only the completion of this book, but also its quality. I also thank my executive editor Jonathan Malysiak, my father, Arthur L. Rizer Jr., who helped me not only edit this book, but also with its conception, and the Hodges Faculty Research Grant for its support of this project. Lastly, I thank my students at the West Virginia University College of Law and Georgetown University, Law Center, who inspire me daily to grow and learn and to be a better teacher.

CONTENTS

PROLOGUE

"We hold these truths to be self-evident, that all men are created equal, that they are endowed by their Creator with certain unalienable Rights, that among these are Life, Liberty and the pursuit of Happiness.—That to secure these rights, Governments are instituted among Men, deriving their just powers from the consent of the governed,—That whenever any Form of Government becomes destructive of these ends, it is the Right of the People to alter or to abolish it, and to institute new Government . . . ."

. . .

"And for the support of this declaration, with a firm reliance on the protection of divine Providence, we mutually pledge to each other our Lives, our Fortunes, & our sacred Honor."

Who was Thomas Jefferson? A Founding Father, a President, a slave owner, and even an inventor? These, of course, are all accurate descriptions of this extremely complex man. But do these descriptions capture the true nature of Thomas Jefferson? Maybe a more meaningful question would ask, What is Jefferson's most lasting contribution? As students today think of Julius Caesar crossing the Rhine, in a thousand years, what will students think when asked, "What did Thomas Jefferson do?"

The answer to this question, with little dispute, is that he authored the Declaration of Independence.[1] We will see in Chapter 7 that this document not only founded a nation, but also is seen as one of the most influential documents in world history, keeping company with the Magna Carta, Martin Luther's 95 Theses, and the US Constitution. Indeed, it is Jefferson the writer that we remember most. Specifically, it was his abilities as a persuasive writer that secured his place in not only the pages of history, but in American lore.

Like all humans, Jefferson had his faults. He was unable to overcome some: he disliked slavery, yet could not free his own; he wrote about wise financial stewardship, but was plagued by financial issues for much of his life. Other problems, though, he overcame: he resolved his problems with public speaking, for example, by dedicating himself to perfecting his persuasive writing skills. Dedication to his craft gave him the confidence to speak with authority on issues he had more than thoroughly thought through by writing and rewriting.

To understand Thomas Jefferson's greatest achievements, perhaps we should begin at the end. On June 24, 1826, Jefferson drafted his last writing. It was a letter responding to an invitation from Roger C. Weightman to attend the 50th anniversary of the writing of the Declaration of Independence. Ill and unable to travel the 116 miles from Monticello, Jefferson was forced to decline, writing,

> I should, indeed, with peculiar delight, have met and exchanged there congratulations personally with the small band, the remnant of that host of worthies who joined with us on that day, in the bold and doubtful election we were to make for our country, between submission or the sword; and have enjoyed with them the consolatory fact, that our fellow citizens, after half a century of experience and prosperity, continue to approve the choice we made.

In the same letter, Jefferson wrote of the Declaration of Independence itself, stating that it would be "the signal of arousing men to burst the chains under which monkish ignorance and superstition had persuaded them to bind themselves, and to assume the blessings and security of self-government." In that tribute to freedom, the Declaration, Jefferson found the words to express ideas that could inspire people all over the world to rise up and restore "the free right to the unbounded exercise of reason and freedom of opinion." "All eyes are opened," he wrote, "or opening, to the rights of man." Indeed, the world's eyes were opening. In just ten short years, France went from an absolute monarchy to a republic, using, in 1789, Jefferson's Declaration of Independence as a guide in drafting their own *Declaration of Rights of*

Man and of the Citizen.[2] Many scholars believe that Jefferson, who served as the US Ambassador to France during its drafting, also helped to write this document.

Just 10 days after drafting his letter to Weightman, Jefferson died. He died on July 4, 1826, the 50th anniversary of the signing of his masterpiece. Coincidentally, John Adams—Jefferson's sometime archrival, sometime friend, and a co-signer of the Declaration of Independence—died only a few hours later on that July 4th. Adams's last words, in fact, were "Thomas Jefferson still lives."[3]

Jefferson's last letter does not mention that he was the drafter of the Declaration, "the preamble to which had established the concept of human rights, for the first time in history, as a basis for a republic."[4] Rather, his letter reiterated his belief in the idea of the United States: that the United States was a nation of principles and ideals, that the Declaration was the blueprint for those ideals, and that those ideals would be exported to the world.[5]

Abraham Lincoln, who was only 17 years old when Jefferson died, recognized Jefferson's contributions to this nation. He said of Jefferson and his Declaration,

> All honor to Jefferson - to the man who, in the concrete pressure of a struggle for national independence by a single people, had the coolness, forecast, and capacity to introduce into a merely revolutionary document, an abstract truth, applicable to all men and all times, and so to embalm it there, that to-day, and in all coming days, it shall be a rebuke and a stumbling-block to the very harbingers of re-appearing tyranny and oppression.

Lincoln recognized, as we will explore throughout this book, that Jefferson helped breathe life into this nation, and that he did so with his pen.

Many books have been written about Jefferson: most about his time in the presidency, many about the Declaration of Independence, some concerning his contradictory roles as advocate of freedom and slave owner. This book does not attempt to replace any of those that laud his tremendous achievements or explore his personal paradoxes. Rather, this book is dedicated to writers of all stripes and its focus is to learn from Jefferson the persuasive writer. We endeavor to analyze and extract some of the lessons his life and his works offer so that we might be able to improve in our own careers. By examining Jefferson's successes and failures, we will highlight the characteristics that made him such a successful persuader and those failures that detract from that success.

Most people would agree that Jefferson was one of the world's greatest persuasive writers. It was in his years as a lawyer that he acquired and honed these skills. Yet Jefferson's years as a lawyer are often overlooked. As one Jeffersonian scholar wrote, the "glamor of his political career and his prodigious versatility in any fields of intellectual endeavor overshadow his achievements in the prosaic realm of law."[6]

Above all, Jefferson's mark on the world was made because of his ability to inspire an audience through the written word. All attorneys and persuasive speakers today—including sales people, those in politics, teachers, and all those who want to learn how to convince others on paper—can learn something from Jefferson. The lessons we draw from Jefferson's life and writings are found throughout the chapters in bold.

The idea for this book started with my first book, *Lincoln's Counsel: Lessons Learned from America's Most Persuasive Speaker*.[7] The Lincoln book started as an obsession with the Gettysburg Address. As I was trained to be a lawyer, I realized that Lincoln's Address was actually one of the greatest closing arguments of all time. I was struck by how many rules of "how to deliver a persuasive closing" Lincoln's Address tracked.

Alas, one cannot close without first opening. An opening lays out the theme for the trial about to commence. When Lincoln spoke of "[f]our score and seven years ago" in 1863, he was not talking about the writing of the Constitution (a "score" is 20 years); he was instead speaking of the signing of the Declaration of Independence in 1776. Thus, as the Gettysburg Address was the inspiration for a book drawing lessons from Lincoln's life and speeches on how to be a better persuasive speaker, it seems fitting that the Declaration of Independence—being Lincoln's opening—should inspire me to write a book drawing lessons from Jefferson's life and works on how to be a better persuasive writer.

Chapter 1 begins the book by providing a brief introduction to what this book is trying to capture: What is persuasiveness? More specifically, What is persuasive writing? We will define this concept in easily digestible bites that will be used to pull out the lessons of Jefferson's life and works identified throughout the book.

Chapter 2 introduces the reader to Thomas Jefferson, attorney-at-law. Really, this chapter describes the education that made Jefferson such a good writer, so good that he was selected to write the document meant to persuade Britain to let America go, to persuade Americans to support independence, and to persuade the world to support a new American state. We look at Jefferson's formative years through his legal training and practice to identify those traits of character, skill, and hard work that made him such a powerfully persuasive writer.

In Chapter 3, we explore Jefferson's political life. We explore how Thomas Jefferson got from the courtroom to the House of Burgesses, up to his time as Vice President under John Adams. This chapter details some of the more practical elements of persuasion, those used in the halls of politics, both domestic and abroad.

Chapter 4, then, discusses Jefferson's time as President. This chapter examines some of the successes and failures of Jefferson's time in office, detailing where the particular persuasive techniques used were effective and where he miss-stepped and could have used a lesson himself.

Chapter 5 outlines three aspects of Jefferson's character that hugely impacted his ability to persuade. First, this chapter looks at Jefferson's pure, innate skill as a writer—he was simply gifted with a pen. Second, this chapter looks at the passion with which Jefferson wrote, injecting meaning and feeling into every syllable he put onto paper. Finally, this chapter discusses what is probably the most useful trait for anyone who wishes to persuade—vision. Jefferson had a vision for this country and that vision drove him in every aspect of his life.

Chapter 6 gets into some of the mistakes Jefferson made over the years and explores some of their potential causes. A persuasive writer should definitely know what *not* to do before he begins the long process of drafting the perfect word, then phrase, then sentence, then paragraph and section, so she doesn't need to revise every word, phrase, sentence, paragraph, and section on day two.

Chapter 7 examines Jefferson's most famous piece and the document that made his name famous the world over. This chapter looks in detail at the Declaration of Independence, highlighting aspects of that document that make it especially persuasive to readers still today.

Chapter 8 looks at several other of Jefferson's masterpieces to further explore just what techniques, what style, and what tone Jefferson used that made him such an effective persuasive writer. Each of these masterpieces is written toward a different end, so the chapter seeks to address the varied nature of persuasion by looking at different texts Jefferson wrote for different purposes and to different audiences.

1

WHAT IS PERSUASIVE WRITING?

What is persuasive writing? What makes writing persuasive? What makes someone a persuasive writer? Although quite similar, these questions lead us to different answers, each of which still only gets at the answer to the question we should be asking: How do I become a persuasive writer?

But to answer that question, we need to know the answers to all those other questions. We need to know what "persuasive writing" is, how to write in a persuasive style, and, perhaps most importantly (especially on larger and more public stages), what an author can or must do to be in a position to persuade others. This chapter aims to provide very general answers to these questions, answers useful to the reader because they are directly related to the lessons we draw from Thomas Jefferson's life and writings in the rest of this book.

To start with the last of those questions, the most essential feature of "persuasion," as such, is the audience's perception of the author. Without the right perception of the author, why would the audience believe or be influenced by the words on the page? Even a well-reasoned, evocative, and otherwise persuasive piece of writing will not gain much traction without a noted author.

Where such a piece does arise, though, it is still not likely to gain traction until the proper authorities have reviewed and "blessed" the material with their own authority.

This characteristic of persuasion is most commonly referred to as "ethos." Ethos is one of three elements of Rhetoric that have been passed down since Aristotle taught his students rhetoric in the fourth century BC. Ethos very loosely translates (though, I think, best translates) as the character of the author. When trying to persuade others, the thing that matters most is the *perception* of the author's character—as opposed to the author's character as she perceives it—so the audience's familiarity with and feelings toward the author are supremely important.

The other two elements of rhetoric that Aristotle handed down are "pathos" and "logos." These elements—ethos, pathos, and logos—are still taught as the foundational principles in any writing course. Ethos translates as the character, and thus the credibility, of the author; pathos best translates as the emotion evoked by the subject and actual text of a writing; and logos, essentially, refers to the logic of the argument presented.

Thomas Jefferson was a master of these elements of writing in an age when writing was the medium of celebrity. He wrote to tug at the heart strings; he wrote to tap into passions and fears; he wrote always for his audience. And as he wrote and gained notoriety as a writer, his celebrity grew. His was an intellectual celebrity, that of a statesman of the highest order in domestic affairs, a diplomat versed in international affairs, and, above all, a principal hand in shaping the ideas that gave rise to our fledgling republic. The popular perception of Jefferson, then, gave him immense celebrity in politics, diplomacy, and philosophy. And that credibility made him persuasive on diverse subjects across those fields.

But an author's credibility is not a static thing. Rather, the perception of that author's credibility will vary with the times, the political winds, and a great many other factors. As you will read over the following chapters, America's perception of Thomas Jefferson ebbed and flowed a great deal with the political tides. That he authored the Declaration of Independence scored Jefferson a lot of points with his American audience. But politics is a fickle business, and Jefferson's celebrity waned for many Americans after the luster of the Revolution wore off. It took Jefferson's semiretirement to Monticello, and letting his opponent's attacks subside, for his stock to rise back up, enabling him to meaningfully reenter public life. That he accomplished so much in such an environment is a tribute to his persuasive power in good times.

One of the most important of the factors playing into an author's credibility is the audience's preconceptions about the author and how well a particular piece of writing fits with those preconceptions—consistency of argument, in short. Basically, does what you say today match what you said yesterday? Or has something changed? If it has changed, is it an important change? This line of questioning goes through every member of every audience's head—albeit generally subconsciously—when evaluating an argument made by someone that audience member knows something about.

Where the audience knows of and approves the author's authority on a given subject, and where the particular piece of writing is about the subject on which the author is an authority, the audience will be open to be persuaded to the author's position. For example, if I read a piece written by Stephen Hawking about the physics errors in *The Big Bang Theory*, I—not a theoretical physicist—will definitely trust the authority of Stephen Hawking—probably the most renowned theoretical physicist—as to any scientific errors that made it into the show.

On the other hand, where the audience knows of and approves the author's authority on a given subject, but the particular piece of writing is about some other subject—something about which the author isn't likely to know—then that audience will be much less likely to be persuaded to the author's position on that other subject. Back to the Stephen Hawking hypo: If I read a piece by Stephen Hawking about Shaggy's new album, I—though still not an expert in the field—will not trust the authority of Mr. Hawking—still a theoretical physicist, not someone we would expect to know much about reggae fusion tunes—about the storytelling aspects of that album.

Jefferson, in this regard, presents an interesting example because he was such a renaissance man, wearing so many hats so very well. In addition to being an attorney, statesman, diplomat, and philosopher, Jefferson was also an architect, a farmer, a philanthropist, and an expert on any number of topics about which he, at any point over his career, needed to know. Therefore, Jefferson would likely have been a credible source on most topics on which he spoke—or, much more likely, wrote.

The consistency of the author's argument will also affect the audience's perception of that author. For example—all too well known to those who ever watch US news during election cycles—where a political candidate switches his position on a particular subject, that candidate's credibility is greatly hurt as he will likely be labeled as something to the effect of a "flip-flopper." Whether an author's position on a particular subject *can* evolve without his being labeled a flip-flopper will be a question of the degree of change to his position, how the author handles the perception of the change, and the author's overall credibility with the audience to date.

If the author can justify his change in position as well as the reasons he held the old position, then he may actually come out looking credible with his new position. For example, if new information becomes available that makes your old position untenable or even moot, an audience is likely to consider the new information to have justified your change in position. If the author cannot justify either his change or his old position, or is simply faced with an unrelentingly loud opposition, he may not come out looking credible on any subject at all. That would probably be an unjustifiable change, giving the audience reason to distrust the author, losing him credibility in the long run.

Importantly, the audience's perception of an author and his work will change over time, regardless of action or inaction by the author, himself. Every time the author issues a new work, every time an old work is critiqued and the audience hears that critique, and every time the audience is exposed to new, relevant information or new circumstances, the audience's perception of the author evolves—or devolves, as the case may be. A positive perception can be reinforced over time where the author maintains the thrust of his position on a subject, where a critique of the author's work is not itself persuasive for any number of reasons, or where new information or new circumstances remain in line with and reinforce the author's previous position on a subject. A positive perception can be undermined, however, where the author materially changes his position on a subject, where a critique of the author's previous work seems to prove that some piece of the author's premise or argument is false or weak, or where new information or new circumstances are encountered by the audience and that new information does not seem to jibe with the author's take on a subject.

Thus far, this has largely been a discussion of character, of ethos. That is because the character of an author matters so very much. One's ethos is a sort of ticket to play. Without establishing it before your audience, you can't even get in the game—the audience has no real reason to read what you've written.

Especially in today's world, where blog posts, tweets, and discussion boards overload our senses without our even seeking out information, establishing your credibility first is absolutely essential if you want the audience to give your piece more than a passing glance.

So, having said all that,

HOW DO I BECOME A PERSUASIVE WRITER?

There are some keys drawn from Aristotle's ethos, pathos, and logos that are taught not only in writing courses, but also in management courses, in psychology courses, in communications courses, and, to a lesser extent perhaps, in most other courses training people to interact with customers, superiors, subordinates, constituents, the masses, the media, the elite, and so on and so forth. In short, the keys presented in what follows are critical to know and understand for anyone trying to persuade others through the written word.

ETHOS

Developed in the first half of this chapter is a very general discussion of some of the concerns a writer should keep in mind regarding her ethos, her perceived character. This first element of rhetoric has been the focus, thus far, not only because it is the ticket to play but also because it is the only element we cannot catch and correct in revising our texts. Therefore, many of the lessons drawn forth from Jefferson's life and writings are simple reminders to "think"—for example, about a choice you are about to make as regards how your audience will perceive you tomorrow. Rather, ethos is something we must cultivate over time; it is something we must keep at the forefront of our minds.

We can refine some of the broad concerns presented earlier and find defined terms that each of us can take practical steps to develop to become more persuasive writers.

First, an author must establish her **Authority**.

There are several ways an author can establish authority and Jefferson was expert at each. One way is to, simply, be an expert in the field in which you write—an easy-enough racket to break in to, no doubt. Here, your level of **expertise** is directly proportionate to your perceived authority. If you are "the guy" in the field, then the people who know that will listen. If you are "some guy" in the field, then you have some work to do—you will most likely need to tap into the second way you can establish authority. For his part, Jefferson was a recognized authority in varied disciplines, so was free to write from a credible position on a number of topics, most notably on inherent rights because it was the realm in which, as we will see later in the book, he really got his start.

The second way an author can establish authority is to **cite to an authority**. Again, the level of expertise of the authority you cite is directly proportionate to his authority, and yours by proxy—so choose wisely. You need not only cite to "experts," however. As long as there have been writers, there have been writers citing to the writers that came before them. Many of the most persuasive speakers and writers throughout history have invoked a higher authority: God, the Prophet, Reason, Laws of Nature, etc. Which you should invoke depends on the particulars of your argument and, most importantly, your audience. It would be a peculiar audience, indeed, who responded equally well to an invocation of God and an invocation of Reason. Jefferson, at different times, invoked both of these. The context, his intended audience, and the time in which he wrote dictated which authority was appropriate when.

Second, an author must be **Consistent**.

If an author intends to have an effect beyond today, he must pay particular attention to the consistency of his arguments over time. As discussed earlier, the author does not really control this aspect of his ethos. Rather, external factors will dictate whether he is able to remain consistent. If new information, new interpretations of facts, or a new argument presents itself to an author, the author is forced to respond if he wants to remain an authority in the field. Those aspects of consistency that are within the author's control, though, must be scrupulously monitored over time. It is tempting to back away from an argument or to go too far with an argument in response to popular opinion. The problem there arises from the nature of public opinion— it swings wildly from one extreme to the other. Therefore, the middle of the road is likely the easiest position from which to remain consistent. Unfortunately, middle of the road positions are, by definition, not novel—reader interest may wane over time. Jefferson, over the course of his career, held a number of positions along the spectrum, frequently changing his position on important matters. We will see in later chapters how this damaged his ethos.

PATHOS

Once an author has established her solid foundation in ethos, it is important to keep in mind that the author's job is to keep the reader's interest. Pathos is the means by which an author does this—it is the means by which an author evokes emotion and feeling in the reader, making him want to read on. The following are some discrete points on which an aspiring persuasive writer can focus in order to improve her writing.

First, an author must demonstrate her **Vision**.

A singular vision can help guide your arguments over time. That vision gives you a stable reference point on the horizon—the place you intend to get. The author should clearly express the grand goals she is advancing, piece by piece, through her arguments. By keeping this vision in mind, an author helps herself to remain consistent. By providing the reader the same vision, an author helps the reader see the true purpose of her argument. Jefferson's vision was that of a grand, expansive America, an idea that held great appeal for his audience. Jefferson's greatest arguments held this vision at their core, persuading his audiences to come along because of the hope inherent in that vision.

Second, an author must be able to **Inspire** her reader toward her desired end.

Hope: An author should inspire hope in her reader. Whether it is the hope of a powerful, independent America or the hope for a little bit better tomorrow, every persuasive argument should inspire the audience in some way. Jefferson's grand rhetoric and appeals to natural law were his means of inspiration; he used them very effectively. Indeed, here as well as by logos, specific points such as word choice and phrasing can help to inspire a reader.

LOGOS

A passionate plea from "the guy" in the field may persuade a reader through sheer force of his will. A stronger, more persuasive argument, though, is coherent and organized to make the argument as logical as possible. An argument that proceeds in a manner the reader expects, and whose points build one upon another, will be easier to follow. A writer's job, here, is to make it easy for the reader to adopt the writer's position. Essentially, a writer "tees up" her points so that the reader, merely by proceeding through the argument, hits the writer's points with the effect the writer desires. Here, too, some discrete points jump out that a writer can focus upon improving.

First, an author should **Structure** her argument so that the reader **Flows** through the work, hitting the writer's points after the desired build-up, in the desired order, and at the desired times.

An author will go through several drafts before his structure is appropriate for his argument. It will go through several more drafts before the piece finds its flow. This process takes time, so plan accordingly. An author must get her thoughts on paper, and then address the argument from the reader's perspective. In what order will your points be best made? What will your audience expect? What will your audience appreciate? Some specific techniques the author can employ are described in detail in Chapter 8: most notably, parallel structure and the rule of three (the triad). These techniques help an author build anticipation into his structure. Then, when that anticipation is released by the author's final point, it is that much stronger for the structure leading up to it.

Second, an author must adopt a **Style** appropriate for the audience and the author's message.

This idea, like that of character, permeates every aspect of persuasive writing. An author must write for his audience. The most eloquent, passionate, logical argument will fall flat if the author does not consider for whom he writes and to what purpose. In this regard, Jefferson was most definitely a master. We will see, over the course of the coming chapters, that Jefferson often wrote to disparate audiences with equally impressive results. He understood what his readers needed to hear, tee'd his arguments up, and let the readers swing through. This skill is the most immediately useful skill to develop. In everyday encounters, the ability to recognize what others expect to hear and adjust your message accordingly will yield immediate results.

A final point to note is that the writings of an author should be concise. Brevity is next to Godliness in persuasive writing. Long-winded authors did not often fit in in Jefferson's day and most definitely do not fit in with today's 24-hour news cycle and sound bites. Even the most articulate and thorough text written today must cater to this trend. People, for the most part, simply will not wait around for you to make your point. By using the techniques described here and in the chapters to follow, though, it is much more likely the reader will choose to read on, follow your points, and come to the conclusion you set out for him.

Obviously, many of these discrete points will overlap the ethos, pathos, and logos distinctions. An author's style, for example, can evoke emotion, can make a logical point stand out, and can make the author seem more credible, simply as an intelligent writer who knows how to present information—just by making the author seem like a smart guy who knows how to write. The rest of the book will give substance to the above remarks—the chapters will put the "meat" on the bones presented here.

Lessons Learned

- Establish your authority.
- Be consistent.
- Demonstrate a singular vision.
- Inspire!
- Make sure your work flows naturally and as you intend.
- Above all else, know your audience!

2

THE PRACTICE OF LAW

EDUCATING A BRILLIANT MIND

Because of the Jefferson family's status as part of the gentry, Thomas Jefferson received a quality education. Jefferson summarized his early education in his autobiography, published in 1821. His father, he wrote, "placed me at the English school at 5 years of age and at the Latin at 9 where I continued until his death."[8] Jefferson studied Latin, Greek, and French with the Reverend William Douglas, and the classics under the Reverend James Maury, whom Jefferson credited as a "correct classical scholar."[9] Jefferson contrasted his own formal education with that of his father, saying that, though his father's formal education "had been quite neglected," Peter Jefferson was of strong mind, sound judgment, and was "eager after information," reading much to better himself.[10] Thomas Jefferson acquired this characteristic from his father, reading and collecting books over the course of his life such that he is known as one of the great bibliophiles of his time—his personal library was, in fact, the foundation for the Library of Congress.

In the spring of 1760, at 17, Jefferson entered the College of William and Mary in Williamsburg, Virginia. At William and Mary, Jefferson studied under a Scotsman named Dr. William Small. Of that experience, Jefferson wrote,

> "It was my great good fortune, and what probably fixed the destinies of my life that Dr. Wm. Small of Scotland was then professor of Mathematics, a man profound in most useful branches of science, with a happy talent of communication correct and gentlemanly manners, & an enlarged & liberal mind. He, most happily for me, became soon attached to me & made me his daily companion when not engaged in school, and from his conversation I got my first views of the expansion of science & of the system in which we are placed."[11]

Jefferson obviously appreciated the value of his own education, and especially of his relationship with a mentor he respected so well. It is also interesting to note Jefferson's acknowledgment of Dr. Small's abilities across the branches of science and his liberal mind. Thomas Jefferson is often acknowledged as a polymath or Renaissance man, well versed across disciplines as varied as philosophy and diplomacy to architecture and horticulture.

It is important to note how one went about "going to college" in Jefferson's day. Jefferson never earned a degree at William and Mary as might be granted today. The gentry class of Virginia observed the English tradition of seeking a "gentleman's education," where the emphasis was on a well-rounded education in art and science, rather than in pursuit of a degree.[12] "Law school" was even less formalized. In colonial America, there were no established formal law schools, but some wealthy colonists would go to London to study at the Inns of Court. Most aspiring attorneys in colonial America, however, simply spent time serving as quasi-apprentices or clerks to reputable attorneys. Before Dr. Small returned to Europe in 1762, he arranged for Jefferson to "read law" under the direction of George Wythe.[13] Wythe was a distinguished lawyer in Virginia, who was known to have liberal views on religion, slavery, and republican forms of government.[14]

In looking at history's greatest individuals, a commonality appears. Most of these greats had someone in their life who acted as a mentor, teaching them the finer points of a given field, influencing their perspectives, often changing the very trajectory of their lives. Alexander the Great had Aristotle; David Thoreau had Ralph Waldo Emerson; Jefferson had Wythe. Wythe was not the only mentor in Jefferson's life, but he was an individual who had profound influence on the then 19-year-old Jefferson.

The point is that most great persuaders **have a mentor or carefully observe a master persuader**. Generally, **the most effective way to get better in any discipline is to learn from someone you respect and trust**, this can be a formal mentor or just someone who has a skill you admire—for Jefferson it started with Wythe.

Wythe's pedagogical approach was to let his students read the law on their own.[15] He saw little reward in the drudgery of formalized legal training and preferred to have his students read law reports and foundational English legal writings.[16] Jefferson was expected to soak in the "black-letter" law from books borrowed from Wythe or purchased for his ever-growing library. After Wythe's students had a solid foundation in what he was teaching, he would spend his limited time with them emphasizing the practical aspects of legal practice.[17] He combined this academic knowledge with the moot-court training he believed was necessary to understand how a Virginia lawyer managed his clients' affairs (typically dealing with property).[18]

Often, the best mentors never tell you what to do; they let you figure it out. They realize that the process of thinking through a problem to a solution is usually more important than the solution itself.

These two facets of Jefferson's legal education training—the study of law as it related to political theory and philosophy and the technical and practical aspects of being a lawyer in 18th-century Virginia—served Jefferson and his gentry clients well. And as we will see later, they also greatly influenced Jefferson's political thinking.[19]

There is some dispute among academics and historians about how long Jefferson actually studied law under Wythe's guidance. The standard account is that Jefferson studied under Wythe for five years, beginning in 1762 when he completed what we would today call undergraduate studies and ending in 1767 when he began practicing in Albemarle and Augusta counties as an attorney. Jefferson himself seems to support this contention, stating, "Mr. Wythe continued to be my faithful and beloved Mentor in youth, and my most affectionate friend through life. In 1767, he led me into the practice of the law at the bar of the General Court, at which I continued until the revolution shut up the courts of justice."[20] Others dispute this account, including Frank Dewey in his book, *Thomas Jefferson: Lawyer*. In that book, Dewey said that five years would have been an extraordinary amount of time to study law, noting that John Adams's two-year legal education was considered long, that Alexander Hamilton spent just six months reading law books, and that Chief Justice John Marshall spent only three. Further, Dewey cites to the fact that Robert Carter Nicholas examined Jefferson in late 1765 for the fitness to practice law.

What Jefferson did between 1765, when he sat for the bar, and 1767, when he started to practice law, is not entirely clear. We do know, however, that Jefferson spent three months of 1766 touring Annapolis, Philadelphia, and New York. Furthermore, the court closed in Virginia for most of 1766 because of agitation over the Stamp Act (which a consensus of colonists considered to be a violation of their rights as Englishmen to not be taxed without representation). That Act ran from March 22, 1765, until its repeal on March 18, 1766.

Unlike most attorneys at the time, Jefferson chose not to ride the circuit and practice in county courts. He chose, instead, to practice at the General Court, "a bar that required another year's wait for admission."[21] He attended his first General Court session in October 1767, becoming the youngest member of this elite group of Virginia lawyers at 24.[22] To put this in perspective, in Jefferson's roughly eight years of practice, only 10 other attorneys qualified to practice before the General Court.[23]

JEFFERSON'S PRACTICE

The General Court consisted of 12 men from prominent Virginia families, appointed by the King of England on recommendation of the governor.[24] The system resembles the Supreme Court today: the members essentially had life tenures and were only removable by the King himself.[25] Lawyers were not permitted to serve both in the General Court and on the circuit (except for the very few attorneys who obtained membership in one of England's *Inns of Court*, a professional association of barristers).[26]

The reality of Jefferson's membership to the General Court bar was that he could "specialize in representing clients with business in the capital, where the court convened."[27] Additionally, of all the lawyers admitted to practice in the General Court, Jefferson, who resided in Albemarle County, was the farthest west, enabling him to serve clients at the forefront of the "Virginia frontier."[28]

This exclusivity allowed for Jefferson's practice to grow rapidly. His first 68 entries in his casebook were from 1767. Of course, that does not mean that he tried 68 cases in his first year; he in fact only tried one. But it does indicate that he had an auspicious beginning.[29] Frank Dewey noted that Jefferson's early years of practice were much better than those of John Adams, who, being admitted in November 1758, found himself "little to do in calendar year 1759."[30]

Obviously, being the only lawyer in western Virginia who could practice in the General Court was an advantage. But Jefferson also comprehended that the practice of law was a business and created other advantages for his practice. One sign of his business adeptness can be seen in his networking abilities. Although the General Court was in Williamsburg, most General Court attorneys would make sporadic visits to different courts to drum up business.[31]

Jefferson traveled to several counties, but he made the strategic decision to concentrate on Albemarle and Augusta counties. Albemarle was an obvious choice as it was his home and base of operations. Augusta, however, seems a peculiar choice because of its harsh terrain and location—on the other side of the Blue Ridge Mountains—other counties were far more accessible. Yet his choice of Augusta demonstrates his canniness as a realistic solo practitioner. Augusta was an enormous county, full of potential business. It spanned from the Carolina border in the south to the Mississippi in the west and the area just north of Charlottesville in the north—it truly was massive. Augusta was also growing rapidly, its population fed by immigrants and eastern Virginians seeking more land to cultivate.[32]

Additionally, Augusta was considered frontier country in the 1760s. Much of the fighting during the French and Indian War took place there, with tribal raids continuing even after the war ended. As a result, large areas of land were claimed by "land exploitists" (a title that did not hold the pejorative connotation it does today), who grabbed land in speculation schemes.[33] This, of course, resulted in imperfect titles, ripe for Jefferson's business model.

As mentioned, a General Court lawyer could not practice in county courts or vice versa. But Jefferson did not simply hang a shingle outside his office, reading "Thomas Jefferson, Attorney at Law, Member of the General Court." Rather, in order to build a robust practice, Jefferson acquainted himself with the different county court attorneys in the areas he visited.[34] He did this by frequently traveling to the different courthouses when they were in session and the local attorneys were gathered.

Jefferson's courtship of Augusta was rewarded. Out of those 68 case entries made in 1767, 41 were from clients who lived in Augusta.[35] Through these cases, Jefferson steadily built a reputation as a persuasive writer who, despite his relative youth and lack of practice experience, understood the intricacies of the General Court in Williamsburg. It was not long before that reputation began to attract a lucrative clientele. A steady stream of county court attorneys, primarily from Albemarle and Augusta (as well as a dozen other counties), began to refer him work.[36]

A lesson to be learned comes from the fact that Jefferson—even with his brilliance, his privileged status, and his persuasive writing abilities—still knew the **utility and, in fact, necessity of networking** and paying attention to his business, of minding his store. He knew his success depended upon more than his abilities: it also depended upon other lawyers', clients', and the public's perceptions of those abilities. **Your success depends upon the entire "package" you present to the world.**

Jefferson also practiced before a body called the privy council. The jurisdiction of that council is not completely clear but included a variety of fields like Indian affairs, the commissioning of sheriffs and justices of the peace, and proceedings related to the acquisition of land patents, the latter of which comprised the bulk of Jefferson's work in front of the council.[37] And, whereas there was a law that forbade country court attorneys from practicing in the General Court and vice versa, General Court attorneys were not prohibited from practicing in the council. Thus, there was more competition. Because there was no maximum fee rule, however, and because the cases were generally simpler "and shorter-lived than General Court cases, the less prestigious council practice was more profitable than General Court work."[38] Jefferson also tried a few cases before arbitrators, typically when the case was particularly complex, requiring specialized knowledge of an area of law.[39]

CASEWORK
PROPERTY LAW

The bulk of Jefferson's cases involved property questions. Jefferson's very first client, Gabriel Jones, was a prominent Augusta county attorney. Jones hired Jefferson to bring a caveat (a legal action used to warn a judge that there is a hidden defect with a particular case in front of them) with respect to a

100-acre plot of land in which Jones had an interest. Jefferson must have been persuasive in his court pleadings because later that year, Jones hired Jefferson again, on behalf of an Augusta resident, for a slander case pending in the General Court.

Jefferson understood a **basic tenet of legal practice: that persuasive representation of clients breeds more clients.**

Jones's endorsement of Jefferson helped him build his clientele, which accelerated Jefferson's legal career.

Jefferson's focus on property cases was more than just a source of immediate work and income. He understood that the colony of Virginia was pushing its boundaries and that property law would be the key to his success in practice. Indeed, most of Jefferson's early cases involved quieting of titles, a property action where landowners seek reassurances that their land titles are legitimate.[40] Quieting required research of property records not only to ensure that the land in question had a sufficient historical paper trail to ensure ownership, but also to ensure that the Crown's taxes on patented colonial lands, called quitrents, were paid. Further, because "taxes" and "colonists" have never mixed well, it was common for Virginia land speculators to avoid paying the quitrent by simply squatting on the land indefinitely, without a patent.[41] Other property owners, who had acquired a land patent, often allowed it to lapse because they could not maintain the stringent land-use requirements, leaving property open to challenge from other claimants who would need a quieting of title—more business for Jefferson.

Jefferson's mastery of property issues came from constant study and practice. He recognized that **finding a niche and becoming a master in that area is key to success.** But Jefferson also knew when to use the expertise of others.

Jefferson often hired experts to conduct the title research, itself. The **lesson** to be learned from that practice is one applicable to us all: **spend your time wisely**.

Of course, one, especially a lawyer, cannot only perform where he is at his best and always use his time most effectively. Whenever a title was challenged in court, for example, Jefferson dutifully represented his client.[42] But Jefferson was not a skilled public speaker, and he knew it. He therefore built his practice primarily on transactional work, where he was best able to exploit his scrupulous attention to detail and his extensive knowledge of English common law.[43] It was not long before Jefferson earned a reputation as an expert in property and estate planning. And, because of his aptitude for precise writing, he was actively sought after to draft wills for his clients and other attorneys who hired him specifically for his writing abilities.

HOWELL V. NETHERLAND

Although property was the focus of his practice, Jefferson represented clients on a wide range of legal issues. In 1770, Samuel Howell, a mixed-race slave, brought a civil suit against his master in the case, *Howell v. Netherland*, to be declared free from slavery. Howell retained Jefferson who took the case pro bono.

Howell's status as a slave was based on a Roman law from antiquity, *partus sequitur ventrem* ("that which is brought forth follows the womb"), often referred to simply as *partus*. The doctrine stood for the proposition that the mother's legal status determined the child's legal status. Howell's grandmother had a black child out of wedlock and was fined for her "indiscretion." Under Virginia law, her child, Howell's mother, was bound into slavery until she reached the age of 31. Because Howell was born before his mother reached the age of 31—the age at which her indentured servitude ended—Howell would be enslaved under the doctrine of *partus*, too.[44]

Jefferson's mentor and teacher, George Wythe, represented Howell's master.[45] Despite facing his mentor, despite facing a biased bench, and despite the uphill battle he would face on the legal issues, Jefferson was not deterred. As a student, Jefferson studied all the major precedents and legal aspects concerning the various statuses of slaves under English law, ultimately concluding that no basis existed for the doctrine of *partus* to be applied in the colonies.[46] Jefferson wrote a brilliant and hyper-technical memorandum of law for the court, maintaining that, if the statute were read strictly, "the plaintiff does not come within the description of the act." Therefore, Jefferson argued, without a positive law dictating his client's status, there was no legal means to continue his slavery.[47] Chapter 6 explores Jefferson's notoriously complex and even contradictory nature on questions of race and slavery. For now, simply note that despite his failings in this respect, Jefferson appears to have worked diligently for Howell in support of his natural rights regardless of his race.[48] That memorandum of law was Jefferson's first known public venture into writing on natural rights.[49] Written five years before he perfected the language in the Declaration of Independence, Jefferson wrote that, under the law of nature, "all men are born free, every one comes into the world with a right to his own person, which includes the liberty of moving and using it at his own will. This is what is called personal liberty, and is given him by the author of nature."

Unfortunately, Howell lost his case; the judge cut Jefferson off during his oral argument.[50] Jefferson represented six other slaves over the years, free of charge. He developed a reputation as a persuasive advocate for slaves by using novel arguments and technicalities to battle a system that was built to keep his clients in bondage.

Today, because of the perception of legal theater associated with the practice of law, people think that a legal victory must be made with a dramatic flourish. We expect the witness to admit he did it on the stand; we expect the lawyer to hold up the lost bloody knife, proving his client's innocence; and we expect the document to be proffered that conclusively proves the insurance company illegally refused coverage to an eight-year-old cancer patient. What Jefferson and other great attorneys and persuasive authors understand, though, is that **a victory is a victory**. Sure, it's preferable (and more fun) to win on the merits of your argument, but winning on a legal technicality is a win, too.

Jefferson had a great ability to see the *edges of the law*—he was able to see through the sometimes obscure facts into the spider web of jurisprudence and identify the diverse implications. He understood that history, the law, and public opinion were all wed and, with that knowledge, he became a formidable force on both the merits and technicalities of the case at hand.

No attorney relishes in the pure procedural win, and Jefferson was no different. However, he considered it a greater travesty and a dereliction of his duty to his client to lose when a technical argument was available. Having undertaken a case, it is a lawyer's duty to array all the facts and to present every phase of the law helpful to his client's cause.

Use every tool in your bag, every weapon in your arsenal. Not using every tool in your bag discredits your client and yourself. It should be noted, however, that when dealing in legal technicalities, it is easy to go from practicing at the edges of the law to practicing in the abyss of the law. If you feel that you are too close to the edge, you probably are. And in some cases, you may have already fallen over. While "play hard, but not too hard" may seem like an impossible standard, it is important to note that 99% of these situations can be resolved by using simple common sense. Most people know when they are being dishonest. If you cannot make that determination, perhaps you shouldn't be making your career in the law. A simple rule is **if you have to justify your actions to yourself, you are likely playing too close to the edge.**

Another **lesson** we can draw from Jefferson's work in the *Howell* case comes from Jefferson's conduct after Howell lost. Not only did Jefferson handle the case for free, but he also gave monetary help to Howell to flee to the North when the court declared him a slave. That decision, although morally correct, was a mistake in light of Jefferson's professional duty and ethical obligations. We will examine that mistake further in Chapter 6 as one of Jefferson's failings.

But Jefferson believed that from justice comes compassion and mercy. It is undoubtedly true that Jefferson believed passionately in the rule of law, as so much of what he has written suggests, but he was also a gentle man in many ways.

In an era of draconian law, Jefferson often found a way to accept extenuating circumstances or extend special considerations. **Though the court is a place of law and order, even in the fiercest legal battles, there is almost always a place for mercy and compassion.** Oftentimes, a display of mercy will have other beneficial effects: people will see you as a moderate, as someone willing to consider the facts of each case instead of blindly following a blanket decision made before all the facts are known.

BOLLING V. BOLLING

Another example where we see Jefferson's brilliance as a persuader is in the 1771 case, *Bolling v. Bolling*. This case was also tried against his former teacher, Wythe, and involved a dispute between two brothers, Robert and Archibald Bolling, over the estate and will of a third brother, Edward, who had died in 1770.[51] The Bollings were an old and prominent Virginia family, descendants of Pocahontas and John Rolfe. Jefferson was associated to the family through his sister, Mary Jefferson Bolling, who was married to a fourth brother, John. On September 13, 1771, Jefferson agreed to represent the defendant in the case, Robert Bolling.[52]

The arguments, primarily written pleadings, were presented to a legally-trained arbitrator rather than the typical lay members of the General Court and have been preserved in a 239-page handwritten manuscript.[53] Jefferson's and Wythe's arguments have been hailed as a "splendid specimen of the professional powers and proficiency of the Virginia bar in the years immediately preceding the American Revolution."[54]

Edward's will gave his older brother, Robert, his plantation named Buffalo Lick and several slaves. To his younger brother, Archibald, he left other property he owned, also designating him the "residuary devisee and legatee," so any property not specifically designated to another person by Edward's will would pass to Archibald.

The first issue before the Court was the brother's dispute as to who owned the crops that were currently growing on the Buffalo Lick plantation. Robert argued that, as the owner of the plantation, they were his. Archibald, of course, argued that, as the residuary legatee, the crops were actually part of his deceased brother's personal property, so were his. The main legal question presented to the arbitrator was, Are crops part of the land, or separate from it?

The second issue presented by the attorneys was who should receive the surplus of money owed to the estate after all debts were paid and funds collected.

Jefferson argued that, as the executor of the estate, Robert had to pay and collect the debts, so they were his. Wythe, on the other hand, argued that the surplus was an undisposed part of Edward's personal property, and therefore belonged to his client.

The case briefs are difficult to understand because of the complex use of English law and language, something he tried to remedy when drafting American laws. In his autobiography, he wrote of his approach to drafting American statutes by referencing the convolution then in vogue in legal writing:

> I thought it would be useful also, in all new draughts, to reform the style of the later British statutes, and of our own acts of assembly, which from their verbosity, their endless tautologies, their involutions of case within case, and parenthesis within parenthesis, and their multiplied efforts at certainty by saids and aforesaids, by ors and by ands, to make them more plain, do really render them more perplexed and incomprehensible, not only to common readers, but to the lawyers themselves.[55]

Jefferson was such a powerful writer because he was able to communicate so effectively. He found ways to convey complex philosophical notions by (relatively) simple means. His means of communicating through the written word—the structure and flow of the argument, the words he chose to use, and his expert citation to authority as well as to current events—are what made him the persuasive writer so sought after that he was chosen to write the Declaration of Independence by his fellow worthies.

In the Bolling case, Jefferson started his argument with a simple Latin proverb: *quicquid plantatur solo, solo cedit* ("whatever is planted in the soil belongs to the soil"). Jefferson argued that the totality of law from diverse sources supported his contention. He then addressed Wythe's claim that the legal authority in question was unfounded because it was not cited by the "judges at Westminster."[56] Jefferson pointed out that some of "the greatest legal jurists' works, such as Coke and Plowden, were published in French and later translated for the English-speaking world."[57] Jefferson's encyclopedic knowledge of the law was not only persuasive to the bench, but also to Wythe, who conceded during the argument that "the common law supposed the owner of the soil to have a right to emblements."[58] Throughout the arguments, Wythe, representing the plaintiff, raised a number of complex legal issues. Jefferson adroitly addressed each, in turn.

The Bolling case demonstrates Jefferson's mastery of the law. Whenever Jefferson took a case, he would study all the laws potentially implicated in the case and study the various directions each could take, until he became expert in those laws surrounding the issue.

A key to persuasive writing is the ability to **master the parameters of your topic** (for lawyers, the law), then to apply your facts within those parameters in easily digestible bites. Jefferson was a master at presenting issues to his audience in ways that were not only comprehensible, but in ways that led his audience to think as he thought and to find the answers he wanted them to find. That, in short, is what persuasive writing seeks to do—and Jefferson was most comfortable in that world.

JEFFERSON CLOSES SHOP

In August 1774, Jefferson transferred his ongoing General Court cases to Edmund Randolph. He had actively practiced law for eight years. Although he did maintain a practice after 1774, he never again appeared in court as an attorney.[59] Randolph sent a letter to Jefferson's old and new clients, reading,

> Mr. Jefferson having declined his Practice in the General Court, and consigned the Business, which he left there unfinished, into my Hands, I find, from his Memorandums that he was retained by you. I shall therefore continue to attend to those Matters wherein you have employed him, and exert myself for your interest, unless you countermand it by Letter.[60]

Randolph received 253 cases from Jefferson, most of which Jefferson had completely prepped and were merely awaiting a court date.[61] Jefferson did retain and accept new caveat cases: they were heard in the Governor's Council and not in the General Court, they paid well, and they were relatively simple.[62] It appears that Jefferson expected to keep a caveat practice continuing.

Before the Council could reconvene in June 1775, however, the courts were closed to civil litigation as a means to enact pressure on British merchants so they would use their influence to address the colonists' grievances with the King. The Governor's Council never reopened.[63] And, as went the Governor's Council, so went Thomas Jefferson's caveat practice. Even the General Court attorneys boycotted the October 1774 session.

The question remains, Why did Jefferson give up his elite position as a member of the General Court bar? Economic considerations definitely played a role in the decision: Jefferson was perpetually upset over his clients refusing to pay their legal bills; he inherited a significant sum of money when his father-in-law died, reducing the need for income from his practice; and he was unhappy with the long travel and costs, in terms of both money and the time spent away from his wife and children that his practice required.[64]

There is no doubt, for me, that Jefferson loved the law and the practice of it. I also have no doubt that he yearned to be back at Monticello, where construction had begun during his days at court and where he had plans for more major improvements (he continued to plan improvements to Monticello until the day he died). Jefferson was a lawyer. But he was also a gardener, a scientist, and a political radical. Frank Dewey summed up the timing of this decision best: "in short, his zest for the practice of law was declining at the same time that his lifelong passions for building and horticulture were beginning to assert themselves."[65]

Jefferson was certainly critical of the legal profession after he left, saying in a letter to a friend seeking advice on whether to pursue a career in medicine or the law that "the physician is happy in the attachment of the families in which he practices. . . . [T]he lawyer has only to recollect how many, by his dexterity, have been cheated of their right and reduced to beggary." Yet I am hesitant to accept this cynicism as his true feeling toward his profession. Throughout his life, he mentored law students and, when he helped to found the University of Virginia, one of his first acts was to establish a chair of law.[66]

We can learn a lot from Jefferson's view of his profession. Chiefly, we should learn that you should **love your job.** Again, I am not convinced that Jefferson disliked his profession. Jefferson certainly had innate abilities, especially in writing; but he became a great attorney the old-fashioned way—through **practice**. He was remarkably young when he joined the General Court bar, and by the time he left, just eight years later, he was renowned as a master of his field. In those eight years at court, according to his case register, he handled 949 cases. He was well known not only as a diligent lawyer, but also as an **inveterate student** of the law. He **gained his experience by reading and listening to the cases of other attorneys**—Wythe foremost among them— **and by identifying and adopting those characteristics that seemed would work well with his particular style.**

An aspiring persuasive writer must understand that **the vast majority of greats become great through hard work and perseverance, not through supernatural talent** (though that sure does help). With a few exceptions, every lesson pointed out in this book is a lesson that Jefferson learned from continual practice and failure until ultimate success. Because that is the usual path, it would be exceedingly difficult to master anything without loving it, especially a profession requiring so much of a person's time and thought. Further, the fact that Jefferson kept his caveat cases tells us that, if not for the Revolution, he would have continued to practice. For Jefferson, and for us, the lesson is clear: **if you love what you do, you will be better at it.**

Still, regardless of his "true" feelings toward his former profession, the nation needed Jefferson the lawyer. Indeed, it was his frustration with the inequity in the law that gave us the Jefferson we needed. Jefferson the radical and Jefferson the republican were born from his frustration at seeing the well-connected benefitting at the expense of those less well-connected, especially farmers, who he thought were the true builders of America. Jefferson the author of the Declaration was born from his days as a lawyer, where he honed his forensic and persuasive writing skills. Jefferson the politician and, ultimately, Jefferson the President were born of his time traveling through Virginia, where he took advantage of opportunities to meet his fellow Americans.

Regardless whether Jefferson fully appreciated his time as an attorney or not, we should. At a critical moment for America, Jefferson learned how to put his personal views down on paper with power, elegance, and persuasiveness.[67] In a letter to George Wythe in 1776, John Adams wrote of the nature of that critical moment, saying, "You and I, dear friend, have been sent into life at a time when the greatest lawgivers of antiquity would have wished to live. How few of the human race have ever enjoyed an opportunity of making an election of government . . . for themselves or their children!" How lucky we are that Thomas Jefferson had established himself as such a persuasive force that he was elected to make the most of that opportunity. The greatest lawgivers of antiquity could not have done better.

Lessons Learned
- Observe those persuaders you respect and trust.
- Observe, but learn by doing.
- Network! Know others and be known.
- Spend your time wisely.
- Use every tool available.
- Master your subject.
- Hard work and perseverance will get you further than mere talent.
- Love what you do—it will show, and it will pay off.

3

POLITICAL PERSUASIONS

In a widely misunderstood line, Shakespeare (*Henry VI*) had Dick the Butcher say, "The first thing we do, let's kill all the lawyers."[68] Dick was a mindless follower of John Cade, the rebel leader whose goal was to overthrow the King—they represented the fall of civilization. In truth, Shakespeare meant the line as a compliment to the lawyers who served as a counterweight to the ex-convict Cade, who was in London to foment mayhem, burn the city, and pillage the nation for his own gain. Cade, and to a lesser extent, the Butcher, appreciated that lawyers think in terms of precedents rather than radical change, and so needed to be dealt with first.[69] The ruthlessness of the revolutionists reveals itself soon after the "kill the lawyers" line is delivered, when Cade orders a law clerk executed for being literate, the ultimate offense against lawlessness: "away with him, I say, hang him with his pen and inkhorn about his neck."[70] Despite how many misunderstand his quote, Shakespeare appreciated that lawyers are a stabilizing force in society. He knew that they help those with the smallest voices to be heard, finding a balance between competing interests and, in so doing, maintaining a functional level of social cohesion for the whole.[71]

Still today, lawyers face persistent ridicule and jokes about their profession—good-natured ribbing for the most part. In spite of the outward perception Americans hold of lawyers, they stand in American history as some of our greatest heroes: a lawyer drafted our Constitution, a lawyer delivered the

Gettysburg address and led us through a civil war, a lawyer steered us through the Great Depression and toward victory in the Second World War. And it was a lawyer who wrote the Declaration of Independence.

The practice of law prepares individuals to bring tranquility from chaos and peaceful resolution from fierce battle. For this very reason, Jefferson's time as a practicing attorney made him a better president. There is no other profession that could have given him a better understanding of the human endeavor. His practice taught him more than the mere letter of the law and advocacy techniques; it provided him a Petri dish in which to view the best and worst of mankind and all its foibles. There is, of course, the counter argument illustrated by the aphorism, "a town with one lawyer has a starving lawyer, a town with two lawyers has two fat lawyers." But the fact remains that whenever we are in trouble, we turn to lawyers for help.

In Norman Gross's book, *America's Lawyer-Presidents*, this idea is well summarized: "[t]hough many people might initially associate the law with legal technicalities, procedure, and documents . . . [it is really] an instructive mirror of the issues, institutions, events, and people that have shaped American history and continue to affect us on a daily basis."[72] Jefferson expressed this same sentiment when he said, "the study of law qualifies a man to be useful to himself, to his neighbors, and to the public."

In writing the foreword to Gross's book, former Associate Justice Sandra Day O'Connor reinforced this theory of a lawyer's utility, observing,

[l]awyers have played a pivotal role in the shaping of the political and civic life of this country. Their role remains a vital one today. Legal education continues to provide the training ground for significant numbers of our nation's leaders. Individuals with law degrees currently occupy roughly half the state governorships, more than half the seats in the United States Senate, and more than a third of the seats in the House of Representatives.[73]

It should not come as a surprise that 26 of our 44 presidents have been lawyers. The nexus between a respect for the rule of law and political ambition helps to explain why each of these men found, through a common profession, their disparate paths to the White House. In the end, each of them, like Jefferson, was made a better president for having been trained as a lawyer.[74]

LAW AS A PATH TO POLITICS

Abraham Lincoln learned to be persuasive by arguing in front of juries. Jefferson, on the other hand, was not a powerful pleader in the courtroom itself. He was less able to sway a trier of fact with oratorical flourishes and turns of phrase than the master, Lincoln.[75] But Jefferson knew that, and compensated for it so well that he came to dominate the courtroom nonetheless. Jefferson was an insatiable reader who became expert in any fields of law implicated in the cases he took. He made a point to do so, in part, so he could minimize his verbiage in the courtroom itself.[76] His voracious appetite for legal knowledge also helped to focus his persuasive writing. Indeed, **reading is a key to good writing.** Jefferson was also concerned with the law beyond his client's immediate interests. He viewed the law not only as a means to a limited end for his client, but also as a means to a much greater end for society: to fight against the injustices and abuses of power inherent in the status quo that the colonial government took pains to maintain.

A DIVORCE CASE STARTS A POLITICAL FIRE

An example of Jefferson's legal practice foreshadowing the path he took in becoming a revolutionist and then President can be seen by his involvement with the *Blair* divorce case. At first glance, this case appears to be unusual for the times, and for Jefferson in particular, because divorce was not possible in colonial America without a *vincula matrimonii* ("from the chain of marriage"). *Vincula matrimonii* was basically a law passed by Parliament declaring a marriage annulled (not even a full divorce) for certain marital crimes, such as adultery. In today's world, the *vincula matrimonii* would be known as legal separation, but one where neither party would be able to remarry.

In the *Blair* case, the Royal British governor, John Murray—called Lord Governor Dunmore because of his title as the Fourth Earl of Dunmore—was having an affair with a woman named Kitty Eustace Blair. The problem with the relationship, beyond the fact that the lovers were not married, was the fact that Kitty was married to another man, Dr. James Blair. The Blair marriage appeared to be troubled from conception (no pun intended), with rumors of Kitty having illicit liaisons with the Royal Governor.[77] Within just weeks of marrying Dr. Blair, Kitty moved out of the marital home and into a boarding house, filing suit against her husband for financial support. Dr. Blair hired Jefferson to defend the suit.

The case originally asked a simple question: Could Dr. Blair divorce his wife of only a few weeks, or would he have to pay "alimony" to a near-stranger who had moved out and who, from all accounts, was having a torrid affair?[78] At the time, there was no precedent for a Virginia court granting a divorce decree, even in cases of adultery.[79] Despite the dearth of legal precedent, Jefferson researched the possibility of obtaining a divorce through an act of the legislature. His written argument in the Blair case included the precursor to what he later referred to as the "natural rights of man," which is acknowledged as a foundational principle in his political thought.

Lord Governor Dunmore

To Jefferson, the issues were larger than Dr. Blair's divorce.[80] The case was about right and wrong, about the freedom of a man being restrained in his "pursuit of happiness" by arcane and unjust laws. Jefferson methodically drew up his argument, listing the pros and cons for both sides. He included in his pros that it would be "cruel to continue by violence by [a] union made at first by mutual love, now dissolved by hatred . . . to chain a man to misery till death" and that the "Liberty of divorce prevents and cures domestic quarrels."[81] Jefferson included among the cons of allowing divorce that "man may get wife at any age—woman cannot when the charms of youth are gone," also asking about the "mixture of fortunes—how to be divided?" and "what is to become of children—divided?"

Jefferson's process, here, provides an important lesson: In persuasive writing, you should **design your argument to address both the strengths and weaknesses of your position**. Not only does acknowledging your weaknesses allow you to frame them so your opponent must work, from his start, within the bounds you set out, but it also **adds credibility to your argument and to you as the argument's author** because you appear honest about the limits of your position. **Conceding a flaw at the start is a great way to focus your audience on the strengths of your argument**.

Before the case had finished, Dr. Blair died, however, mooting his argument. The focus of the case then shifted to the legal question of whether Kitty Blair should inherit part of her late still-husband's estate. Jefferson agreed to handle the estate with another attorney, but hired two others to argue the case before the court. Although the historical evidence provides no clear answer as to why Jefferson hired other attorneys to give the oral argument, a strong possibility is that he understood where his true strengths lay, shopping out his oral advocacy to others with strengths different from but complementary to his own.

Know what you are good at. Utilize hired guns to pick up where your skill set leaves off. The ability to acknowledge your limits and appreciate others' abilities is key to success in lawyering or any business. You aren't that persuasive if you aren't that good.

The case of *Blair v. Blair* came before the General Court with a shocking twist—Lord Dunmore was one of the judges presiding over the case. Jefferson may have known that this was the case beforehand, perhaps giving rise to his hiring other attorneys to pursue the case before the court. Jefferson would not have wanted to argue that Kitty Blair had an affair with the Royal Governor before that same Royal Governor acting as judge. Jefferson also very likely would not have wanted to argue the issue publicly, regardless of who presided, because of the Royal Governor's influence across Virginia. Jefferson knew, in short, that it was not worth threatening his ability to fight tomorrow to fight the wrong battle today.

Of course, Jefferson also knew where the line should be drawn, moving him to threaten everything of tomorrow to fight for independence today. Ben Franklin's famous statement expresses what the American revolutionaries risked by declaring their independence and choosing to fight: "We must all hang together, or assuredly we will all hang separately." Jefferson knew where to draw the line, and the Blair case was not it.

There may be times when being your persuasive best would be professional suicide. At those times, you must weigh the benefits against the costs to yourself. **Sometimes, you will decide it is worth it to push on. Other times, though, you may simply have to eat it.**

Patrick Henry, opposing counsel at the *Blair* trial, masterfully set forth a persuasive, yet delicate argument. Instead of arguing that the marriage was consummated—which could be key in deciding if she inherited from the estate—he argued that Kitty had "tendered herself but there was a want of readiness in the doctor." Henry basically argued that Dr. Blair was impotent.[82] That argument apparently pleased Lord Dunmore. Henry's tact allowed Lord Dunmore to not have to hear (1) an argument that Kitty was having an affair, which would have indirectly implicated the Lord or (2) details of his lover's sexual relationship with another man, regardless that that "other man" was her lawful husband.[83]

Jefferson's legal team lost that case. But the case is important beyond the salacious facts—Jefferson learned here and through some of his other work as a lawyer just how corrupt the system actually was. Specifically, he learned that, under British rule, the natural rights of man came to nothing when they conflicted with the interests of the elite, such as the powerful Lord Dunmore. Moreover, this was an obviously unjust result, one which Jefferson remembered throughout the revolution. Indeed, Jefferson made Lord Dunmore America's first supervillain when he cited to some of Dunmore's more reprehensible actions in his list of grievances of the Crown in the Declaration of Independence. As unlikely as it is that a divorce case would be the venue for two of the most prominent architects of the Revolutionary War to work with one another, it truly foreshadowed what was to come—the "divorce" case of *United States v. Britain*.[84]

A LEGAL RIGHT TO PROPERTY

Jefferson viewed the law as an intellectual, particularly when it came to property law. Not only did he see the law as an avenue to help his client, but also as a method to improve life in the colonies and, ultimately, to create a political dynasty. Jefferson saw the American frontier as central to his vision of a great American Republic because it provided acreage to sustain farmers, which would lead to the development of the middle class. Additionally, Jefferson believed that the idea of land ownership provided the communal interest that could band the colonists together under a single identity—Americans.[85]

However, as a lawyer, Jefferson saw how the elites tried to monopolize power over property as they had done in the tidewater area of Virginia and throughout Europe. In Virginia, the old-moneyed elites obtained enormous tracts of land from the royal government in the colony. Other wealthy spectators of this practice were able to acquire dozens of smaller tracts and assemble them into estates that resembled those of the European land barons. And while Jefferson did represent some of these land barons of colonial Virginia, his practice primarily focused on the representation of smaller landowners. Better than four out of five of his clients worked tracts of 400 acres or less. That number may seem largish today, but not when compared to the land barons who sat atop thousands upon thousands of acres—Jefferson himself owned over 10,000 acres.

When Jefferson said, "Those who labour in the earth are the chosen people of God," he was speaking from his core belief that the personal autonomy of the land owner was essential to creating a thriving American empire.[86] Jefferson understood that property "served as more than an economic commodity. It had a social and political purpose."[87] By concentrating huge tracts of land under only a few elites, the colonial government threatened to bring European-style politics and structures to the new country and, with it, European domination and subjugation of the vast majority of the colonists. Under the European model, only a few land barons would rent to the masses. Because voting rights depended on land ownership in many areas, most Americans would be dispossessed of the American dream—and it would all be done legally.[88]

The passage of laws of *primogeniture* and *entail* solidified this concern. Primogeniture refers to the right to succession belonging to the firstborn son, the whole estate passing solely to the eldest male. Entail, also known as fee tail, is the legal restriction on the sale or inheritance of property, forcing real estate to pass to certain of the owner's heirs by an operation of law. Together, these laws, which are rooted in feudal rule, utterly destroy upward progression by anyone other than the already-elites.

Jefferson complained that the result of these laws was the "accumulation and perpetuation of wealth, in select families." He believed that the European land system had to be fought not only to prevent the concentration of power in the few, but also to encourage the land to be used and worked by those who cared most, the owners who needed it for their family's survival. To circumvent these old laws "required a skilled lawyer such as Jefferson, who could disencumber large blocks of land for clients."[89] Jefferson's fight against feudal property law did not end when he left practice. Once elected, the experience his law practice brought him helped him to draft statutes to ensure primogeniture and entail could never take root in the United States. With Jefferson's help, entail was abolished in 1776, primogeniture in 1785.[90]

JEFFERSON'S ROOTS IN NATURAL LAW

Jefferson's awareness of the "natural law" of man, as opposed to the King's law, dates to his early years as a law student.[91] While studying under Wythe, Jefferson systematically took notes on different English judges and their writings.[92] Here, Jefferson found himself attracted to the jurisprudence of a group of judges who had been writing in the tumultuous 17th-century England.[93] Their writings dealing with the philosophy of rights particularly engrossed Jefferson. Jefferson's "philosophy on rights" is typically viewed, as he wrote in the Declaration of Independence, as "Laws of Nature."[94] As the Jeffersonian scholar, Professor David Konig, pointed out, however, "he actually drew far more heavily on an English 'whig' tradition of resistance to arbitrary power."[95] Later in life, Jefferson explained how this way of thinking took root. He described how he would write summaries of the relevant legal decisions and mix in his own reflections on the subject. He explained further that those reflections "were written at a time of life when I was bold in the pursuit of [knowledge,] never fearing to follow truth and reason to whatever results they led, [and] bearding every authority which stood in their way."

Jefferson was greatly influenced by Sir Edward Coke, who reinterpreted the 1215 Magna Carta. The Magna Carta was tremendously important as an early guarantor of freedom, but it was weak in that these freedoms were only guaranteed for wealthy baronial families. Coke argued that this thin layer of rights proved that even the King was subject to common law—a powerful first step in proclaiming individual rights. Jefferson wrote of Sir Coke in a letter to James Madison: "a sounder whig never wrote, nor of profounder learning in the orthodox doctrines of the British Constitution, or in what were called English liberties."

Another authority to influence Jefferson was Sir John Holt, the Chief Justice of the King's Bench from 1689 to 1710. Jefferson called Sir Holt "the greatest lawyer England ever had, except [for] Coke." It was principally from the writings of these two great minds that Jefferson assembled "his own principles of government based on personal freedom and limited government."[96] As we will examine in Chapter 8, in the *Summary View of the Rights of British America*, Jefferson rejected feudal law in America. Instead, citing natural property law, he argued that Americans were born with certain rights. Thus, as individuals with inherent rights, their interests in their own property were held in "freehold and beyond royal demands."[97] Further, as he declared in the Declaration of Independence, King George III violated these natural rights and, therefore, had forfeited his place as trustee over the colonies.[98]

LEGAL REFORM

Jefferson did see the important role that judges, generally, play in the prevention of tyranny and mob rule. At the same time, though, he was critical of those judges who stepped too far afield from the strict application of the laws set forth by the legislature. He also sharply criticized the drafters of Virginia's Constitution for not including a specific, defined list of individual rights (a bill of rights), because he believed a constitution written without such a listing of rights would give the legislature potentially unrestrained power.[99] Because of these and other fears developed primarily during Jefferson's years practicing, Jefferson—throughout his law practice, presidency, and time as a statesman—continually worked for reform.

Jefferson cannot solely be commended for his role in slavery reform, of course—not by any stretch of the imagination. Yet his role in the slavery debate was not as simple or as transparent as one would assume at first glance.

It is true that he was considered an expert in slavery law—he did own more than 200 slaves over the course of his life. It is also clear that he advocated for the legal ownership of human chattel (his role in the slavery debate is discussed in Chapter 6). But Jefferson did prepare a draft of the Virginia Constitution that would have prohibited not only the "introduction of any more slaves to reside in this state," but also "the continuance of slavery beyond the generation which shall be living on the 31st day of December 1800; all persons born after that day being hereby declared free."[100]

Although that draft of the state constitution was not adopted, it does stand as one of the few legal assaults on slavery in the Commonwealth of Virginia, apart from individual freedom suits, in which Jefferson was also involved. As discussed, Jefferson was a member of a small and unpopular group that would take these freedom suits, doing so *pro bono*.

When Jefferson returned to Virginia after the colonies declared independence, he was convinced that the entire Virginia legal "code must be reviewed [and] adapted to our republic form of government." Jefferson viewed many of Virginia's laws as "vicious," needing immediate repeal or redrafting. Jefferson identified "lawcraft" with "priestcraft" (the scheming and machinations of some church leaders), realizing that the laws were written by the legislators of olde and were aimed to hobble the colonists' natural rights.[101] With these motivations, he accepted an appointment to the General Assembly's committee tasked with revising the code and separating out what was good for the people from what was good for the old institutions the colonists were fighting against.

Jefferson focused on three reforms in his position. First, he pushed for the abolition of primogeniture and entails, as discussed above. Second, he lauded the need for a bill of religious freedom, eventually drafting such a bill (the Virginia Statute for Religious Freedom, examined in Chapter 8). Lastly, Jefferson argued for the reform of public education with the specific goal to produce a well-informed citizenry—something he considered absolutely essential for a meaningful and functional republic.[102]

Jefferson ultimately prevailed on his first and second proposed legal reforms. As to the third, however, Jefferson was unable to develop the vast state-funded education programs he envisioned. Later, as a member of the Board of Visitors for the College of William and Mary, Virginia's only college, Jefferson did effect some of the reform he envisioned when he "purged the College of William and Mary of its chair in theology," replacing it with a Chair in Law and appointing his mentor George Wythe as its first holder.[103] Forty years later, he broke ground on one of his life's *chef d'oeuvres*, the University of Virginia. The University was so important to Jefferson that he left explicit instructions to have "Father of the University of Virginia" inscribed on his tombstone, one of only three achievements he felt it necessary to so memorialize (the other two achievements that "made it" were "Author of the Declaration of Independence" and "of the Statute of Virginia for Religious Freedom"). At the University of Virginia, Jefferson planned to "include among the school's faculty a professor of law whose mission was a summary of Jefferson's own career: to use the law to contemplate the proper republican principles of government and to inform how those principles are enacted in the real world."[104]

One of the keys to Jefferson's success as a persuasive force is evidenced by his lifelong attempts at shaping the education system in America. He simply had a vision for the future and he worked every day toward America's realization of that vision. Even as such a persuasive force in revolutionary and early America, he was unable to accomplish that reform quickly. Over years, however, because he stuck by his vision, some of his hopes for education in America became realities—realities that still shape us today. **Having a vision for the future will give you a fixed target. It will also give others hope for a better tomorrow. And hope is a powerful thing for anyone who wishes to persuade.**

JEFFERSON THE VIRGINIAN

In 1768, Jefferson was elected to Virginia's House of Burgesses. While not much is known about his first election, we do know that the legislative body met part-time and was made up solely of members of the gentry class. Jefferson had a quiet demeanor, generally, but was said to have been quite eloquent in small groups. As the newly elected representative from Albemarle County, he took his place sitting on the back bench in the hall. He was slim but not waiflike; he stood ramrod straight at six feet two inches, with a slender face and dominant nose.[105] Although he was only 25 when elected, Jefferson took the responsibility of representation seriously, intending to use his time and office to better the lives of ordinary Virginians.

One of his first tasks as an elected official began what became a pattern of interest, perhaps an obsession, over the course of his life. Over the years, Jefferson constantly returned to the idea of westward exploration and expansion, an idea ultimately leading to Manifest Destiny and, some say, the Monroe Doctrine. Jefferson personally explored the Rivanna River. He was determined to document its obstacles in order to replace the onerous route that tobacco farmers were forced to take over land to the more traversable, but farther, James River. That adventure paid off—the river was made navigable in the late 18th century. The Rivanna River exploration was an early glimpse at another facet of his national dream: finding a transcontinental water route to connect the continent. It also anticipated his later obsession with the Mississippi River.

In May of 1769, the House of Burgesses passed several resolutions condemning Britain's deployment of troops in Boston. Those resolutions also stated that only the governor and legislature could tax citizens of the colonies. Obviously, this did not sit well with the British Royal Governor who immediately dissolved the body for insubordination. The House of Burgesses thus officially disbanded; its members, including Jefferson, removed to the Apollo Room of the Raleigh Tavern—how very American!—to conduct the former House's business. That body reconstituted as the "Nonimportant Association" and vowed to support the Massachusetts (and now the Virginia) cause by boycotting British imports. Although this micro-rebellion quietly subsided within a year, the strategy of using economic warfare in the form of boycotts and embargoes was firmly planted in Jefferson's mind.[106]

Although this first rebuff of the British yoke by the Virginia leadership was tame when compared with what was on the horizon, it did spark within Jefferson the idea that resistance was not futile. More critically, the brush with British authority brought him in closer contact with full-fledged revolutionaries like Patrick Henry. Within just six years of the Nonimportant Association's first meeting at the Raleigh Tavern, Henry convinced the Virginia legislators to send troops for the Revolutionary War effort with one of the most famous lines in American history: "give me liberty or give me death."

Being near these oratory masters during the "dress-rehearsal rebellion" reaffirmed for Jefferson that he would never be a revolutionary speech-master. But he knew that his talents in organization, strategic planning, and writing were just as, and often more, important as fiery oratory.

This is a lesson worth repeating. No one is good at all things, but almost everyone is good at something. **Learn what you are good at, hone it, and then deploy it.** Understanding your strengths is a key to being persuasive. Understanding your weaknesses, though, is just as key.

Jefferson was noted for his articulate speech in small groups. It is true that he was often quiet in crowds, but he was always engaged. He always appeared inquisitive, poised, and confident. Because he always appeared so engaged, and because he was regarded as such a powerful writer, whenever he did choose to voice his opinion, his peers listened. After all, if Thomas Jefferson, the quite gentleman in the back, felt a point was important enough to speak to, it was worth listening.

It is not the man that speaks most or speaks loudest that persuades a crowd. Rather, it is the man that knows when and how to speak that makes his point best.

Despite his abilities with small audiences, he never considered himself and was never known as an accomplished speaker. The HBO miniseries, *John Adams*, presented a fictional, but insightful, exchange between Jefferson and Adams:

Jefferson: I would gladly lend my hand to sink the whole island of Great Britain into the ocean.

John Adams: I have not heard you say three words together in the last Congress. With such passion, I regret that you have not made your mind more plainly known!

Jefferson: I have no gift for oratory, Mr. Adams.[107]

Jefferson was a soft-spoken man, no doubt. After the first dissolution of the House of Burgesses, though, he recognized that although his voice was weak, his hand was strong. He was an excellent draftsman, fusing legal and political arguments and synthesizing complex and often disparate ideas into cohesive and persuasive bills and resolutions.[108] His ability to write, allied with his voracious appetite for the written words of others, caused him to be in constant demand as the mounting crises with the King developed.[109] In 1773, he became one of the founding members of the Committee of Correspondence, in fact drafting the resolution to establish the Committee. The Committee served as a shadow government for the colonies, organized by different patriot leaders in the 13 colonies as the revolution approached in order to coordinate responses to Britain and to share plans among the distinct colonies. The Committee also acted as the germ for the Continental Congress.[110]

On December 16, 1773, the Sons of Liberty in Boston boarded ships and destroyed tea sent to the colonies by the embattled East India Company.[111] The British government responded by closing the port of Boston and passing punitive laws known at the Coercive or Intolerable Acts. The most notable provision of the Acts stripped Massachusetts's right to self-government. The Virginia legislators passed a resolution to express their solidarity with the people of Massachusetts. As a result of this insolence, the Royal Governor Lord Dunmore again dissolved the House of Burgesses. And, once again, its members strolled down to the Apollo Room in the Raleigh Tavern to partake of political debate-inducing beverages. This time, the body reconvened as a "rump" House of Burgesses.[112]

At around the same time, Jefferson was drafting one of his masterpieces, the *Summary View of the Rights of British America*, a hugely important document (discussed in Chapter 8). Jefferson's *Summary* was seen as polemical: it was a combative publication, meant as a last ditch effort to warn the King that his subjects' patience in America was very nearly exhausted.[113] The

Summary, which was printed and distributed throughout the colonies and in Britain, made "Thomas Jefferson" a household name—some considered him famous, others infamous. When he arrived in Philadelphia to claim his seat in Congress in 1775, his name carried great weight—he was perceived as a writer of persuasive force and as a thoughtful negotiator of competing interests.[114]

JEFFERSON THE REBEL

By 1776, Jefferson had completed his transition from diplomatist to all-out revolutionary. The crowning achievement and his very public announcement of that transformation was the Declaration of Independence (discussed in Chapter 7). In September 1776, he felt that he could do most for the revolution at home in Virginia. Resigning his seat in Congress, he returned to state politics and immediately found himself embroiled in the drafting of the new Constitution of the State of Virginia.[115] The proposed constitution that he found upon his return contained many of the entrenched feudal features that he had been battling against for much of his career. To Jefferson, these offensive proposed features in what was to be the new supreme law of the land for his home state were proof that Virginia was not free from royal influence, despite the war for independence raging in the colonies. Defeating these sections of the new constitution became his priority; he even declined a prestigious invitation to accompany the American delegation (which included his friend Benjamin Franklin) to Paris to help secure a treaty between his new nation and a European superpower.

In 1779, Virginia's new legislative body, the General Assembly, elected the 36-year-old as its second governor, Jefferson succeeding Patrick Henry. War was still raging against Britain, a fact that dominated his tenure as governor.[116] Jefferson had the capital moved from Williamsburg to Richmond in order to remove it from the reach of the British navy. Benedict Arnold, though, marched into and seized the more inland Richmond in 1781. At this treason, the capital once again packed up and moved, this time to Charlottesville, which was subsequently also overrun by British forces. Jack Jouett—the southern version of Paul Revere, in short—rode 40 miles overnight to warn Jefferson and his government that royal troops were coming, by land and fast.

Jefferson, who oversaw the evacuation of the government, barely escaped before the red coats arrived. Thomas Jefferson might have been a minor footnote in history but for Jouett and his ride.

Jefferson's term as governor ended on June 2, 1781. He stayed in office an additional 10 days as "acting" governor because the British invasion disrupted the election. At the time, Jefferson worried that the 10 days would allow others to condemn him as a usurper, but that fear turned out to be the least of his worries. During the British attacks, Jefferson left the capital and escorted his family to safety. His enemies used this excuse to question his "abandonment" of the capital. Although he defended his actions well and the inquiry was almost immediately dropped, the label "coward" followed him for the remainder of his days as it proved a useful weapon for his political rivals.[117] The allegation of cowardice may be the reason for his brief withdrawal, in 1781, from public office. A reasonable analysis would conclude that Jefferson acted honorably.

Mistakes, and perceived mistakes, will be remembered. Remember that.

Indeed, soon after Jouett gave his warning, Jefferson ordered a carriage for his family and sent them to a neighboring farm—he remained behind to gather important government documents. Christopher Hudson, a neighbor, found Jefferson in the capital organizing the government's evacuation. Hudson gave Jefferson a second warning that the red coats were ascending Monticello. Hudson recounted that Jefferson remained "perfectly tranquil, and undisturbed," despite the news that a light horse unit was a mere 10 minutes away. Jefferson, knowing the land intimately, stayed off the main road and caught up with his family by traveling through the woods.

The British caught seven of the rebel members of the General Assembly, but the vast majority of the assemblymen escaped to the town of Staunton. After the group reconvened in Staunton, they inquired into Jefferson's abandonment of his post. Jefferson then insisted on appearing before the

Assembly to defend his actions. He explained that it was understood that the commander of the state militia, General Nelson, would be appointed governor once Jefferson's term ended. Jefferson explained that, although he was a sound administrator, Jefferson was "unprepared for the command of armies," and, because of the dire situation in Virginia, having one man able to lead both the army and civil government "would greatly facilitate military measures." Nelson was named Jefferson's successor and capably led Virginia's government and military through the end of the war. Cornwallis's surrender at Yorktown in October 1781 was the beginning of the end of British rule in America.

Two lessons can be garnered from the evacuation incident. **First, the ability to remain calm when the pressure is on will allow you to remain persuasive, rather than merely emotional. Cooler heads will prevail.** Chances are, no one reading this will ever be in the situation where a hostile army is literally chasing you out of your home. But other high-intensity situations arise in all sorts of contexts. For example, many, including me, have served in the military. I served in Iraq as a combat arms officer. There were dozens of times when I felt the pressure—and the dread—creeping up my spine. Some of those times, I was "perfectly tranquil, and undisturbed." Other times, though, I am positive that the men I led saw me as a bit panicked, to say the least. I am confident that during those times when I remained tranquil, I used better, more reasoned judgment and provided better leadership to my soldiers.

As an officer, I *should* have been listened to in either case. As just one man among many, however, I was much more persuasive when I appeared calm in the face of pressure. To put this in terms of persuasion as such, although I had authority over those men because of our respective ranks, the authority I exuded and, in turn, earned was much greater when I was able to step back and approach the high-pressure situations with a cool head. I was, simply, more persuasive at those times.

The second lesson the evacuation teaches us might seem a bit counterintuitive. **Know when to give up even hard-won authority. And know who to give it to.** We are taught, properly, from a very early age in the United States that our civil and military leaders must be different people. Hence, Jefferson's desire to place complete control of Virginia's leadership in the hands of just one man may seem contrary to this belief system, that of limited government, separation of powers, and control of our armed forces in the hands of an elected official. But there were no such doctrines in 1781, at least not in practice. And Virginia, like the rest of the colonies, was in a fight for its very survival. Jefferson, understanding his limitations and that his best qualities were no longer what was needed, saw what else was necessary and helped get the right person with the right set of skills into the right position at the right time.

Too often people get in over their heads and refuse to acknowledge when they are outmatched. The ability to see through your own shortcomings, to **recognize what or who is needed**, and to cede authority is admirable and will likely only make you **more credible in the long run.** Plus, the more quickly you can make those hard, but necessary, decisions, the less heartache and wasted effort you will have to suffer. And **if you are working on behalf of a client, their freedom or fortune can depend on it.**

The following year, on September 6, 1782, after his besmirched governorship had ended and the Revolutionary War was coming to an end, Thomas Jefferson's cherished wife, Martha, died. Her death affected Jefferson immensely. He removed himself from society almost entirely. Two months later, he wrote to his friend, the Marquis de Chastellux, that he was "slowly emerging from a stupor of mind which had rendered [him] as dead to the world as [she]."

Shortly thereafter, he was again asked to join a diplomatic mission, this time as envoy to England and France to help negotiate the Treaty of Paris, which would officially end the hostilities with Great Britain. Jefferson likely wanted to remove himself from the fresh memory of his wife's death, so agreed to take the post. Because of inclement weather, however, he was delayed and the treaty negotiations concluded before he set sail. Under the treaty, Great Britain recognized the United States of America as a sovereign nation, acknowledged some American commercial rights (mostly fishing), and conceded the territory that lay between the Allegheny Mountains and the Mississippi River.

The treaty officially brought forth a new nation and gave Jefferson new purpose. He was elected a delegate to the federal Congress, where he worked fervently to ensure that his new country would have a solid foundation. He was instrumental in ensuring that the other colonies, now states, ratified the treaty. He further helped General Washington prepare the stirring speech in which he started the American tradition of the commander-in-chief stepping down peacefully. The peaceful transfer of power was no foregone conclusion until George Washington, the great war hero, set the precedent. That stands as a truly proud day in American history. It is reminiscent of the Roman dictator (a word intended without the pejorative connotation attached to it today), Lucius Quinctius Cincinnatus, stepping down after the enemies of Rome were vanquished, making him a model of Roman, and now American, civic virtue.

After Washington did step down as General and de facto commander-in-chief, he was elected President and became the de jure commander-in-chief envisioned in our Constitution. As President, he appointed Jefferson the Minister Plenipotentiary to France (French Ambassador). In the summer of 1784, then, Jefferson embarked for France. He would return to the United States four years later—a changed man.

JEFFERSON THE DIPLOMAT

Jefferson presented his credentials to the French Court of Louis XVI on May 17, 1785. From that date until his return in 1789, Jefferson practiced persuasion at the international level. He, along with his revolutionary compatriots John Adams and Benjamin Franklin, was charged with finding banks willing to lend to the new nation. The triumvirate found it difficult to negotiate commercial treaties as many nations simply did not think this new America would be around long enough to repay whatever credit was extended. Despite these difficulties, "Jefferson's absence in France between 1785 and 1789 was very useful to his subsequent political rise. It won him opinions as a diplomat and negotiator but, no less important, it kept him out of, and to some extent above, the domestic fray."[118]

That is not to say that Jefferson made the absolute best of his opportunities while abroad. Back in the United States, much to Jefferson's chagrin, the Constitutional Convention was taking place, once again assembled at Philadelphia. As he relied solely on whatever information reached him, Jefferson was upset about the secrecy of the proceedings, writing to Adams, "I'm sorry they began their deliberations by so abominable a precedent as that of tying up the tongues of their members." Jefferson wanted to be part of the process and was distressed that he was being kept in the dark while performing his duties as Minister Plenipotentiary, an ocean away. He concluded his letter to Adams with what can be perceived either as high praise or passive aggressive sarcasm, stating that he was secure of their work because it really was "an assembly of demigods."[119]

The events of 1789 would not only change the course of history in Europe, but also dominated Jefferson's political outlook for years to come. On July 14, 1789, Jefferson witnessed the Bastille fall. Though he did not support the mob mentality of those early days, he did identify with the larger principles of the movement. His opinion of the French Revolution metamorphosed over time. Jefferson originally identified himself as a Lafayette liberal and, like most Americans at the time, he praised the battle of natural law against tyrannical Kings. As the French Revolution ramped up, however, he hesitated in his support, finally recoiling from it in all but original principles.

As Jefferson was influenced by the French Revolution, so too were the French influenced by the American War of Independence. Gilbert du Motier, known in history as the Marquis de Lafayette, was a pivotal figure in advancing liberal ideas in France. The Marquis de Lafayette had two picture frames displayed prominently in his library on the Rue de Bourbon: one frame held a copy of Jefferson's Declaration of Independence, the other lay empty. When visitors asked why the frame was empty, Lafayette responded that the space was reserved for the "French declaration of rights."

When Jefferson first sailed to take up his post as Minister Plenipotentiary, he left a confederacy of United States. When he returned, though, he returned to a United States now federalized under a new Constitution. Upon his return, President Washington appointed Jefferson to be Secretary of State. Jefferson took up his new post in March 1790 in New York, which served as the capital city until a new city could be founded. Almost immediately upon assuming his duties, Jefferson began to worry at what he perceived to be a pseudo-monarchism growing around the Washington administration.[120]

It is not clear whether his suspicion was directed at Washington himself, but most likely it was not.[121] Rather, his fear probably came from what he perceived as a too-courtly administration. He was convinced that a sycophantic entourage was quietly installing a feudal-esque system of aristocracy.[122] As evidence of this, Jefferson cited Adams proposed title for the President, "His Highness, the President of the United States of America, and Protector of their Liberties," which Jefferson called the "most superlatively ridiculous thing I have ever heard of." One of the many gifts Washington's humility gave America was a result of listening to James Madison and selecting the title, "Mister President," making "Mister" the highest rank in America.

When Jefferson became President, he was constantly aware of avoiding any practice that he considered monarchical. He broke with the tradition of delivering the State of the Union in person, a tradition started by Washington and passed down to Adams. Jefferson saw that speech before Congress as too parallel to England's Speech from the Throne, a part of a traditionally lavish affair opening Parliament where the King would appear and read out his agenda. Jefferson, instead, simply delivered his statement, carefully written and revised, to Congress, a practice followed for over 100 years until Woodrow Wilson gave an oral speech in 1913.

Overall, Jefferson's time as Minister Plenipotentiary and, then, as Secretary of State was the perfect rehearsal for his time as President.[123] Not only did the posts provide him the practical skills to maneuver between and influence foreign powers and political rivals, but the postings also allowed him to make mistakes in a setting somewhat insulated from public opinion by the bureaucracy and the towering respect that his boss, George Washington, commanded.

Jefferson was already known as a patriot because of his authorship of the Declaration and participation in revolutionary governance. But his time as Secretary of State proved him to be a master politician, as well. As Secretary of State, Jefferson had three primary goals: (1) to encourage the continuation of the rivalry between Great Britain and France, and to exploit it; (2) to ensure that he acted as a counterweight to Hamilton, who had identified himself with strong British post-war interests; and (3) to continually look to secure American dominance at the frontier, especially toward the Mississippi River, which he knew would be critical for America's westward growth.

The greatest crisis that the United States faced during Jefferson's tenure as Secretary of State was a debt crisis. Although national finances were the concern of the Secretary of the Treasury (Alexander Hamilton), as part of Washington's inner circle—along with Vice President John Adams, Hamilton, and Madison—Jefferson involved himself wherever he thought he could be of use.[124] The question of how to handle debt was one of the first real political battles between Jefferson and Hamilton. Hamilton proposed to consolidate the national debt into a new centrally-controlled federal bank.

Jefferson acknowledged that this made some economic sense, but he took pains to caution against giving Britain too favorable a bargaining position. He understood that such a scheme as Hamilton proposed would give even more power to Britain, who maintained a favorable trade deficit with the United States and owned most of America's debt. Despite Jefferson's reservations, however, Hamilton persuaded him that the question of how to handle debt was not simply a question of politics, finance, and wealth; rather that it was essential to the survival of the nation. Jefferson agreed to broker a deal between Hamilton and Madison, a powerful congressman at the time. The agreement was that Madison and Jefferson would ensure Hamilton got the necessary votes in Congress to pass the statute creating the bank. In return, Hamilton guaranteed that a southern state would be the site of the new capital, a site on the Potomac being the likeliest choice. To mollify Pennsylvania, which was lobbying for the capital itself, it was negotiated that the capital would be in Pennsylvania until the new capital was established.[125] The deal was a boon for Jefferson and Madison, both Virginians. The establishment of a capital city would create contracts and jobs for their constituents—legislative pork began early in American history.

Jefferson's involvement with Hamilton's national bank provides us a lesson. **Always look out for the best interests of your constituents/ clients. But be willing to adjust your position.** It is clear that Jefferson had reservations about the bank. It is equally clear that he wished for the new national capital to be established in Virginia. To get the one he had to give on the other. Jefferson listened to Hamilton's expert plea and found himself willing to change his mind. He balanced his interest in defeating Hamilton's bank against his interest in bringing money, jobs, and power closer to Virginia. Hamilton was surely persuasive in arguing for the bank, and Jefferson likely saw the writing on the wall. So Jefferson saw an opportunity to be seen giving a little. In exchange, he gained a great deal for Virginia—for his state and for his constituents.

To be persuasive, you must be able to absorb new, potentially detrimental information, and **make the best decision based on all the facts. By arguing a losing point, you not only don't help your current case, but you hurt your credibility for the argument sure to come tomorrow.** For Jefferson, getting a capital city built in his back yard was simply the cherry on top.

Jefferson also learned how to control information while Secretary of State. He was perpetually worried about the press, understanding that perception is just as important—if not more important—than reality. He knew that the press could easily undermine his or the Washington administration's power. One of Jefferson's duties was to control news coming out of France. As a French supporter, he ensured that some of the gruesome details of their revolution didn't make it into the American press. He thus controlled perception.

At the same time, however, he made some incredible blunders, despite his agility and adeptness at controlling information. Several times, his "private" letters became public, causing him both personal embarrassment and political turmoil. One such letter, addressed to a printer in Philadelphia, referred to two members of Washington's cabinet as "political heretics" (Adams and Hamilton took offense as the likeliest "two members").[126] That got out. He later wrote to the President himself, apologizing for the letter and claiming that he did not mean to offend the Vice President. That incident widened the rift between his one-time ally, Adams, who rejected Jefferson's claim that he was not the target of the comment.

The lesson here is apparent. **Never write down what you don't want the world to see** (or, as a college professor told me once, "what you don't want your mother to see"). In Jefferson's time, the offensive language had to have taken a particular route to be published to the public—there simply weren't that many avenues for publication. Today, however, the means by which "private" communication can become public are too numerous to name. Plus the line between what is "private" and what is "public" is blurred: what once were private e-mails between you and a work colleague could be part of a Freedom of Information Act request and, therefore, published to the world.

A related lesson drawn from the paragraph above is, simply, **know when to keep quiet** (or, as any number of elementary school teachers tell children every day, "if you don't have anything nice to say, say nothing at all"). Strategically keeping your mouth shut is a key to successfully maneuvering through the political world. One example of this is provided by the Federalists (who named themselves the "Federalists" in order to term Jefferson and his ilk the "Anti-Federalists"), who attempted to curry favor with Britain by coming out heavy-handedly against the citizens of France in claiming their own natural rights. Americans well-remembered their recent struggles against the British and the fervent assertion of the natural rights of Americans. Public sentiment, thus, began to turn against the Federalists. In response, Jefferson did not take the easy route: he didn't just join the mob and kick the Federalists while they were down. Instead, he took a more nuanced stance, painting the Federalist opposition to France as fanatical and unrealistic. And by using Madison as his proxy voice, he was able to remain, in the public's perception, above the fray, maintaining the level of decorum expected of a member of Washington's cabinet.[127]

In 1793, the armies of revolutionary France repelled the invading armies of European monarchs and exclaimed that they would export democracy through revolution "on republican bayonets." America's popular support for France was full-throated, even when King Louis was executed in February 1793—Americans saw the event as the result of "natural justice."[128] Jefferson was ecstatic over the possibility of democracy spreading throughout Europe. He was even more encouraged by the prospect of a close and lasting European ally—alas, this did not come to pass.

America had entered into a treaty with France in 1778; it was a seal of Franco-American fraternity. France had spilled blood and spent gold to help the Americans drive King George out of America.[129] The United States also had a commercial accord with France, "which mandated that French belligerent vessels would receive favored treatment in American ports."[130] These relations were attenuated, however, when President Washington sent diplomats to Britain. Those diplomats were sent to try and end the practice of impression—the practice of British navy ships kidnapping American sailors and impressing them into service—as well as to negotiate for more favorable trading rights with Britain.

Those in the administration who favored Britain argued that the French treaty was made with King Louis, and that, as the King was now headless, the treaty with the monarchical regime was no longer legally binding with the succeeding French revolutionary government. Those who identified themselves as republicans began to form societies and clubs and unofficially recognized Jefferson as their patron.[131] This was, in essence, the beginning of Jefferson's distinct political party, his patronage of which put him forever at odds with the Federalists—most notably, Adams, Hamilton, and Washington.

It was at this critically sensitive time that the inept, but flamboyant, French Ambassador to the United States, Edmond-Charles Genet, arrived and almost single-handedly destroyed public support for France, settling the question of with whom the United States would ally. Genet made a series of truly stunning blunders for a foreign minister. Instead of presenting himself to Washington immediately upon arrival, he tarried in South Carolina to stir up Americans for ventures against the British at sea. He encouraged Kentuckians to fight the Spanish in Florida, which would have helped France but not necessarily America. He commissioned several ships as privateering vessels, including a captured British ship, without so much as revealing the fact to Washington. Each of these actions endangered the carefully crafted neutrality America was playing for with Britain, France, and Spain (itself France's ally). At first, Jefferson ardently supported the Ambassador, but the feckless Genet damaged Jefferson's own prestige and credibility. Jefferson was eventually forced to write to Paris, demanding Genet's recall.[132]

In 1793, Jefferson announced his resignation as Secretary of State, and returned to Monticello. He let it be known that he was intending to abandon his political career for life. In what could be seen as his retirement letter to James Madison, he wrote somewhat despondently,

The motion of my blood no longer keeps time with the tumult of the world. It leads me to seek for happiness in the lap and love of my family, [and] in the society of my neighbors and my books .... What must be the principle of that calculation which should balance against these the circumstances of my present existence—worn down with labors from morning to night, and day to day, knowing them as fruitless to others as they are vexatious to myself; committed singly and in desperate and eternal contest against a host who are systematically undermining the public liberty and prosperity, even the rare hours of relaxation sacrificed to the society of persons in the same intentions, of whose hatred I am conscious even in those moments of conviviality when the heart wishes most to open itself to the effusions of friendship and confidence, cut off from my family and friends, my affairs abandoned to chaos and derangement, in short giving everything I love, in exchange for everything I hate.

Jefferson's time in the Washington administration, clearly, had been "deeply wounding and frustrating."[133] He had, however, learned how to play the political game at the national level. It is not clear if he fully recognized that he had left the government in a quasi-stalemate between the Federalists and the Republicans, between Britain and France, and between the "putative heirs" of President Washington.[134] Most scholars believe the turn of events in France weighed heavily on him. For Jefferson, those events slowly drowned his hope of republicanism spreading via the American Revolution, catching fire in France, and taking off throughout Europe.

Jefferson went back to Monticello and, from all accounts, was serious about his retirement, refusing even, in 1794, to help with negotiations between Spain and the United States. But Jefferson was eventually drawn back into the nation's political life. Although his reasons for venturing back into the public's scrutinous eye are not clear, one reason is likely related to the November 19, 1794, John Jay Treaty between Great Britain and the United States. When the terms of that treaty reached Monticello and the rest of the country, "a huge patriotic and populist reaction was ignited," largely stirred by the Jeffersonian republicans.[135]

Among the treaty's provisions, the British agreed to evacuate certain areas of the Northwest Territories (what are, today, the states of Ohio, Indiana, Illinois, Michigan, and Wisconsin). That provision was already a part of the Treaty of Paris, but British troops had yet to remove from the Territories because, in part, America's own obligations under the Treaty of Paris had yet to be fully honored. The Jay Treaty also lifted some of the trade restrictions between American and British holdings, but did not lift the restrictions on the more lucrative West Indies trade. Most of the disagreements over debts were settled in favor of British creditors by the treaty's provisions. The most egregious aspect of the treaty, however, was not found in the treaty's provisions; rather it was found in what had been ignored. The British refused to address the kidnapping of American seamen and impressing them into British naval service—an omission that later led to the War of 1812.[136]

The treaty certainly boiled Jefferson's political blood. But the event that most likely was the real catalyst in propelling him back into public life was George Washington's retirement. When that announcement was made, every American immediately realized the immensity of the vacuum in leadership, power, and stature his retirement would create.[137]

By all accounts, Jefferson realized that John Adams would be the next president and actually supported the idea. His support was not just because he could not beat Adams, but also because he recognized that the person who immediately succeeded the larger-than-life character of George Washington would never be able to escape his shadow.[138] It is also likely that Jefferson understood popular American sentiment at the time—the Vice President was simply seen as the President in waiting. Jefferson, ever conscience and cautious of popular opinion, did not want to be seen as too eager or ambitious—after all, it was ambition that killed Caesar. Jefferson knew that he would get his turn, but it would not be in the 1796 elections.

The lessons here are important: **Be aware of the political "temperature." You can't persuade an audience if you don't know what that audience does and, importantly, does not want to hear.**

Also, generally, **don't appear overeager,** and **respect that the audience expects certain outcomes.** Appearing overly eager and not giving the audience what they expect, at least to some extent, may earn you the animosity, rather than the support, of those you intend to persuade. This is not to say that you can't change an audience's mind—not at all. It is meant to say that, if an audience expects something to proceed from A to B to C, you need to address that process, at the least, if you don't want to alienate your audience from the start.

Still, when James Madison arranged for Jefferson and Aaron Burr to be the Democratic candidates to run against Adams, Jefferson did not refuse. In 1796, the Twelfth Amendment (providing that the President and Vice President would run on a ticket) had not yet been adopted. Then, electors were chosen by each state legislature, each legislature having two votes. One vote had to be cast for a candidate from another state. The two individuals with the most votes were elected President and Vice President, irrespective of party alliances.

Jefferson, for his part, did not engage much in the election. He did, however, receive a series of vitriolic assaults on his character and politics.[139] Despite the negative "ads" run against him, he easily came in second place, losing to Adams by only three electoral votes. Jefferson was to become the second Vice President of the United States.

JEFFERSON THE VICE PRESIDENT

When George Washington left office, the political landscape became even more fractious. John Adams initially offered an olive branch to Jefferson, proposing that Jefferson accept another prestigious posting to France to repair US–French relations. The French felt betrayed by their fellow revolutionists after the announcement of the Jay Treaty. Jefferson declined that invitation, instead choosing to preside over the Senate, a somewhat powerless, but Constitutionally-provided for, position.

When Jefferson declined to lead the mission, Adams appointed another in his place who, along with two others, sailed for France. By this point, Adams's distrust of the French had morphed into a Nixonesque suspicion or paranoia, foreshadowing the Red Scare 150 years later. Adams saw French spies and sympathizers lurking around every corner. At first, public support was against Adams for promulgating his "Franco Scare." After an obscene diplomatic blunder by the French, though, the public came over to his way of thinking. These events are known, colloquially, as the XYZ affair and led to the first American cold war.

The French Foreign Minister, Talleyrand, through informal agents, demanded tribute (a bribe, simply) before negotiations with the American diplomats could begin. Although such demands were not unheard of in European politics of the late 1700s, the American contingent, relatively new to the "game of thrones" without Jefferson's presence, took offense and left without engaging in formal negotiations. The commission sent its dispatches back to Adams who had them published for the American public's consumption. Though Adams's publication of these dispatches was not the most diplomatic of moves, he did redact the French actors' names, replacing them with X, Y, and Z, though this had the added benefit for Adams of not even offering the French actors the dignity of referring to them by name.

Adams took advantage of the public's outrage over the affair to promote his "spy fever" and expanded the armed forces.[140] Like Senator McCarthy in the late 1940s and 1950s, Adams pushed to have laws passed to seek out the spies, saboteurs, and seditionists he believed were plotting against the fledgling United States. In 1798, Congress passed, and Adams signed into law, the Alien and Sedition Acts. These four bills tightened the conditions for naturalization, authorized the president to arrest and deport aliens posing a national security threat, and criminalized subversive actions aimed at the government. Adams rode this wave of public opinion against the French too far, apparently not realizing that public opinion may change. When it did change and the pendulum of popular opinion swung back to center and beyond, the resulting outrage against these Acts ultimately led to Adams's defeat in his run for a second term. The Alien and Sedition Acts were widely criticized as infringing upon the rights of individual states to act in areas reserved to them by the Tenth Amendment to the Constitution.

Jefferson disagreed with the Acts in principle, but he also recognized the pettiness of Adams's political swipe at him in the statutes themselves. One of the Acts made it a crime to undermine the government or its officers, specifically excluding the office of the Vice President—Jefferson, in person—from its protection. The Acts were unpopular for any number of reasons with the general public, but it was Adams's use of the legislative process for political gamesmanship that appeared to be the most spiteful aspect to most voters. Jefferson understood Adams's conduct as the political move it was. He also knew, however, that his prestige had been seriously tarnished by his unpopular support of France while Secretary of State. He decided, therefore, not to attack the Acts, himself, fearing that any public reprisal on his part would turn the public's ire back toward him and away from Adams. Instead, he used the states as proxies in his personal fight against the Acts and helped both Kentucky and Virginia to pass resolutions that openly denounced the statutes. Those resolutions even called for other states to "annul" the federal legislation. Hamilton, for his part, poured fuel on the fire by suggesting that Adams should march troops into Virginia to take control of the situation, words that surely resonated with the former colonists as reminiscent of those of an English King so recently deposed their side of the Atlantic.

In December 1799, George Washington passed away. The divisions exposed when he left office were only expanded at his death. The Federalist party, especially, felt these divisions widen. And the somewhat downtrodden-of-late Jeffersonian republicans saw this as an opportunity to remake their mark.[141] Meanwhile, in Europe, Napoléon Bonaparte became the undisputed ruler of France. That event, it appears, was the point at which Jefferson no longer felt any alliance with revolutionary France.

The election of 1800 was a defining moment for this nation, signaling a new epoch for the United States.[142] Jefferson was clearly the best choice (vis-a-vis electability) as the Democratic candidate, a point that someone should have disclosed to Aaron Burr, who was also aligned with the Democrats. The early election results made it clear that John Adams would be the first sitting president to be voted out of office, rather than bowing out voluntarily as Washington had done. The real shock was that Aaron Burr actually tied Jefferson in the electoral vote count. That meant that the Federalist-controlled House of Representatives then sitting would choose the next president. After 35 ballots, the House was still stalemated. In the end, it was Hamilton, Jefferson's long-time rival, who decided the fate of the election. Believing that Burr was an active threat to the union—a fact proven later—Hamilton put his political weight behind Jefferson. On the 36th ballot, then, Delaware and South Carolina abandoned Burr and cast blank ballots, Vermont and Maryland abstained, and Jefferson was chosen as the third President of the United States.

Lessons Learned
- Read! Reading is a key to good writing.
- Acknowledge your weaknesses: Conceding a flaw at the start is a great way to earn the trust of your audience. It also is a great way to focus your audience on the strengths of your argument.
- Know your strengths and use hired guns to pick up where those strengths leave off.
- Know when to stubbornly push forward and know when to yield or pivot—obstinately arguing a losing point hurts today's argument and all others down the road.
- Show your vision: demonstrating your vision of the future gives others hope for the future.
- Know when and how to speak. And know when and how best to shut up.
- Remember that mistakes will be remembered, so think and use caution.
- Be calm, especially when the waters around you are not.
- Know when and to whom to pass the reigns—but not the buck.
- Never say what you don't want remembered—and *never write* what you don't want remembered.
- Know the audience's expectations.

4

JEFFERSON THE PRESIDENT

As a teenager, I remember seeing two photographs of the White House side by side. Under one, the caption read, "the night before Richard Nixon resigned as President of the United States"; under the other, "the night after Richard Nixon resigned as President of the United States." The pictures were identical. Even back then, I noticed that there was something missing from those otherwise serene images of the President's home. I noticed that the President was nowhere to be seen. I noticed that the most powerful man in the world was basically removed from office, and I noticed that there was not a single soldier, not a tank, not even a policeman on the grounds.

When John Adams learned that he had lost the election, he simply said to Jefferson, "Well, I understand that you are to beat me in this contest." We can be proud of the American tradition of peaceful transitions of power, something that occurs in this country even when the parties have been in heated opposition. Such peaceful transitions were rarely seen in the world in 1801, and are still rare in much of the world today. Our first presidents—simply by stepping aside for another revolutionary they respected—created a process that has contributed to the greatness and the lasting power of this nation. It may be true that John Adams was not overly cordial, was probably even rude, when he left the capitol before Jefferson was sworn in. The more important fact, however, is that he left, and he left peacefully.

With wounds still so fresh, Jefferson's inauguration address, delivered on March 4, 1801, was a speech of reconciliation. Because of Jefferson's weak voice, most people had to read the speech. Like Abraham Lincoln's second inaugural address, given in the midst of the Civil War, Jefferson's first was a full-faith attempt to ameliorate the political factions and coax them into co-operation. Jefferson said, in part,

> [E]very difference of opinion is not a difference of principle. We have called by different names brethren of the same principle. We are all Republicans, we are all Federalists. If there be any among us who would wish to dissolve this Union or to change its republican form, let them stand undisturbed as monuments of the safety with which error of opinion may be tolerated where reason is left free to combat it. I know, indeed, that some honest men fear that a republican government can not be strong, that this Government is not strong enough; but would the honest patriot, in the full tide of successful experiment, abandon a government which has so far kept us free and firm on the theoretic and visionary fear that this Government, the world's best hope, may by pos-sibility want energy to preserve itself? I trust not. I believe this, on the contrary, the strongest Government on earth. I believe it the only one where every man, at the call of the law, would fly to the standard of the law, and would meet invasions of the public order as his own personal concern. Sometimes it is said that man cannot be trusted with the gov-ernment of himself. Can he, then, be trusted with the government of others? Or have we found angels in the forms of kings to govern him? Let history answer this question.

Even as President, Jefferson distrusted government. But as President, Jefferson gave the nation a unitary focus, something to bring the disparate political groups together and focus the national energy. Jefferson set his sights on nation-building, not in the way that term is used today (that is, supporting foreign nations), but in defeating those who threatened her citizens at the frontiers and abroad and expanding the boundaries of the United States. Five of Jefferson's goals for America came to fruition while he was President: (1) the Barbary Pirates were defeated; (2) New Orleans was secured; (3) America's land holdings were explored; (4) Britain's efforts to keep the United States subjugated were thwarted; and (5) Aaron Burr—a dangerous political rival and constant thorn, generally—was contained and controlled.

PIRATES

The first sentence in *The Marines' Hymn* is an unofficial salute to the Third President of the United States. "*From the Halls of Montezuma to the shores of Tripoli*" is a reference to America's first foreign war, one conceived by Jefferson even while he was in Paris as a young diplomat.

From the 1500s until the time Jefferson took office, it is estimated that over a million Europeans and Americans were kidnapped and sold into slavery by Muslim Autocracies in North Africa. This trade involved ransom and piracy by Barbary pirates who raided the coastal towns of Europe, mostly England and Ireland.[143] The entire population of one such town, Baltimore, was said to have been completely kidnapped or killed in a 1631 raid.

The European solution was to pay tribute to the Barbary powers in exchange for agreements of immunity from their raids.[144] The newly minted American nation could not afford to handle the emergency with such equanimity because it simply did not have the funds to pay; it could not fight against the practice because it simply had no real navy.[145] Trade had declined since the Revolutionary War because relationships with lucrative British trading partners had ended or been strained, which further pinched the purse. That is not even mentioning that some particularly spiteful British elements actually encouraged Barbary attacks on American ships as reprisal for American insolence.

When Jefferson was in Paris, he developed a loathing for not only the pirates themselves but also the European practice of appeasement, which encouraged if not sanctioned the practice outright.[146] In 1784, the American ship, *Betsey*, was captured and its ten crew members were sold into slavery—soon thereafter, the *Dauphin* and *Maria* were also captured. In response, John Adams and Jefferson were ordered to "follow the European example and make treaties with the abductors."[147] They were authorized to borrow money from Dutch bankers to pay the tribute and secure the sailors' release.

When meeting in London with the ambassador of Tripoli, Ambassador Abdrahaman, they were offered a deal for the sailors' release at a staggering price—the Ambassador's stated price for a perpetual peace was even more. The Ambassador did propose that he, as part of the price, sit down with the Americans and broker the negotiation himself. Jefferson asked the Ambassador under what law could Tripoli kidnap Americans and ransom them back to their home country. (The irony is not lost on the reader, I'm sure, that the same question could be asked to Jefferson with regard to black slaves stolen from Africa.) Ambassador Abdrahaman's response is detailed in a letter Jefferson wrote to the Secretary of State, John Jay:

> The Ambassador answered us, that [the aggression] was founded on the laws of their Prophet; that it was written in their Koran, that all nationals who should not have acknowledged their authority, were sinners; that it was their right and duty to make war upon them wherever they could be found, and to make slaves of all they could take as prisoners; and that every Mussulman who was slain in battle was sure to go to Paradise.

A better summary of all that Jefferson loathed both about religion and monarchy could not be described.[148] He recommended that his government refuse to pay the bribe and, instead, raise an American navy. Adams, who was the more senior envoy, agreed that the United States should begin to build a navy, but in the meantime said that it "was wisest for us to negotiate and pay the necessary sum without loss of time." It was then that Jefferson decided that there would someday be a reckoning with the Barbary corsairs.[149] This determination can be seen in Jefferson's unedited first draft of the Declaration of Independence: he accused the King of "piratical warfare, the opprobrium of infidel." The line was cut from the final document, but its place in the first draft gives us a clear reference to Jefferson's odium toward the Muslim Barbary pirates.

The situation with the pirates only worsened from the time Jefferson was in Paris through to his presidency. One positive effect of Adam's Franco-spy-fever was that President Jefferson found himself equipped with a new Navy and a Marine Corps. Jefferson had long thought about how to wreak American justice (or perhaps revenge) on the Barbary powers. He went as far as proposing to capture their sailors and sell them into slavery in retaliation. Jefferson's opportunity to act came almost immediately upon taking office and was in response to the arrogant actions of Tripoli's ruler.

The Pasha, Yusuf Karamanli, sent an ultimatum to the United States, threatening war if an exorbitant tribute was not paid.[150] Karamanli, no doubt, expected the government to simply negotiate the price down, as the European powers did. But he underestimated the new President. Jefferson took the threat as a quasi-declaration of war. With Congress in recess, and only three months after his inauguration, he gave orders to the new American squadron to set sail and make war—the first projection of American power abroad.

Over the next four years, the US Navy, via constant bombardment, pacified the entire Barbary Coast.[151] In February 1804, Captain Stephen Decator sailed the American fleet brazenly into Tripoli's harbor, set fire to the captured American ship *Philadelphia* to prevent it from being used by the pirates, and rescued the *Philadelphia*'s crew. A year later, Captain William Eaton led a detachment of Marines on a march across land and captured Derna, a city under Tripoli's control.[152] This was the first time the American flag flew over foreign soil. It was not long before each of the Barbary States signed treaties promising to stop the practice of piracy and ransom against American vessels and crew.[153]

The lesson here is that there are times when it is best to simply **be bold**. Jefferson acted without a clear legal mandate. Congress was in recess; the Constitution was clear that the President was the Commander-in-Chief; and, although Congress had the power to declare war, this was only a "little war"—and what about those? Jefferson took a chance and did what he thought was right. The Federalist oppositionists did protest his supposed abuse of power, **but it is hard to argue against results**. It just worked out, that time.

Taking chances is sometimes necessary when persuading. One should always remember, however, the maxim, "the bigger they are, the harder they fall." Had Jefferson failed, it could have spelled the end of his presidency altogether. These were the nation's formative years, and it was not unheard of to depose a leader for simple miscalculations. It certainly would have lessened his ability to persuade. Today, we call a president in his second term a "lame duck" because he is on his way out and simply does not have the leverage he had with another election by the masses looming. Jefferson's calculation, if it had missed, would have made him a lame duck and ineffective at persuading congress to vote as he wished and ineffective at persuading the public to perceive world and national events as he wished. In America, it turns out, we just don't trust losers to make the right choice next time.

The point is, if taking a risk is necessary, take measures to make sure you are right. In short, **think first**. They say you should not respond to messages that stir up emotions without waiting 24 hours (they actually say don't send angry e-mails immediately, but I think it holds true where any emotions are involved). Think through the potential consequences. If, after thought, taking the risk is worth it, take the risk. And if you take the risk, own it.

Being persuasive is a critical skill to have, but you may not be able to persuade all people at all times. On occasion, you need to take bold, decisive action, in the face of opposition. At times, you may even be operating outside the true range of your authority. Although you probably shouldn't make a habit of flying in the face of opposition and operating beyond your authority, sometimes, the situation calls for just that. Do think, though. Do plan and, at least, justify your actions beforehand. The risks can be high, but the rewards can be even greater.

The term for this is "leadership." As a prosecutor, I didn't have the ability to take unilateral action and put the "bad guy" in jail on my own initiative, but I did have (and took) the opportunity to "push the envelope" and apply existing laws in new and creative ways, often against the "inertia" of the bureaucracy.

LOUISIANA PURCHASE

A little background is necessary to understand just how the Louisiana Purchase actually happened. It began, to some extent, with the Haitian rebellion, an unprecedented event begun in 1791. A brilliant slave general, Toussaint L'Ouverture, took charge of rebel forces, organized a formidable resistance movement, and formed the first black republic in history. Needing the revenues derived from selling Haiti's sugarcane crop to fuel his imperial ambitions, Napoleon sent a fleet and army to retake the island and quiet unrest in the region.[154] The French forces were annihilated, and Napoleon's plans for French dominion in the Caribbean, crushed.[155]

In 1803, France and Spain entered into a treaty. Among its terms, Napoleon took control of all Spain's holdings in the southeast fringes abutting America. Knowing that Napoleon was desperate for cash, Jefferson seized the moment. He saw an opportunity to secure the Mississippi, which he saw as critical for American prosperity. The President sent envoys to negotiate with Napoleon to purchase New Orleans and, with it, control of the Mississippi. One of the envoys, James Monroe, offered France $10 million dollars for the city of New Orleans. The French countered with $15 million for all of the American territory in France's possession—almost a million square miles. That worked out to be four cents an acre. Jefferson was willing to pay $10 million for control of the mouth of the Mississippi; for only $5 million more, he doubled the size of the United States. The treaty won overwhelming support in the Senate and was easily ratified.

Jefferson saw an opportunity and seized it. The purchase not only increased the size of the United States, but also increased Jefferson's prestige at home. Jefferson understood something that every successful persuader knows—**strike when the iron is hot.** Jefferson negotiated his treaty at what some considered the fringes of his authority; he obligated the United States to spend millions of dollars and then asked the Congress to find a way to make it happen. Given Jefferson's conservative political leanings, he was acutely aware that what he was doing may not have been clearly within his powers. But he knew the value of his actions and trusted that the ends would justify the means.

The opportunity presented itself because Napoleon miss-stepped. Jefferson saw it and knew what to do with it. **Know what you want and recognize when your opponent's own needs can help you get it.** It is much easier to press an advantage than to create one.

LEWIS AND CLARK

The terms of the Louisiana Purchase were not clear as to the boundaries of the territory just acquired. The treaty merely stated that the Missouri River was the northern boundary; just how far the Missouri ran, though, was a mystery. Jefferson wanted to solve that mystery. Unfortunately, the treasury had been depleted by the Louisiana Purchase and the campaign against the Barbary pirates. Jefferson thus knew that an exploration would not be funded unless he included broader goals than mere scientific and geographic study.

Jefferson took the problem of the depleted coffers and turned it to his advantage. He set the parameters of the mission to focus on commerce. With the fur trade booming in the interior of the country, it was an easy argument for Jefferson to make. "The interests of commerce," he said, "place the principal object within the constitution powers and cares of Congress, and that it should incidentally advance the geographical knowledge of our own continent cannot be but an additional gratification." Over some hostility, he was able to secure $2,500 from Congress for the expedition.

Frame the debate as you wish it to be framed. Jefferson saw a problem in having no money to pay for an expedition. So when asking Congress to fund the expedition, he framed the expedition as economic in nature, promising good returns to refill the Treasury. By setting the conversation up in this way, Jefferson effectively shut down the naysayers who would otherwise have raised the bad economics of the expedition. **Anticipate the opposition's arguments, get the first word on those issues, and make that first word what you want it to be.** Then, the opposition is forced to react to what you have said rather than attacking on their own terms.

To lead the momentous mission, Jefferson chose Captain Meriwether Lewis and his close friend, Second Lieutenant William Clark. Before the expedition left, Jefferson ensured that the men had the proper education to fulfill their mission. For example, there is evidence that Jefferson advanced Clark's ability to read and write.[156] He sent Lewis to Philadelphia to study with Jefferson's American Philosophic Society under the tutelage of such remarkable scientists as Dr. Benjamin Rush. There, Lewis was instructed in the rudiments of astronomy, navigation, and the natural sciences.[157] The explorers were introduced to inoculation against smallpox and taught how to reproduce the inoculation so they could teach the technique to the tribes they encountered.

As much of the journey was through territory controlled or populated by the French, Jefferson taught Lewis a code to convey sensitive information. From its inception, the expedition was created as a project of "enlightenment," with one of its goals to share the knowledge acquired from the excursion, rather than a project of attaining knowledge for the power that knowledge conferred.[158]

Politically, the Federalists further damaged their place in American politics by describing the expedition, which was becoming a matter of national pride, as outlandish and akin to searching for mythical giants and monsters.[159] As news updates of this extraordinary trek were being published in the States, the Federalists' censures were publicized to make them look like small thinkers, a task made easier by their earlier critiques of the wildly popular Louisiana Purchase itself.[160]

The lesson here is evident: **don't fight just for the sake of fighting**. Sometimes—often, really—it is much better to remain silent or concede your opponent's successfully landed point than it is to fight tooth and nail on every issue. Not only will fighting on every point seem petty to an audience at large, but it wastes your resources on losing battles. And your battles lost will be perceived as points won by your opponent. A great scene comes to mind as an example: in *A Few Good Men*, a passionate attorney objects to an expert witness's testimony. When the judge overrules her objection, she remains standing, raises her voice, and tells the judge that she "strenuously objects." The judge shouts her down in a great, patronizing manner, overrules her again, and states explicitly that the witness is an expert, giving his own weight and credibility to the witnesses' testimony. Further, by drawing attention to small points and losing those fights, you may actually help your opponent by giving him momentum in the eyes of the audience.

The Federalists did have some legitimate complaints against the Jeffersonians, but their resentment at losing power overshadowed those legitimate complaints. In a too-quick, emotional response, the Federalists forgot that, in order to regain dominance, they had to be perceived as credible and as better alternatives to the Jefferson Republicans. By abandoning reason for partisanship, they lost the public's trust for nearly 30 years. It also appears that they refused to learn from their mistakes—a lesson we all must learn but too often forget. They ridiculed the Louisiana Purchase and were proven wrong. Instead of trying to regroup and attack methodically, they simply attacked the next proposal, the exploration of the land acquired by that purchase—incredibly short-sighted politics.

Lewis and Clark's adventure was officially known as the Corps of Discovery Expedition. And while it was not the first expedition across the continent, it was the first American expedition to cross the western portion of the United States. Lewis and Clark and their band departed in May of 1804 from what is now a suburb of St. Louis, on the Mississippi River. The journey ended in September of 1806 and was hailed as an enormous success. They met their primary objective of exploring and establishing an American presence in the acquired territory, as well as establishing trade with native tribes. The campaign's secondary mission to collect plants and animal specimens was also quite successful. A third effect, though not an objective necessarily, was to popularize exploration and to reinforce in Americans the idea that theirs was a land of boundless opportunity. As Jefferson ended his first term in office, he too was seen as an enormous success.

THE HIGH SEAS

In 1807, the British were little less domineering than they were in 1776. The British maintained that they had the right to capture American civil and military ships to "impress" new sailors in the British Navy. On June 22, 1807, the British HMS *Leopard* fired upon, boarded, and kidnapped four crew members. One of the crew members was a British Navy deserter, the other three were American citizens who had fled from being impressed into Royal service and were retaken. The deserter was hung as a traitor; the other three were forced to enlist in the British Navy. Jefferson, along with the American public and Congress, was outraged by the mistreatment. He easily could have asked for and received a declaration of war because of the popular outcry. Instead, however, he decided to be patient, understanding that further British aggression could be tempered by Napoleon's successes in Europe.

Despite his recent successes and the high regard in which he was generally held at that particular point in time, he was remarkably levelheaded about his own limited powers on the international stage: "I suppose our fate will depend on the successes or reverses of Bonaparte. It is really mortifying that we should be forced to wish success to Bonaparte and to look to his victims for our salvation." But as he said, the British Navy was "as tyrannical at sea as [Napoleon] was on land." He resolved to play for the long game. He prepared for an eventual war against Britain, but waited to see just how the conflict between Britain and France played out.

There are two lessons that we might learn from Jefferson's handling of this issue. First, **try to avoid conflict when your opponent is at his strongest.** Second, **don't engage in battle needlessly; if your opponent might be "taken down" by another, let him.** Both lessons are made more impressive considering that Jefferson chose not to act at a time when he could seemingly do no wrong. Many who experience success get into the mindset that they can conquer anything. Often, those people fall far and hard because they have grown more and more accustomed to gambling with bigger and bigger stakes at each success. Recognize reality as distinct from perception. And recognize that luck plays its part as well.

Rather than acting rashly, Jefferson began to develop the system of resistance that would "stamp his closing years in office" when, in December of 1807, he asked Congress to pass the Embargo Act.[161] He had seen economic warfare's effectiveness during his time in the House of Burgesses (the colony had refused to import goods from any British merchant). The Act made it illegal to export any goods from the United States to Britain or France. The goal was to force both Great Britain and France to respect American neutrality during their wars. By using economic coercion and by punishing British and French merchants, the theory ran, pressure would be put on the governments to respect American rights.

The embargo may seem like an extreme measure, but French war ships were seizing American cargo and the Royal Navy, which also seized American goods as incidental to war, actually increased their use of impressment. It is estimated that over 10,000 American sailors were kidnapped and forced onto warships (a huge number, considering that America's population was fewer than six million, including slaves). To Jefferson, these were extreme problems that called for extreme measures.

The bill passed Congress quickly, which is a testament to the influence of the Democratic Party and not the law's popularity; it was, in fact, highly unpopular. Ports in New England were almost entirely shut down and the regional economy went into a depression. When the ban was ignored along the Canadian border, Jefferson went a step further, pushing to have the Enforcement Act passed in 1808. This law enforced the embargo of all American goods carried by land or sea, regardless of destination, and mandated that port authorities were to seize cargoes without a warrant and prosecute the merchant that attempted to violate the embargo.

The success of the embargo is a question for historians to debate. It did have a terrible effect on the US economy, maybe more so than it helped by hurting Britain and France. But it also had an unforeseen positive advantage; it forced the United States, which previously had an economy based mostly on producing raw materials, into the world of manufacturing. This switch in focus not only directly helped certain states (Pennsylvania was a big beneficiary) but also sparked what would become the American industrial revolution, which radically transformed the entire country and, in fact, the world.

Politically, the embargo was a stain on Jefferson's presidency. Not only did it highlight the hypocrisy of Jefferson's arguing for a government with little intervention while his policies gave his government extraordinary powers, it also weakened his entire party and gave strength to the Federalists, who had all but been extinguished by that point. Before leaving office, Jefferson signed the repeal of the Embargo. After James Madison won the election, the Embargo Act was replaced with the much-diluted Non-Intercourse Act, which was signed into law as the last act of President Jefferson and allowed for some trade so long as it was not with France or Great Britain.

AARON BURR

An entire book could be written about the complex relationship between Thomas Jefferson and Aaron Burr. Burr, a man who lives in American infamy, killed the bigger-than-life Alexander Hamilton in an illegal duel and was later tried for treason—the retelling makes him almost into a caricature of a villain. At the same time, though, he was a darling of the Democratic Party, serving as its first Vice President. This is, of course, not even to mention that he was a revolutionary war hero.

For Jefferson, however, Burr was nothing but bad news. Jefferson knew that Burr was unpredictable. Jefferson compared him to "a crooked gun or other perverted machine, whose aim you could never be sure of." Yet, despite this, to Jefferson's detriment, it was not until 1804 and his second run for office that he distanced himself from Burr—and by that point it was too late.

After Burr killed Hamilton, on July 11, 1804, Burr's days in politics were over (two indictments were issued for his arrest), but his scheming had only just begun. It is likely that this is when Burr decided to lead a secessionist revolt in the Western States. Burr approached Merry, the British Ambassador who Jefferson had scorned when Jefferson was first in office, and made a case for British support. Essentially, the plan was for Burr to lead a force with British help, to take Florida from Spanish control, and then to invade Mexico. This would have been a blow to Jefferson, who had plans to acquire Florida for the United States, and it would have destabilized Jefferson's plan to establish American dominion over the Louisiana Territory.

In 1805, Burr set out on a mission of reconnaissance and made plans for rebellion. He reported to Merry that if they did not take advantage of his scheme, he would reach out to the French. Evidently, the British were more concerned with Napoleon's endeavors in Europe than in America, because Merry was unable to convince London to dedicate vessels to Burr's plan. Burr also involved General Wilkinson, who commanded American forces in the Southwest of the United States. However, after his plot was discovered (likely by General Wilkinson notifying Jefferson after he calculated that Burr's plan was unlikely to succeed) in November 1806, Jefferson issued a presidential order to arrest Burr for treason.

Jefferson erred, though, by reporting to Congress that Burr's guilt was "placed beyond question," something he would regret saying before long.

Chief Justice John Marshall, a longtime Jefferson rival, was the presiding judge in Burr's trial. Almost as soon as the trial began, Marshall threw out the most serious charge of treason, finding that, because there was no direct testimony concerning the overt act, the charge was impossible to prove. The partial dismissal emboldened Burr. Burr then subpoenaed President Jefferson as a witness to the remaining charge that he had conspired to invade the territory of a friendly Mexico. Marshall granted the subpoena request. Jefferson was furious at the legal gamesmanship of all this, and so refused to appear (this was the first time Executive Privilege was invoked). The law was not settled on the matter of noninterference with a friendly power, and the jury who faced the legal ambiguity returned a verdict of "not proven to be guilty under this indictment by any evidence submitted to us."

Two lessons can be drawn from Jefferson's interactions with Burr. First, **don't overstate your case.** Jefferson lost some credibility by offering that a guilty verdict for Burr was a foregone conclusion. He also erred by setting the public standard so high. Jefferson's words gave the Congress and the jury pool one idea about Burr's guilt. What came out at trial, however, gave the jury a very different idea. When faced with competing and, in fact, contradictory stories, your audience is forced to either agree or disagree with your version wholly, leaving little room for nuanced persuasive techniques to have their proper effect.

Second, **your reputation and, thus, your credibility are built not only upon your own deeds but also on the deeds of those with whom you associate.** While this surely isn't fair, it is fact. An argumentum ad hominem may be a fallacy, but it can still be very persuasive, especially to the masses. It is clear from Jefferson's correspondence that he had never trusted Burr. Still, his long association with Burr made Jefferson seem like a political schemer like any other. That idea not only tarnished Jefferson's reputation but it allowed people to dismiss many of his better-intentioned actions as mere scheming, as well.

JEFFERSON THE STATESMAN AND EDUCATOR

The French philosopher, Joseph De Maistre, said, "every nation has the government it deserves." In December 1807, Thomas Jefferson announced that he would not be a candidate for a third term, leaving the nation's leadership to others. He never left Virginia again. He focused on his passions for agriculture and the improvement of his beloved Monticello. A longtime political animal, he did not remain completely out of public life: improving higher education occupied his final years. Christopher Hitchens described what the University of Virginia meant for Jefferson: "[t]he University . . . culminated . . . the proselytizing interest in general education that he had shown when he was a young Virginian politician. I choose the word *proselytizing* deliberately, because it was his plain intention to found a campus that would be independent of all priests and denominations."[162] The architectural style was that of Palladian, derived and inspired by the Venetian architect, Andrea Palladio. He insisted there would be no chairs of divinity or theology, and, while Christianity would be taught as part of the curriculum, it would be taught as part of the study of evolution and ethics.[163]

Jefferson sought professors from around the world and reserved only the chair of law and government for an American scholar. In 1825, when his *tour de force* was finally completed, he said, "this institution will be based on the illimitable freedom of the human mind. For here we are not afraid to follow truth where it may lead, nor to tolerate any error so long as reason is left free to combat it."

His dedication to education in his later years is also demonstrated by his transfer of his impressive personal library to Congress after the British burned their collection in the War of 1812. Jefferson put his money where his mouth was and sold virtually his entire library, which the *National Intelligencer*, a prominent D.C. newspaper at the time, noted, "for its selection, rarity and intrinsic value, is beyond all price." Some have criticized Jefferson for this sale because he received $23,950 for the books. They argue that, because of his perpetual debt problems, it was not at all an altruistic act. But if one understands how much a bibliophile like Jefferson valued his library—truly a life's work to assemble—it would be clear that this was likely one of the most difficult and generous decisions Jefferson ever made. Jefferson believed down to his bones that "an educated citizenry is a vital requisite for our survival as a free people," and that an educated Congress was, of course, key to that formula.

Jefferson's mission to educate also included religious education, but not in the traditional sense. He did write that he had no opinion on his neighbors' belief systems because "it does me no injury for my neighbor to say there are twenty gods or no God. It neither picks my pocket nor breaks my leg." But he was openly aggressive toward what he considered religious oppression. When he was elected in 1800, he was attacked by what we would call today the "religious right," who called him an atheist. Despite the religious freedom this nation was founded upon, a charge such as "atheist" was still pretty damning. Jefferson returned fire, writing that "the returning good sense of our country threatens abortion to their hopes, and [the clergy] believe that any portion of power confided to me, will be exerted in opposition to their schemes." Jefferson assured his opponents that their fears were correct, concluding that "they believe rightly; for I have sworn upon the altar of God, eternal hostility against every form of tyranny over the mind of man."

Jefferson went further than mere political banter. He "was resolved to write about the life of Jesus, separating fact from myth and allowing for the distortions of legend and the exaggerations of oral history, and thus to arrive at something like an ethical minimum."[164] Jefferson published *The Philosophy of Jesus* in 1805, which its cover described as "an abridgement of the New Testament for the use of the Indians." Near the end of his life, he went further with this project, writing, "I have performed this operation for my own use, by cutting verse by verse out of the printed book, and by arranging the matter which is evidently His, and which is as distinguishable as diamonds in a dunghill." This version was published in 1820 as *The Life and Morals of Jesus of Nazareth, Extracted Textually from the Gospels* and is now known colloquially as *The Jefferson Bible*. In this version, he excised any mention of angels, miracles, and even the resurrection, and intended the book to sift out reason from faith.[165] His goal was to educate its readers of the glory of Jesus's genius as a man before his time, a philosopher, and a teacher.

As Jefferson was preparing to leave Washington, he wrote a friend and described his feelings about leaving public office for good. In a powerful passage showing, again, the unique nature of peaceful transitions of power in the United States, he wrote,

But all these concerns I am now leaving to be settled by my friend Mr. Madison. Within a few days I retire to my family, my books and farms; and having gained the harbor myself, I shall look on my friends still buffeting the storm, with anxiety indeed, but not with envy. Never did a prisoner, released from his chains, feel such relief as I shall on shaking off the shackles of power. Nature intended me for the tranquil pursuits of science, by rendering them my supreme delight. But the enormities of the times in which I have lived, have forced me to take a part in resisting them, and to commit myself on the boisterous ocean of political passions. I thank God for the opportunity of retiring from them without censure, and carrying with me the most consoling proofs of public approbation. I leave every thing in the hands of men so able to take care of them, that if we are destined to meet misfortunes, it will be because no human wisdom could avert them. Should you return to the United States, perhaps your curiosity may lead you to visit the hermit of Monticello. He will receive you with affection and delight; hailing you in the mean time with his affectionate salutations, and assurances of constant esteem and respect.

To understand the immensity of Jefferson's Presidency, one cannot look at a single year or a single event; it must be examined in its totality from start to finish. In 1800, the United States had just over five million residents. That same year, Great Britain had 15 million residents; France, roughly 27 million. With two centuries of European–American history preceding him, "the land was still untamed; forest covered every portion, except here and there a strip of cultivated soil; the minerals lay undisturbed in their rocky best, and more than two thirds of the people clung to the seaboard."[166] By the time Jefferson left office, however, the nation was building canals, great rivers were opened to navigation and connected by roads, universities were built, the nation nearly doubled in size, the Barbary pirates were smashed, and the road to the industrial revolution was mapped. Jefferson had ushered America across a bridge from a settlement of loosely connected colonies into nationhood.[167]

Lessons Learned
- Know what you want and recognize when your opponent's own needs can help you achieve it.

- Frame the debate as you wish it to be framed: Anticipate the opposition's arguments, get the first word on those issues, and make that first word what you want it to be.
- Try to avoid conflict when your opponent is at his strongest.
- Don't engage in battle needlessly; if your opponent might be "taken down" by another, let him.
- Don't overstate your case.

5

SKILL, PASSION, AND VISION

Thomas Jefferson's ability to persuade came from his skills as a writer, his passion for his ideals, and his vision for the future. He was a model idealist who seized upon the drafting of the Declaration and the revolutionary cause to change the fundamental assumptions of the human endeavor the world over. Jefferson looked at the process of writing much as an artist looks at a blank canvas. He knew that the words he chose were not ends, but means to greater ends achievable only by reaching and convincing his audience. He invested his words with lyrical power, and he structured his words to make them impactful. Much as a piece of classical music will start with a single violin and end with the power of a full orchestra, Jefferson's prose could begin simply and then soar, stirring his audience's emotions to his will. In this chapter, we look at Jefferson's skills, passion, and vision, and examine how we can replicate those traits to become more persuasive writers ourselves.

SKILL

Jefferson had a knack for words, to say the least. He understood that words matter, that labels matter. When he was in a political battle with those he perceived as "the elites," he chose to label them as "aristocrats" and "Anglomaniacs" (i.e., someone who excessively admires English customs). He chose these words because of their roots in the feudal ruling system. He knew the baggage those terms carried with them. He knew their connotations would resonate with the public as words of regal rule, implying that these new elites were just new versions of the rulers cast out by the Revolutionary War. The Anglomaniacs were the British sympathizers (and worse) that American brothers, sons, and husbands fought and died to secure the nation's freedom. When it came to describing his opponents party, the Federalists—he labeled them "the party of England."[168]

Akin to the lesson of framing the debate, the lesson here is to **use the terminology that best advances your position.** Choosing labels for your opponents and the issues with just the right nuances in meaning is the first step in persuading an audience that yours is the right path and the other is just that—other, foreign, less than your own.

Jefferson's use conjured historical elements, giving them weight beyond the current parameters of the debate. By associating his opponents with the hated British, the baggage the British legacy carried with it was implicitly carried onto the backs of the Federalists. Once that link was made in his audience's minds, Jefferson had to say little more on the issue as the audience was now predisposed to link the Federalists with that British legacy and its attendant history of malfeasance.

Historically-charged labels can be very powerful, echoing in the minds of your audience long after the piece is read or the speech is heard. We must all be careful, however, not to overuse such labels for fear of losing the effect. We must also **be careful not to use terms with too much baggage**. For example, in debates involving human rights abuses, persecution, religious freedom, and any number of other issues, it is not uncommon to hear someone make the inevitable comparison to Nazi Germany or the Holocaust. Unless there is actual genocide occurring, however, such a comparison or labels as Hitleresque generally do more harm than good to the author's position. That is so because that comparison is too often made—and audiences know that—and because terms such as those are much too politically charged in the vast majority of cases.

Jefferson also had the advantage of being naturally pithy, a powerful skill for any persuasive writer. He was great at the "hook," that line that catches a reader's eye and makes him want to keep reading. "We hold these truths to be self-evident, that all men are created equal, that they are endowed by their Creator with certain unalienable rights, that among these are Life, Liberty, and the Pursuit of Happiness." Does it get better than that? Jefferson took somewhat novel concepts and set them down clearly and concisely as facts. His evocative summarization of philosophic notions crystallized ideas that had been developing in the public debate in much rougher terms. Thus, he took an "already mobilized" audience and focused their ideas by his inexorable logic and the momentum of his delivery.[169] Jefferson draws the reader into the Declaration with a high-minded, deceptively modest, and polite preamble, then roundly declares that the truths to follow are "self-evident."[170]

Jefferson's almost lyrical prose allowed his works to be memorized and read aloud on street corners throughout the colonies. This is one of the most difficult skills for the aspiring persuasive writer to develop: **Write for the reader.** We should write so the reader wants to read on. For Jefferson, that meant utilizing his natural abilities. For the rest of us, that means understanding what our audience expects in terms of both substance and form, and giving it to them. It means reading the works of good writers and practicing emulating the styles you like.

Jefferson's style was also very effective because of the times in which he wrote. Because his works were easily memorized and read aloud on street corners, his words reached a huge number of people from those corners. His style thus made him more popularly known than most writers of his day.

The style of the preamble to the Declaration honored the expectation that a gentleman should be courteous. Jefferson then set the boundaries of his argument and followed that with his list of grievances. This evolution made the Declaration powerful because Jefferson moved the reader from gentlemanly manners through to a listing of grievances every colonist recognized.

Students of history have long admired Jefferson's persuasive style of indulging in sentimental idioms. He complemented this skill and style with a powerful imagination and passion for the written word. Unlike most writers of his time—Madison for example, who was a master at deliberative and direct writing—Jefferson was always concerned with style.[171]

A key lesson is that **persuasive writing involves more than simply delivering information effectively**, though that is certainly important. **It also involves delivering and evoking the right emotions.** Jefferson would use nuanced, meaningful words, charging them with feeling by the context in which he used them. While Madison was valued for his candor in writing, Jefferson was valued for his ability to inspire others with his vision.[172] And he inspired others by his word choices and the sheer force of his writing. It was a driving force for Jefferson to construct the right sense of our nation and, at that, Jefferson's skill was unmatched in his time.[173]

There is no doubt that Jefferson had the ability to use powerful emotional language, but he also knew how and when to tone it down—he knew when boring was better. In his *Summary View of the Rights of British America*, he explored the legal theory that the American Englishman and the Englishman living in England were equals and based that appeal on ancient tribal history, on cold logic. Specifically, he argued that, because the ancient Saxon settlers of England had voluntarily removed themselves from the main continent, and because Americans had voluntarily removed themselves from the home island, both peoples had established self-ruling autonomous societies.[174] In the case of both migrations, the rights of the people came with them. There-fore, the inherent rights of Americans could not be forfeited to the King any more than they could have been surrendered by the preceding Saxons to Germany.[175]

To Jefferson, an Englishman was an Englishman—anywhere. Once he es-tablished this basis of reasoning, Jefferson was able to demonstrate that the King was treating two groups of people, who he had proven had equal rights, by different standards. He levied taxes without the legislative consent of the taxed, he restricted commerce, and he extended the jurisdiction of remote courts to pass judgment upon Americans.[176] He then pointed to the people of Boston who had been penalized for asserting their rights as Englishmen, stating that they were "devoted to ruin, by that unseen hand which governs the momentous affairs of this great empire." Jefferson was clear in his interpretation of the ancient laws of England. He knew that the liberties enjoyed by the original Saxons were not lost by the invasion of William the Conqueror at Hastings in 1066. Rather, he pointed out, the "whole of subsequent English history had been a slow but inexorable battle to reaffirm those same rights," citing to the 1215 Magna Carta and the forcible suppression of the English King's claim to divine rights as evidence of his analysis.[177]

That *Summary* showcases Jefferson's unemotional, logical analytical techniques, with which he was equally able to persuade, though to a different audience and on different points than his popular appeals. That *Summary* had its intended effect on his intended audience. **A persuasive speaker should always care more about the *effects* of her words than the *style* in which they are presented.** Sometimes a simple, somewhat boring, written argument will go further than a much more forceful one written as if it should be shouted to the masses. There is a time and place for many things: sometimes the most effective communication is the powerful, evocative argument; sometimes working "under the radar" will be the most persuasive strategy.

Where did Jefferson learn this skill of persuasive writing? He obviously had significant natural talent, but he also sought out other persuasive authors and absorbed the lessons they had to teach. At the time, Jefferson had one of the most extensive and diverse libraries on the continent.[178] He loved books, viewing them as some of life's greatest treasures and their content as the key to elevation. He constantly searched books for new and different perspectives, evaluating issues from all angles. He would reach out not only to older intellects but also to younger men with different life experiences. Each, he knew, could bring a unique perspective and new information to bear on matters that, but for his constant search for knowledge, would have remained foreign to him.[179]

Jefferson was more than just an insatiable reader; he was also an exceptional record-keeper. He would write down passages from his favorite authors and reread them until he had them committed to memory. He kept virtually every letter he received and even made copies of ones he had written. Jefferson often reused passages he had written that he found especially worthy.

The lesson here is that **if cutting and pasting was good enough for Thomas Jefferson, it should be good enough for us**—especially as it is much easier than it was in Jefferson's quill pen era. Sometimes, the thing you want to say has been said so perfectly, so succinctly, so eloquently, that to change it would only do your position harm. If you wrote the passage to end the writing of all new passages on a subject, by all means reuse it. If those words were written by another, by all means use those, too—just cite them. In fact, citing an author who is especially well-known and respected in a field will only lend credence to your argument as it shows you do not stand alone on the position. In short, don't be afraid to ride the coattails of another's credibility.

Thomas Jefferson also kept track of the details of the goings on of the government while Secretary of State, Vice President, and President. Reflecting upon these notes aided his understanding of the finer points of the administration he worked for and eventually those of his own administration. Keeping track of the details and reviewing them for opportunities to improve is also a sign of good leadership—and good leadership requires the ability to persuade above almost all other skills.

Jefferson's leadership did not rest entirely on his persuasive ability, though. We will read in the next chapter that Jefferson had a petty side; he was often vindictive and could hold a grudge. However, Jefferson was also known for appreciating candor from his subordinates, even inviting officers into his inner circle whose opinions differed greatly from his own. As a lawyer, he gained the ability to avoid personal conflicts with other attorneys, despite the adversarial system. He was also able to mend wounds necessarily inflicted and deal with strong egos. And this was in the legal community—where it is well-known that attorneys' egos are huge. Today's legal community is known for its gladiator, no-holds-barred style. In Jefferson's time, gentlemanly manners often ruled, but in politics, especially, those manners could easily give out, requiring an ability to assuage the ill-will held on both sides of an argument.

Attorneys, especially, can learn a lot from Jefferson here. **You can represent your client zealously without stepping on your brothers and sisters of the bar.** At the least, you can step lightly on your brothers and sisters and then apologize profusely (and sincerely) afterward. The nature of opposition makes it somewhat difficult to mix cordially with opponents. Being able to do just that, however, as Jefferson knew and practiced, expands your horizons and makes you a better opponent in the future.

Jefferson's legal training and practice taught him to think of his client first and his own ego second; as President, his client was the nation. Jefferson's appointments to his cabinet show his selfless dedication to the good of the country. This aptitude for containing his own ego for the good of the cause may be the most difficult skill for anyone to master. When he was first elected, Jefferson knew that the country was in the middle of a political awakening: it was the first time power transferred to a different party. More than that, it was a transfer to a party that held very different ideas on how to govern and the very nature of American government itself.

Realizing the politics at play, Jefferson ensured that his cabinet was filled with quality individuals, regardless of affiliation. He also made sure that his personal feelings did not interfere with the process of selecting the best individuals for the posts.

The lesson is obvious: **never let your personal feelings interfere with doing the job.**

To distinguish his administration from that of John Adams from day one, Jefferson let it be known that no office would be given to even distant relatives.[180] This demonstrates Jefferson's commitment to the business proverb that first-rate people hire first-rate people and second-rate people hire third-rate people. Jefferson would have understood and supported General von Hammerstein's eponymous adage about leadership:

> I divide my officers into four classes; the clever, the lazy, the industrious, and the stupid. Each officer possesses at least two of these qualities. Those who are clever and industrious are fitted for the highest staff appointments. Use can be made of those who are stupid and lazy. The man who is clever and lazy however is for the very highest command; he has the temperament and nerves to deal with all situations. But whoever is stupid and industrious is a menace and must be removed immediately!

In addition to ensuring that the best people filled his administration, Jefferson banished protocols and systems of formalities that Washington and Adams paid such close attention to, seeing them as forms of subjugation.[181] To Jefferson, pomp and circumstance ranked well below merit and quality of character. He also simply hated those customs that reminded him of British monarchy and domination. By removing the customary formalities passed down from ancient structures—ranks, titles, and degrees—Jefferson was able to weaken the entire edifice of his era's hierarchies.[182]

Through his appointment policy and removal of ornamentation and ostentation from the Office of the Presidency, Jefferson strengthened the Republican Party. The crucible of politics burned away the old system in which gentlemen ruled those below from ivory towers. This movement turned into a national party.[183] Jefferson's opponents lashed out at all of Jefferson's policies, even the ones they once supported. They often resembled the boy who cried wolf, criticizing his administration in such hyperbolic terms that their criticisms actually gave Jefferson and his officers little reason to try and work with them—and political cover for not doing so.[184] Yet Jefferson still attempted, publicly at least, to stay above the fray. And that gave him an aura of dignity as rare in politics then as today.

We will see in the next chapter that, many times, Jefferson failed to stay above the mudslinging. But at a time when partisan politicians were described as "ravenous wolves," Jefferson did his best to lead the nation by persuading those in Congress and the American people to buy into his vision for a greater America.[185]

PASSION

The key to Jefferson's ability to persuade was his passion for his cause. In 1813, he said of Meriwether Lewis's trek across the nation, "Of courage undaunted, possessing a firmness & perseverance of purpose which nothing but impossibilities could divert from its direction, careful as a father of those committed to his charge, yet steady in the maintenance of order . . . I [had] no hesitation in confiding the enterprise to him." Even from this single passage, we feel the power of his convictions come through these words. From those words, his utter and total belief in what the expedition had accomplished is apparent.

Jefferson, above all things, wrote for his audience. Then, as today, Americans appreciate leaders with passion. Jefferson did not write as he did to cater to the masses, explicitly, but he did write what he earnestly felt *to* them. Even in a writing to Robert Livingston, detailing how Livingston was to treat with Napoleon regarding Louisiana and New Orleans, Jefferson wrote with a larger audience in mind. He knew from experience that the letter could find its way into American newspapers and so ensured that the letter was written with both American and French readers in mind. His letter was passionate, yet resolute, his logic clear and thorough. That letter suggested that France cede Louisiana to the United States to eliminate any possibility of war between the two nations. The letter went further, boldly and passionately declaring that, if France landed troops in New Orleans, the US Navy would "marry" itself to the "British fleet and nation" with the goal of sinking every single French ship.[186] Jefferson evoked the ghost of the American Revolutionary War to drive home the point that this was a serious matter to the United States, one that she would fight for, when he wrote that "perhaps nothing since the revolutionary war has produced more uneasy sensations through the body of the nation."

This letter was exactly the type of blunt talk that Americans wanted in their new president.[187] It also carried weight because it was based in reality and was supported by facts known to the key players in the audience. Jefferson knew that Napoleon's forces were crushed in Haiti and that he could not reconquer that colony, let alone fully occupy New Orleans. Thus, the letter gave Napoleon an out—a politically feasible means to abandon a losing fight and while appearing to have gained something at home. Napoleon knew that, if the United States joined forces with Britain, they could sink every French military and merchant vessel. The bottom line was that Napoleon could not defend what he owned—France would lose Louisiana.[188] The letter presented a great case for its sale.

Part of Jefferson's genius in writing came from his ability to know, and write to, his audience. Even when the audiences were complex, Jefferson was able to turn the right phrase and use the right words. In the case of the Livingston letter, it was written with very different parties in mind—both Napoleon's ministers and average American citizens—and it hit the mark with both audiences. Jefferson wrote so that each reader saw what he wanted to see in the letter. Decades later, Mark Twain observed, "The difference between the almost right word and the right word is really a large matter—it's the difference between the lightning bug and the lightning."

Jefferson's passionate writing was also effective in other ways. When Boston was occupied by British forces at the cusp of the war, Jefferson and his fellow members of the Virginia House of Burgesses called for a day of fasting and prayer to show their support. He issued a plea to the colonies to be of "one heart and one mind" in answering "every injury to American rights."[189] The passion of that plea had the intended effect, and the Royal Governor of Virginia dissolved the legislative body shortly thereafter—highlighting the unfair treatment of "American Englishmen."

VISION

In an age of imperialism, Jefferson was motivated by the vision of building a great American empire.[190] He developed grand goals and, through his writings, he projected his will onto the nation. From conception, he envisioned a United States that would stretch from one great ocean to the other.

A persuasive writer must have vision—goals to focus her writing. Sometimes, goals are ambitious and grand (e.g., declaring independence from the most powerful nation in the world) and sometimes goals are small, but all need to be articulated if they are to be achieved. Articulating your goals will focus your writing. Each writing can then serve as an incremental step toward that large or smallish goal.

Jefferson's vision for the nation was something he recognized at our founding. Every policy he suggested, every paper he drafted, was directed, to some extent, toward continental dominance and westward progression. Early in his career, he suggested westward territories be brought gradually into the union (although, thankfully, his suggested state names of Cherronesus, Assenenisipia, and Metropotamia were rejected).[191]

Jefferson's vision grew from his intellectual curiosity. Dr. Samuel Latham Mitchell, a prominent member of society and congressman, stated that Jefferson was "more deeply versed in human nature and human learning than almost the whole tribe of the opponents and revilers."[192] Jefferson had an omnivorous curiosity and was known for his "enlightened enthusiasm and liberal views."[193] He was a scientist first and a politician second. His studies included botany, crop cycles, and zoology. His curiosity drove him to take copious notes on his observations, which led to inventions, such as a new plow head that could cut deeper into the soil. He discovered early on that tobacco farming was devastating to the land and so experimented with ways to improve the harvest and heal the soil. He was "fascinated by the invention of air balloons, which he instantly saw might provide a new form of transport as well as a new form of warfare."[194] In a time of rampant pseudoscience, Jefferson was able to see through many of the quackeries (save for his own views on slavery) and advocate positions based on science. One such cause was his support for the smallpox vaccine, which he had administrated to all comers at Monticello.[195]

Jefferson's intellectual curiosity only added to his ability to persuade. From his days as an attorney, he was respected for his thought, preparation, and writing. From his days working toward independence, he was respected as a patriot. And from his days in politics, he was respected as a leader and worldly diplomat. But his insatiable need for knowledge earned him respect across disciplines. Jefferson could speak from immense knowledge in any number of fields, from botany to architecture to law. The lesson we should all take from this aspect of Jefferson's character is to **never stop learning**.

History knows the third President as the one who transformed the democratic process, the author of the Declaration of Independence, an ardent advocate for religious freedom, and the one who acquired and explored the Louisiana Territory.[196] Perhaps his greatest gift, though, was the vision he imparted to our nation. Each of the achievements listed above are products of his imagination and vision.[197] It was his vision for America that drove him to dismantle the old social order, to the horror of the Federalist regime, and teach the people who were disenfranchised that they were not, by God's nature, doomed to that fate.[198]

His vision built a political program on the foundation of enlightenment, self-improvement, and independence from an intrusive government.[199] He said on the latter topic, "We both consider the people as our children, and I love them with parental affection. But you love them as infants who you were afraid to trust with nurses, and I adults whom I freely leave to self-government." Jefferson's imagination assumed that Americans were innately benevolent and would naturally flourish. All that was needed, he thought, after shedding the yoke of the British Empire, was to abandon the colonial tradition of "gentlemen" monopolizing power under the guise of parenting the people.[200] In Jefferson's words, he sought to develop a "system by which every fibre would be eradicated of ancient or future aristocracy, and a foundation laid for a government truly republican."

The Federalists, to show some contrast, would have designated the clergy to articulate national values and thought that "proper" families would provide leaders to the nation.[201] Jefferson, on the other hand, taught his followers to ask themselves what the national values ought to be and to look to themselves for the nation's leadership. Jefferson was proud of the climate of political empowerment he had helped to create. He would "impress" foreign visitors by ensuring newspapers that were critical of him were on display around the White House. When they would question the audacity of the press to criticize a sitting president, he would tell his visitor to take the paper and "show [it to your countrymen] and tell them where you found it."

Jefferson's writing was truly beyond his time; he addressed the nature of civilization and the psychological poverty that was a result of British rule.[202] But it was not all talk for Jefferson; he put his political vision to the test, "arriving at a lively and quotable manner of presentation as he made the embrace of liberty a daring proposition. Less well-known in his pique: severe and judgmental in private communication, Jefferson spoke his mind to his friends but refused to debate his adversaries in public."[203] As always, he knew his true strength lay in his manipulation of the written word, not the oral debate so popular among his contemporaries.

Jefferson was courageous in his stance against religious radicalism and subjugation, even editing his own bible, which was something unheard of at the time (and still not something altogether encouraged). Jefferson was a leader in the field of crime and punishment reform and was heavily influenced by Cesare Beccaria's *Dei delitti e delle pene* (On Crimes and Punishment), published in Milan in 1774. In 1778, he put forward a "Bill of Proportion in Crimes and Punishments" in the Virginia legislature. In that bill, he argued against capital punishment and favored replacing it with punishment by hard labor—the measure was rejected by a single vote.[204] He continued to study prison sentences as a scientific matter and advocated a graduated sentence scheme based on the crime—a common idea today, not in 1778.[205]

The motives for his vision were many, but primarily can be traced to his desire for a strong-enough nation so that the country could speak with one voice, but in which the states were the sovereign. His vision reached beyond the expanding borders of the United States, too. He wanted the principles of the Revolutionary War and Republicanism to spread throughout the world (save for Haiti, perhaps).[206] In American history, Jefferson has been memorialized as a philosopher king, willing to martyr his values for the larger goal of making America a nation to last.[207] He is one of the few whose very name is associated with "democracy."[208] One must understand that the word "democracy" was not common in his day—and when it was used, it was not in a positive form. John Adams, for instance, would use the word "democratical" when he meant to talk of a subversive form of government.[209] The idea that government came from the people, and was not imposed upon them for their own good, was radical to say the least.

Jefferson compared his vision of government with clothing, an image he borrowed from Thomas Paine, when he said, "Government, like dress, is the badge of lost innocence."[210] It was a reference to Adam's and Eve's feelings of guilt upon discovering they were naked in Eden—the dress is representative of lost innocence. Paine's version went on to say that our "society is produced by our wants and our government by our wickedness." To Jefferson, there was a balance to be struck between the necessary evil of government and the rights of the people to be free of government interference.[211] That balance was best struck by parties advocating for either side negotiating a compromise between them. This launched his idea of consent of the governed—and the experiment we call America.[212]

Lessons Learned

- Use the terminology that best advances your position.
- Don't use terms with too much baggage (don't analogize to Hitler, Nazi Germany, and the Holocaust unless genocide is actually occurring).
- Write for the reader.
- Do more than just deliver the right information; evoke the right emotions.
- If it works, keep using it: copy and paste.
- Represent your client with zeal, but do not do so by stepping on your colleagues.
- Think about what feelings you let into your work and do not let your personal feelings interfere with the job.
- Never stop learning!

6

LEARNING FROM THE DARKER SIDE OF THOMAS JEFFERSON

In many cases, it can be said that Thomas Jefferson was a man who learned from his mistakes, correcting his course according to a moral, ethical, and philosophical compass. In other cases, however, it may be said that Thomas Jefferson simply changed his course to make the best use of the prevailing political winds. There is ample support for both positions.

It often took time, but Jefferson did eventually learn from some of his mistakes and political defeats.[213] He made use of the Hamilton banking system that he had earlier railed against. He made use of a Navy that he had earlier argued violated the Constitution. He found use for laws making certain statements against various officials illegal, though he had vehemently opposed the Sedition Acts those laws so closely resembled.[214]

Some of Jefferson's contemporaries, and many historians over the years, accused Jefferson of being an opportunist because of these major reversals. Others defend his actions as Jefferson having learned from his past mistakes. There is no doubt that Jefferson did learn from mistakes and could adapt when that would be useful, but he was also quite capable of holding a contrarian position in the hopes that he would eventually be vindicated.[215]

Jefferson was also at times contradictory, even hypocritical, beyond those stances he based in principle. He was known for his grand rhetoric about freedom and liberty. But his policies toward women, Native Americans, and slaves definitely did not match up to that rhetoric. And some of his actions lead us to question his ethics and character, even toward some of his close friends. Jefferson also struggled with narcissism and pettiness, as is often the case with brilliant and powerful men. This chapter examines some of these flaws. The goal is not to defame a man with great gifts and accomplishments, but to learn from some of these "great mistakes" that great men too often make. By analyzing Jefferson's blind spots, perhaps we can prevent ourselves from making similar mistakes in the future.

A SEA OF CONTRADICTIONS

A lazy way to analyze Jefferson would be to say merely that he was filled with paradoxes, struggled with theories of right and wrong, and often made decisions based on greed or false logic. I say lazy because that describes every human to some extent; Jefferson is in the spotlight, here, so those flaws are brought into starker relief. Jefferson was not simply a man who held beliefs that battled for logical harmony. No, Jefferson was, himself, a contradiction.

WOMEN

Jefferson enjoyed the company of intelligent women and ensured that his daughters had a superior education. But he taught them that they were created purely for the "pleasure of men." While in France, he was critical of what he perceived as Frenchwomen's independence, stating that women in the United States knew their place, which was in the nursery, and not "gadding frivolously about town as Frenchwomen did, chasing fashion or meddling in politics."[216] To Jefferson, American women were "'tender and tranquil amusements of domestic life' and never troubled their pretty heads about politics."[217]

Jefferson even went as far as blaming the French Revolution on Marie Antoinette, describing her as "haughty," and later, "proud, disdainful of restrain, indignant at all obstacles to her will, eager in the pursuit of pleasure, and firm enough to hold her desires, or perish in their wreck." In his opinion, the Queen had "an absolute ascendency over" King Louis XVI, resulting in the King receiving sound advice in the morning but having it "reversed in the evening by the influence of the Queen and court."

There is no doubt that Jefferson would have been disapproving of modern women's involvement in government and politics: at the time of this writing, women hold 3 seats in the US Supreme Court, 20 seats in the US Senate, and 84 seats in the US House of Representatives; there has been a female US Attorney General; and there very well may be a female President of the United States in the near future. Indeed, as President, when his Secretary of the Treasury wrote Jefferson suggesting that he hire women to fill some of the remunerative positions in his Department, Jefferson replied with a curt note stating, "the appointment of a woman to office is an innovation for which the public is not prepared, nor am I." Many of the positions went un-filled because of this policy.

Foreigners who traveled to Virginia often found American women "dull and insipid,"[218] noting that American women were denied any significant role in the management of the plantation, would surround themselves with a small circle of house slaves, and had become "indolent, self-indulgent, frustrated, and unhappy."[219] One such commentator described the American situation: "[n]othing has surprised me more than the cold, melancholy reserve of the females, of the best families. . . . Old and young, single and married, all have that dull frigid insipidity, and reserve, which is attributed to solitary old maids. Even in their own houses they scarce utter anything to a stranger but yes or no."

Jefferson's attitude toward women intertwined with his views on slavery. While still a practicing attorney, he addressed the question of laws against cross-racial sex. Jefferson wrote that the laws were meant to "deter [white] women from the confusion of species which the legislature seems to have considered an evil."[220] For a man as precise with words as Jefferson, he seems to have fully considered and come to an opinion about these laws.[221] It ap-pears Jefferson was "making light of the legislative judgment that sex across the color line was inherently evil or even that it was ever an evil at all."[222] After Jefferson became a prominent figure, however, his language about cross-race sex came more into line with the expectations of the very legislature he mocked as a young lawyer.[223] This back-pedaling only adds to the confusion on this topic as this is the same man, who—as may be known to the reader and as will be discussed—fathered children with one of his slaves.

In this, and many other incidents, Jefferson seems to have "unlearned" some of the better principles he earlier held. We must be cautious that short-term expediency and negative experiences don't sway us in the wrong direction. Sometimes, our first reactions are the right reactions. **Do not be swayed by popular opinion or the needs of today when you know you are right**.

NATIVE AMERICANS

Jefferson's attitude toward Native Americans is more complex than his attitude toward women. He believed that Native Americans were equal to whites and that all that was necessary to bring them fully into the American culture was to teach them "agriculture, relieve their women from drudgery, intermarry with Europeans, and throw off the pernicious doctrines of their priests, shamans, and witch doctors."[224] Thus, in Jefferson's eyes, Native Americans were equal *if* they gave up their culture and religion and, preferably, bred themselves into the European race and out of their distinct existence. Put differently, the red man would be equal just as soon as he became white.

Jefferson's hypocrisy ran further than his personal beliefs; it ran through his official policies as well. Indeed, Jefferson, along with his predecessors in office and most Americans, adopted the "join us or get out of our way" stance toward Native Americans.[225] In contrast to his beliefs regarding blacks, he believed that Indian Tribes could assimilate. And while his "Indians are equal" attitude was different from the first two presidents, it was only different in rhetoric—practice remained consistent. In action, Jefferson took every opportunity to take land from tribes east of the Mississippi and was prepared for tribes west of that river to suffer the same fate in the white settlers' search for pelts and land.[226]

This begs a question: How could Jefferson, the man who is known across the globe as a champion of human dignity over tyranny, be so indifferent to a group who were so obviously being oppressed by a greater power? To Jefferson and his contemporaries, though, this wouldn't have even been a valid question.[227] "In their view, Indian ideas about land ownership were a lot of foolishness."[228] Land was wasted on the tribes; the only proper use of land was to develop thousands of farms with tens of thousands of settlers.

Regardless of Jefferson's confessed compassion toward Native Americans or his belief that they could fold into American society, the frontier was wild—there, might made right. "On this question, the people, not the government, ruled. Americans had but one Indian policy—get out of the way or get killed—and it was nonnegotiable."[229] Jefferson's public ideals did differ from those of settlers in that he wanted to buy the land from the tribes rather than simply drive them out. But even Jefferson's relatively enlightened approach had a dark side: Jefferson wrote to a friend that the true plan was to buy lands from the tribes with items valued by Native Americans (such as metal cooking pots), rather than the hard currency valued by the rest of America. With that land, trading posts could be established that would, in turn, extend credit to tribes, which they could use to buy more western goods. As the Native Americans were largely unable to pay their debts, they would "become willing to lop them off by a cession of lands." Jefferson concluded, "in the whole course of this, it is essential to cultivate their love. As to their fear, we presume that our strength and their weakness are not so visible that they must see we have only to shut our hand to crush them."

Jefferson's attitude toward Native Americans bordered on the edges of promoting genocide. It is easy to criticize his policies with the hindsight that history provides—in fact, his approach was more "compassionate" than the approach most Americans of his day advocated. However, the same cannot be said of his attitude toward African-Americans. In this context, we can judge Jefferson without that cover—it is all too clear that Jefferson acted with his eyes wide open.

BLACKS AND SLAVES

In 1775, one year before Jefferson declared that "all men are created equal," Dr. Samuel Johnson—a famous English writer, poet, and moralist during Jefferson's days—asked an embarrassing question: "How is it that we hear the loudest yelps for liberty from the drivers of Negroes?" On one hand, Jefferson did more for progressing the rights of man in a single lifetime than all the generations that had preceded him—among his many gifts to mankind were the Declaration of Independence, Virginia's Statute for Religious Freedom, and the University of Virginia.[230] On the other hand, however, few men profited from the buying, selling, and exploitation of human beings more than Thomas Jefferson.

All Talk

If one were simply to read Jefferson's letters containing references to slavery, it would clearly appear that he was a staunch opponent of the institution. He maintained until his death that the United States could not maintain its democracy while some lived as slaves and others as masters. Knowing that, he still absolutely believed that blacks were an inferior race; he specifically mentioned this in his book, *Notes on the State of Virginia*. At the same time, Jefferson believed that liberty was inherited from the "Laws of Nature" and that "Nature's God entitle[d] them" to it. Hence, for Jefferson, the "inferior" slave was entitled to liberty because of his birth and not because of his intelligence. Jefferson did appoint the black astronomer and mathematician Benjamin Banneker as the surveyor for the development of the capital city. Yet Jefferson, even while writing of a belief in the intrinsic rights of man, treated his slaves as chattel. He sold slaves, whom he considered lazy or insubordinate, when he needed money. He drafted statutes that provided for severe physical punishments and was very matter-of-fact about the nature of the slave economy as a business model, preferring slaves to white workers because, though the latter could be hired for manual labor, they were "often less docile, had to be paid wages, and "their nourishment [was] much more expensive."[231] He valued female slaves over males, stating, "I consider a woman who brings a child every two years is more profitable than the best man of the farm. What she produces is an addition to the capital, while his labor disappears in mere consumption." That is very cold logic.

It was only when Jefferson talked about slavery as an institution that his rhetoric really soared on principles.[232] Jefferson *could* have removed himself from the slave business, but chose not to. One cannot deny, however, that Jefferson's rhetoric on the institution of slavery had a huge impact over the course of American history. The original draft of the Declaration of Independence railed against the King's involvement with slavery. That draft, in fact, outright blamed the King for slavery in the Americas, stating,

> He has waged cruel war against human nature itself, violating its most sacred rights of life and liberty in the persons of a distant people who never offended him, captivating & carrying them into slavery in another hemisphere, or to incur miserable death in their transportation

thither. This piratical warfare, the opprobrium of INFIDEL powers, is the warfare of the CHRISTIAN king of Great Britain. Determined to keep open a market where MEN should be bought & sold, he has prostituted his negative for suppressing every legislative attempt to prohibit or to restrain this execrable commerce. And that this assemblage of horrors might want no fact of distinguished die, he is now exciting those very people to rise in arms among us, and to purchase that liberty of which he has deprived them, by murdering the people on whom he also obtruded them: thus paying off former crimes committed against the LIBERTIES of one people, with crimes which he urges them to commit against the LIVES of another.

That passage was deleted for political reasons discussed in the next chapter. That the passage was in Jefferson's original draft, though, is evidence of Jefferson's understanding of the horrors of the slave trade and his hatred for it. Also significant is his use of the word "obtruded," showing that he understood how to "appeal to a certain self-righteousness in his audience and looking further ahead—that he saw no future for free black-people in America."[233] It also shows Jefferson's deflection of blame for the sin of slavery. He profited from slavery and profited from his slaves, particularly. But he made sure to blame the nature of the system: the King during colonial times, the politics of passage in the independence debate, and the dependence of the American economic system on the institution once statehood was achieved and America was growing.

In that passage, we see Jefferson clearly charging the King, but also the Barbary powers for the slave trade (the reference to "piratical" and "infidel powers" is a reference to the Barbary states). Jefferson also blamed other southern states, specifically Georgia and South Carolina, for the continuation of slavery, saying, "who had never attempted to restrain the importation of slaves, and who, on the contrary, still wished to continue it." He said all this, despite Virginia's having almost 300,000 slaves (which accounted for 40% of all American slaves in the 1790 census; Georgia and South Carolina had 30,000 and 100,000, respectively). He also blamed the northern states, saying, "our northern brethren also, I believe, felt a little tender under these censures; for though their people had very few slaves themselves, yet they had been pretty considerable carries of them to others."

While Jefferson was adept at using the lawyer's tool of deflection and using the "you're one too!" defense, it doesn't seem he ever examined his actions in this ethical and moral cesspool, though he surely would have profited from that, if not at the time, then surely in the eyes of history. We must learn to examine our own positions. Even if your opponents are "evil," your own hands might be dirty, too. **Think about how others will see your own position if you are arguing a point that implicates your own practices.** This is especially true where you have a financial interest in either side of the thing being argued.

Jefferson did make some attempts to strike blows at the institution of slavery (it should be noted, however, that none of these blows would have affected his personal ownership of slaves and that none of these blows quite landed). He wrote, "I made one effort in that body [Virginia's House of Burgesses] for the permission of the emancipation of slaves, which was rejected: and indeed, during the regal government, nothing liberal could expect success." He also introduced a law that would have prohibited any further importation of slaves to Virginia, with its goal, as he put it, "to stop the increase of the evil" and to "leave to future efforts its final eradication."[234] Ultimately, Jefferson believed the real method by which slavery would end would be to set a cutoff date, where anyone born after that date would be born free and, importantly, deported. Not a completely charitable solution, obviously. He wrote, "Nothing is more certainly written in the book of fate than that these people are to be free. Nor is it less certain that the two races, equally free, cannot live in the same government. Nature, habit, opinion has drawn indelible lines of distinction between them." He concluded that they still had the "power to direct the process of emancipation and deportation peaceably and in such slow degree as that the evil will wear off insensibly . . . . If on the contrary it is left to force itself on, human nature must shudder at the prospect held up."

Haiti

Jefferson's hypocrisy toward black slaves didn't end at the US border. Almost as soon as the French Revolution began, it spread to the island of Hispaniola (now

Haiti). Run by wealthy white planters with the labor of African slaves, Haiti was an important colony for Spain, and then France, because of its lucrative sugar crop. In 1791, a slave revolt broke out, culminating in 1804 in not only the elimination of slavery but also in the founding of the Republic of Haiti. It was the only slave revolt in the 19th century that led to the founding of a nation. When the revolt began, Jefferson thought of it only as a skirmish against "monocrats." However, as the revolt developed into a full-blown black rebellion—less than a thousand miles off the Florida Coast, leading to French refugees coming to the United States—Jefferson's attitude changed. He wrote to James Monroe in July 1793 that he felt pity for the white slave masters fleeing Haiti and was further upset that he, as Secretary of State, could not "devote money from the federal government to help these poor slave owning souls."[235] He went on to urge states to provide support to the aristocratic refugees to not only protect the planters but also to build good will with France. Jefferson reveled in the French Revolution because he saw it as the spread of liberty. When it came to Haiti, however, he saw revolution as a threat to the slave holding caste.

Later, Jefferson referred to the free Haiti as "another [potential] Algiers in the seas of America," a reference to the notorious Barbary pirates.[236] That attack was harsh, but not as harsh as when he referred to the free blacks as "cannibals of the terrible republic." What was Jefferson saying? Because they are black they must be pirates? That's how it plays, at least. Because they wanted to rid themselves of the boot of tyranny, just as the colonists had done, must they be cannibals? Jefferson, a man who loved freedom, limited that freedom when it was politically convenient—he loved democracy most of the time; but sometimes, in some cases, he wanted not too much of it.

His hypocrisy runs deeper when you consider that his grand plan for the American slave problem was emancipation and colonization, meaning their deportation to another African or West Indies nation. Of course, for this plan to work, there had to be an African or West Indies nation willing to take close to a half a million slaves. Yet, right in front of Jefferson was a new black republic where the American slaves could go. Jefferson went out of his way, however, to deny their claim to freedom, going so far as to even propose that England and France make temporary peace and combine forces to restore the slave state in Haiti.

To this author, this is sufficient evidence of Jefferson's short-sightedness on this issue. The rebellion in Haiti threatened his way of life, so, despite it being counter to his rhetoric of freedom and liberty and even his own plans for slaves in America, he tried to crush it.

When the Haitian slave Toussaint L'Ouverture led his people to freedom, he formed the first black republic in history—based partly off of Jefferson's own ideals. It was the Haitian defeat over the French at the 1803 Battle of Vertières and the corresponding loss of income from sugar that forced Napoleon to sell the Louisiana territory to the United States. In a sense, then, the slave revolt helped shape the United States and helped to define Jefferson's presidency.

Sally

In addition to inheriting masses of land from his father-in-law, Jefferson also inherited his father's illegitimate daughter from a slave relationship—his wife's half-sister—Sally Hemings. Sally was certainly a slave, for the simple fact that she was Thomas Jefferson's property, but she was not subjected to many of the humiliations and the anguish of field work or punishment by the lash.[237] She and her brother, James, began receiving wages in 1788, a practice Jefferson had never done before. By all accounts, she was a beautiful woman[238] and was reported as being very "nearly white" in appearance.[239] Later in life, Jefferson would "compose an insanely complicated ethnographical diagram to show how, after a certain number of "'Crossings' between black and white, the paint of Africa was removed": Jefferson would have described Ms. Hemings as a "quadroon."[240] She and her three sons were able to register as white in the 1830 census.

To say that cross-racial sex or miscegenation was taboo would be to trivialize the social stigma. The practice was much more than just "taboo."[241] There has been much debate on the Jefferson/Hemings relationship. The most reliable evidence suggests that the two did have an affair starting in 1788. The controversy surrounding the affair was really put to bed when the scientific journal, *Nature*, published a detailed DNA analysis, in which they used three totally separate laboratories. The testing was conclusive: a Jefferson male fathered at least one of Sally Hemings's children. The remaining question, "Which Jefferson male?" was solidly put to rest with evidence that each of Sally's children were born almost exactly nine months after Jefferson visited Monticello, and several when his brother was not in the area at the time of conception.[242] The details of the relationship are unknown, but theories have ranged from a loving quasi-marriage, to Sally simply being Jefferson's live-in concubine. The prominent Jefferson scholar Gordon-Reed wrote that most historians have refused to consider "whether Sally might have had a mind of her own. Or might shockingly have made that mind up—and favor an affair with a rich, famous, powerful, and fascinating man."[243] This may be true, but it is this author's opinion that in the late 1700s, a slave—even an attractive nearly white slave—had so small a voice in society that even if the "love affair" story is true, the power imbalance between the two "lovers" washes away any attempt to justify the relationship. The same is true for a relationship between a high school teacher and his willing 18-year-old student. It matters not that they are both consenting "adults"; it is an abuse of power and seedy, no matter how much perfume you spray around.

The affair came to light after James Callender, a political pamphleteer and journalist, wrote a series of articles that detailed the affair and accused Jefferson of fathering Sally's children. Callender, who was once a Jefferson supporter, was angered by condemnation from Jefferson's supporters who asserted that Callender had abandoned his wife to die of a venereal disease (it seems that the nastiness of politics in America has been here since our founding). Callender's reporting on the Jefferson/Hemings relationship was vicious—he referred to Ms. Hemings as a "slut" and her children as a "litter." He wrote that Jefferson, on his visits to Monticello, would summon Sally from the "pigsty."[244]

We are all human. All of us make errors—some, of the heart. But Jefferson opened himself up to attack, both vitriolic personal attacks and good old-fashioned political attacks, by not being sufficiently discrete and by tasting of the "forbidden fruit." Rumors and stories, such as his earlier attempts to seduce a married woman, were fodder for his enemies in a time when upper-class people were especially careful to keep up appearances. **Don't open yourself up to attacks, personally or professionally.** Make your opponents address the issues, not your character.

Additionally, though modern times are somewhat more forgiving of turpitude, circumspection in this regard is always warranted.

He Knew

Probably the most frustrating aspect of Jefferson's stance on slavery was the fact that he knew better. Many contemporaries in his era truly believed that blacks were inferior and whites were put on earth to hold dominion over them—true ignorance. Jefferson's rhetoric, though, leaves no room to doubt that he not only understood it to be a barbaric practice, but that it would eventually lead to bloodshed and threaten the existence of the Union—yet he did little to try to stop it. From our place in history, it is easy to see General Lee's army forming up even then.[245]

Jefferson's *Notes on the State of Virginia*, written and published in several editions between 1781 and 1785, states,

man is an imitative animal. This quality is the germ of all education in him. From his cradle to his grave he is learning to do what he sees others do. If a parent could find no motive either in his philanthropy or his self-love, for restraining the intemperance of passion towards his slave, it should always be a sufficient one that his child is present. But generally it is not sufficient. The parent storms, the child looks on, catches the lineaments of wrath, puts on the same airs in the circle of smaller slaves, gives a loose to his worst of passions, and thus nursed, educated, and daily exercised in tyranny, cannot but be stamped by it with odious peculiarities. The man must be a prodigy who can retain his manners and morals undepraved by such circumstances. And with what execration should the statesman be loaded, who permitting one half the citizens thus to trample on the rights of the other, transforms those into despots, and these into enemies, destroys the morals of the one part, and the amor patriae of the other. For if a slave can have a country in this world, it must be any other in preference to that in which he is born to live and labour for another: in which he must lock up the faculties of his nature, contribute as far as depends on his individual endeavours to the evanishment of the human race, or entail his own miserable condition on the endless generations proceeding from him. With the morals of the people, their industry also is destroyed.

Jefferson tried to spin his stance on slavery away from his own selfish motives. He also tried to justify his idea that the blacks, if freed, would have to be deported when he said, "if a slave can have a country in this world, it must be any other in preference to that in which he is born to live and labour for another." It is true that he hated slavery and regarded it as a curse on the slave states, but he also profited from the institution, and it was clear that he did not want it to end in his lifetime, believing that his generation was yet not ready for such progress.[246]

The most damning statement from Jefferson, also from his *Notes on the State of Virginia*, demonstrates that he knew that slavery was evil and needed to be stamped out: "Can the liberties of a nation be secure when we have removed a conviction that these liberties are the gift of God? Indeed I tremble for my country when I reflect that God is just, that his justice cannot sleep forever." Jefferson went on to write that the "[c]ommerce between master and slave is despotism. Nothing is more certainly written in the book of fate than that these people are to be free. Establish a law for educating the common people. This it is the business of the state and on a general plan." After Jefferson's proposal to end slavery by a gradual fading of the institution lost in a vote, he wrote, "we [saw] the fate of millions unborn hanging on the tongue of one man, and Heaven was silent in that awful moment!"

Jefferson did not—indeed, could not—believe that slavery was justified because of the perceived inferiority of blacks. When he heard such an argument, he would rebut that under this logic: "white fools" should be slaves; in fact, under his logic, any "white person who could prove he was more intelligent [with] more education than they," should take dominion as master.[247] Jefferson wanted freed slaves deported because of his fear of retribution. He warned, "10,000 recollections, by the blacks, of the injuries they have sustained; new provocations; the real distinctions which nature has made; and many other circumstances, will divide us into parties, and produce convulsions which will probably never end but in the extermination of one or the other race." Jefferson predicted that, if freed, the blacks and the whites would inevitably engage in a race war.

And he was considered progressive by some.

At the same time, Jefferson also purported to believe that blacks lacked basic emotions, stating that "their griefs are transient." He broke up families, believing that their love for each other lacked "a tender delicate mixture of sentiment and sensation." That has to be complete self-deception. It is simply unbelievable that Jefferson could be the brilliant and rational man we know him to be, a man who fathered children with a black woman, and actually believe that blacks lacked even rudimentary emotional faculties. Jefferson obviously cared for Sally, paying her a salary and setting her and her children free at his death. So how was Jefferson able to hold such insanely contradictory views?

Greed and selfishness explains much of it; an enormous capacity for hypocrisy provides most of the rest. Jefferson wanted to sell slaves when he needed money. Moreover, he wanted to build his home, Monticello, and so he needed slaves to work for free in order to get it done. In order to get what he wanted, he had to justify it to himself. He had to convince himself, or simply pretend, that blacks were less.

These conclusions are not merely the author's conclusions. Jefferson's actions demonstrate the point. He denied blacks' abilities in the arts, yet all three of his "slave" children learned how to play the violin and were likely taught in part by Jefferson, himself.[248] His youngest child by Sally Hemings, Easton Hemings, later became a violin maestro. The evidence available to Jefferson, this intellectual who questioned the nature of everything in his world, suggests that Jefferson's rhetoric about the lesser nature of blacks was meant to justify his actions toward his slaves. Jefferson's writings on the relations (read *sexual relations*) between master and slave evidence his understanding of the nature of the relationship: the "whole commerce between master and slave is a perpetual exercise of the most boisterous passions, the most unremitting despotism on the one part, and degrading submissions on the other. Our children see this, and learn to imitate it; for man is an imitative animal." Jefferson perfectly understood the power imbalance and the unfairness of the relationship, yet he partook all the same.

Jefferson predicted that slavery would eventually cause a civil war between American peoples. When the Missouri Compromise was finalized in 1820, he wrote a letter to John Holmes, one of its architects, stating that the Compromise's passage was

like a fire bell in the night, [which] awakened and filled me with terror. I considered it at once as the knell of the Union. It is hushed indeed for the moment. But this is a reprieve only, not a final sentence. A geographical line, coinciding with a marked principle, moral and political, once conceived and held up to the angry passions of men, will never be obliterated; and every new irritation will mark it deeper and deeper. I can say with conscious truth that there is not a man on earth who would sacrifice more than I would, to relieve us from this heavy reproach, in any practicable way. The cession of that kind of property, for so it is misnamed, is a bagatelle which would not cost me in a second thought, if, in that way, a general emancipation and expatriation could be effected: and, gradually, and with due sacrifices, I think it might be. But, as it is, we have the wolf by the ear, and we can neither hold him, nor safely let him go.

Jefferson concluded that letter on a despondent note, one fearful for tomorrow's Americans:

I regret that I am now to die in the belief that the useless sacrifice of themselves, by the generation of 1776. To acquire self-government and happiness to their country, is to be thrown away by the unwise and unworthy passions of their sons, and that my only consolation is to be that I live not to weep over it. If they would but dispassionately weigh the blessings they will throw away against an abstract principle more likely to be effected by union than by scission, they would pause before they would perpetrate this act of suicide on themselves and of treason against the hopes of the world.

It is easy to sum up Jefferson's contradictions by simply declaring that he was a victim of his times. But it appears to be more complex than that. He wrote about black people lacking consciences because they had "that immovable veil of black, which covers the emotions of the other race." In essence, he was saying that because you could not see a black man blush, he was prone to bad behavior. As a man of science, however, Jefferson most certainly knew this was not true. Jefferson often called out the various fads as the quackeries they were. This "veil" argument would not stand up under any reasoning at all to a man of such logic. Perhaps his attitudes changed with time. If that is the case, he never admitted his mistakes on this issue.

Admit when you are mistaken and adopt the right position according to your new understanding. This is essential for any person in any field who desires to persuade people. Stubbornness may take an advocate far, but it will not take him far enough if his position is just wrong.

Additionally, the issue of slavery hurt the United States on a strategic level. Britain was quick to point out the great contradiction. The *Pennsylvania Packet* asked only weeks before the First Continental Congress met, "Can we suppose that people of England will grant the force of our reasoning, when they are told that every colony in the continent is deeply involved in the inconsistent practice of keeping their fellow creatures [note that they did not say "man"] in perpetual bondage?"[249]

Patrick Henry addressed this contradiction with his fellow slave owners in Virginia at a time when natural rights were being defined by the "great men" of the time. He "understood with precision, in a country above all others fond of liberty [that] we find men professing religion the most humane, mild, gentle, and generous, adopting a principle as repugnant to humanity as it is inconsistent with the Bible and destructive to liberty[.]" Henry was not talking in the abstract; he was talking about himself and his fellows, Jefferson, Madison, and Washington, among them. "Would anyone believe I am the master of slaves of my own purchase! I am drawn along by the general inconvenience of living here without them. I will not, I cannot justify it."[250]

While the central intent of this book is not to proffer a personal opinion concerning Jefferson's philosophies, it is important to point out that when the law dictates *over* us instead of acting as a buffer *between* us, we are no longer a society of law, rather we are a "police state." Jefferson was conflicted over the issue of slavery; he knew it was morally repugnant. He predicted the slaves would inevitably be freed because, simply, they must be. He predicted that when that happened, they would seek retribution for the many and severe harms done to generations of their ancestors.

Generally, a civilization will only prosper when its citizens obey the law, whether or not they agree with it. Elections are held to select representatives who will enact just laws to be enforced with the "consent of the governed," who implicitly agree to follow them. However, resistance against the transparently unjust is a human responsibility.

As St. Augustine said and Dr. Martin Luther King, Jr. quoted, "an unjust law is no law at all." This is the legal conundrum that has plagued nations since laws were first written: Unjust to whom? During Jefferson's time, a person who hid runaway slaves thought he was helping subjugated people. To others, those that helped were outlaws. The point is that it is easy for us from a distance of two-hundred-plus years to criticize Jefferson for his position on the slavery issue, knowing as much as he did about the natural rights of all men, and knowing all that we know about the history that has followed. Was his position on slavery wrong? Unequivocally, yes. Was he a brilliant man trying to create a better world for all mankind? That, too, we answer yes. With all that said, however, one can't help to ask, Was Jefferson "trembl[ing] for his country" when he took a slave lover and kept slave children, when he wrote laws allowing for horrendous punishment for defiant slaves, or when he did not support the spread of democracy in Haiti from selfish motives? Those answers are more complex, and confusing.

Jefferson was a wonderfully capable, persuasive writer. In reading any individual work written to any individual reader or collective audience on almost any topic, Jefferson's message comes through clearly. In reading his collective body of work, however, his persuasiveness seems to falter on some issues, fail outright on others. Vision was earlier discussed. Related to that concept, Jefferson's varied stances provide us a lesson: **Keep a focus on the future and work consistently toward it.** In everything you do, think of your long-term goals. Ask yourself, on large projects and seemingly insignificant tasks, how does this fit the larger scheme? Jefferson "talked a big game" about the rights of every man. His large projects show his passion, vision, and logic toward that end. His lesser writings and actions, however, show us a different Jefferson. That Jefferson, because of his innate abilities and skills developed in persuasive writing, seems equally passionate if not as visionary or logical toward very different and, often, contradictory ends. The overarching themes in Jefferson's works—and lack thereof in many regards—show us that this lesson is one he can teach, but is one he never learned.

MONEY

The inheritance from his father-in-law "haunted Jefferson for the rest of his life (although he didn't know it at the time) because it "brought with it more debts and responsibilities than he was capable to managing."

Money problems were the direct or indirect cause of many of Jefferson's errors in judgment and gave plenty of ammunition to his opponents. Like a major league baseball player who signs for tens of millions and spends it all within a short time, Jefferson never seemed to learn proper money management. Despite having huge plantations with rich soil, a lucrative law practice, and hundreds of slaves, he managed to consistently outspend his income. He felt unable to free his slaves because of his issues with money, then tore families apart when he needed cash, pretending to himself that that didn't matter because they had only transient feelings. His expensive tastes (he purchased over 2,000 bottles of French wine between 1802 and 1804) and work on his fabulous house (the ever-growing Monticello) just added to the total. And there were the books—so many books. Some of his problems were not self-inflicted: he did incur debt from his father-in-law's estate; he suffered through a panic (depression) in 1819 and lower-than-expected profits from the crops in his plantations; and he cosigned on a loan for a friend who very shortly thereafter died. Bad luck, to be sure. But for such a brilliant man, Jefferson seems to have lacked any financial sense.

ETHICS

During Jefferson's career as a lawyer and politician, he faced many ethical dilemmas. For a man revered as a Founding Father, one who, in American lore at the least, held to the utmost principles in the face of a tyrant and his army, we do, upon examination, see that Jefferson occasionally made serious ethical mistakes, both professionally and personally.

PROFESSIONAL RESPONSIBILITY

In 1769, several of Jefferson's clients in Augusta County devised a get-rich-quick scheme that came to an inglorious end in just a few short years.[251] Although there is no evidence that Jefferson actively participated in the plan, he was the lawyer acting with the understanding that his fees were contingent on the success of the scheme. For perception's sake, at a minimum, he was implicated.

The plan "involved a large-scale use of caveats and petitions for lapsed lands, types of legal proceedings that constituted over half of Jefferson's business during the eight years of his practice."[252] A person could obtain a patent for land in Virginia with only an obligation to cultivate the land within three years of obtaining the patent. If the farmer failed to harvest the land within the time period, then the farmer could lose his land through a legal proceeding in the General Court brought by "informers" who would show why the land should be forfeited.[253] These informers, who established the delinquency of the older patent, could then obtain a patent for the land in question. These civil suits were necessary at the time because government enforcement of the three-year rule was almost nonexistent.

Typically, at the start, Jefferson's clients would bring him the delinquency cases one at a time. Later, though, a group of his clients began to bring cases to Jefferson on a wholesale basis. The scheme manifested itself in 1769 when Jefferson filed 14 petitions at one time for James Greenlee.[254] Later that year, Jefferson filed 49 caveat cases in Augusta County in the name of a client, "Waterson and company." In July of 1769, Jefferson sent a list of 270 potential cases for screening to an employee. Out of that 270, 190 caveats were filed. In September of 1769, an additional 127 were filed in the name of Andrew Johnston. By April of 1770, the "company" had filed a total of 450 caveats.[255] The good citizens of Augusta County, not to mention the actual defendants in the cases, were outraged over the unprecedented land grab. One commentator at the time referred to Jefferson's clients as "villains" because they were exploiting a loophole in the law that allowed the "caveators" to take land from its owner without putting down any security or proving their ability to cultivate the land.

As rules are made to be broken, so too are loopholes made to be closed— but only when abused such that attention is called to them, making it a political issue. The plan thus fell apart in the summer of 1770 when the General Assembly passed a law that required the plaintiffs in such cases to pay a security deposit to bring the suit sufficient to pay the defendant's legal costs if the plaintiff lost. If a security deposit was not paid, the case would be dismissed. The new law was promptly applied to Jefferson's clients, requiring them to provide security deposits for their opponents' costs. When those deposits were not paid, the cases were simply dismissed and Jefferson's fees dried up.

Why did the General Assembly thwart the plan? There are two likely reasons. First, the scheme should be considered unethical from its conception. The legal action being exploited, caveat was designed for exactly the purpose for which the plaintiffs were using it—enforcement of the patent requirements where the government could not. The suits were designed to keep land speculators honest. The full-scale attack that Jefferson's clients launched on the system, though, "threatened the fabric of frontier society." Second, the plaintiffs could not cultivate all the land they attempted to seize. Rather, the plan likely called for the informers simply to "flip" the property to others or exact a tribute from the original owner to drop the suit. That practice, today, is called legal extortion.

Jefferson skated close to the ethical line at other times during his tenure as a practicing attorney, too. We have already talked about Jefferson's providing "escape money" to Howell (his client who sued his master to be declared free), a clear violation of the law and thus of his legal ethical duty. In addition, although there were no ABA Rules of Professional Responsibility at the time, there was general consensus among Jefferson's bar that lawyers owed certain minimal duties to their clients. Included in that was the duty not to engage in cases where the attorney would face a conflict of interest, the duty to put forth a good faith effort for your client, and a duty to be loyal to your client. Jefferson, at one point or another, broke each of these basic rules.

The most common ethical breach Jefferson committed was his violation of his duty to avoid conflicts of duty between his clients and his own personal interests. In the case, *Jameison v. Hubard*, Jefferson left his client, Hubard, to represent the other party, Jameison. In another case, *Harrison v. White*, Jefferson was hired to bring a caveat case for Harrison only to abandon the case within a year to represent White. What is even more amazing is that it is clear that he understood these conflicts to be prohibited. In other cases, he noted a case conflict in his case book and refused to represent the client, noting the conflict of interest. Perhaps his most egregious breach came in the case of *Wilkinson v. Fitzpatrick*, where Jefferson actually noted the conflict in a letter to Fitzpatrick: "note I am emploied by Wilkerson . . . so cannot do anything here but as a friend." He then proceeded to give his friend Fitzpatrick information to help his case and hurt that of his real client. Even without reading the Model Rules, that conduct should sort of jump out as probably unethical.

In the case of *Donaghe v. Leeper*, Jefferson brought a frivolous claim against a landowner, not in order to actually take control of the unused land (it was, in fact, in use), but only to draw the individual into the jurisdiction where he could be arrested for another matter. In *Waterson v. Allen*, Jefferson appeared for his client in the hope that the client would then have enough time to get out of the jurisdiction. In both the cases of *Hyneman & Co. v. Fleming* and *Bland v. Fleming*, he brought legal action for the sole purpose of "protract[ing] the matter."

Jefferson would also play legal games to avoid rules he didn't like. In the 1700s, a party to a lawsuit was expected to be hostile and therefore was not allowed to testify in court. Jefferson would therefore name witnesses as defendants to prevent them from testifying. In one case, Jefferson breached his fiduciary duty by warning his friend, John Walker, that Jefferson's client was about to bring a case against Walker over uncultivated land, violating the lawyer's duty of confidentiality, among others.

But how should we judge the professional responsibility of 18th-century attorneys? In order to fully understand Jefferson's actions, it is important to note that the bar for the General Court where he practiced was very small. It never had more than ten attorneys admitted at one time.[256] Perhaps all the attorneys engaged in such practices? Perhaps that was just custom. It is likely that that does not provide a full explanation; it definitely is no justification. Additionally, today we have sophisticated filing systems that allow us to see if there are potential client conflicts; no such system existed when Jefferson was practicing. Yet, it is clear that Jefferson violated some basic rules, while acknowledging their existence, because it was convenient or profitable to bend the rules. The cornerstone of professionalism, here, is doing the job even when it is not in your self-interest. Clearly, Jefferson didn't meet that standard.

The lesson here is that you must **follow basic precepts**, at the very least. Even if every other General Court attorney engaged in the same practices, which would make for an interesting bar, Jefferson's actions are still being judged unethical by us, today. Minimal standards did exist and Jefferson often did not meet them. It is likely that, even in the case where the other nine members of his bar played by similar rules, members of bars adjacent did not. Those attorneys would see the conduct and think less of Jefferson for violating even the most basic rules under which attorneys operate, and those attorneys would tell other attorneys who would tell clients, and so on and so forth. That, in short, is how a reputation gets ruined and how one's credibility erodes.

LOYALTY

For a man who often talked about honor and loyalty, Jefferson had a habit of breaching his friends' trust. Elizabeth Walker, known as Betsy, was the wife of his lifelong friend John Walker.[257] The couple was married in June 1764 with Jefferson in attendance. Walker referred to Jefferson as "the friend of my heart" and as a "groomsman."[258] But this did not stop Jefferson from trying to seduce his friend's wife. In 1768, it appears that, while Walker was on a delegation in New York, Jefferson fell in love with Betsy. From all accounts, she resisted Jefferson's advances, but he was persistent.[259] Betsy kept Jefferson's pursuit hidden from her husband, but began protesting Jefferson's involvement with her family. Specifically, she objected to Jefferson being named as John Walker's executor, asking her husband how he could "place such confidence in him."

For years, Jefferson kept up his campaign to entice Betsy Walker. On one visit to the Walker estate, he went as far as slipping a note in the cuff of the sleeve of her gown. Her husband was later to recall of the letter that it was "a paper tending to convince her of the innocence of promiscuous love." Jefferson, knowing his skills as a writer, likely hoped to woo her with soft, written words. That ploy failed, though, because Betsy, "on the first glance tore [the letter] to pieces."[260] In another failed attempt, while at a house party of mutual friends, Jefferson "pretended to be sick, complained of a headache and left the gentlemen." Jefferson went to Betsy's room, who was "repulsed with indignation and menaces of alarm and ran off." The Walker story was revealed and confirmed years later, after the two became political rivals. It is not clear that the failed affair was the reason the two friends fell out, but one could guess that Jefferson's repugnant behavior did not help the friendship. Jefferson admitted to his actions, but said merely that it was "an incorrect thing to do."[261]

Unfortunately, this was not the single incidence of Jefferson's lapse in judgment. Maria Cosway was also the focus of Jefferson's attention and, while the depth of their relationship is not certain (most historians believe it was physical for a period, with a friendship that lasted until his death), what is perfectly clear is that she was married. The longest letter written by Jefferson to have survived the ravages of time was to Cosway.[262] Not only was this his longest letter, but he wrote it with his left hand because he had broken his right wrist (some report the injury as a broken hand) jumping over a fence to try and impress her in the *Cours-la-Reine* in Paris, France (this injury is of note because he suffered from pain for the rest of his life). The letter, which is known colloquially as the "Head, Heart, and Wrist" letter, was a passionate farewell, where he admitted he should not have fallen for her but was happy that he did. In 4,000 words, he wrote what Alfred Lord Tennyson summarized 60 years later: "Tis better to have loved and lost than never to have loved at all." The Head, Heart, and Wrist letter was not the only one written to Mrs. Cosway. In another letter, Jefferson made jokes about the length of a man's nose (perhaps a subtle reference to his own long nose), which in the 1700s was apparently a euphemism for the size of a man's penis—early American smut.

Jefferson not only displayed a lack of loyalty by his pursuits of his friends' women, he also alienated political allies and friends with other breaches of loyalty. Jefferson, throughout his life, had a hard time understanding the nature of things public versus things private. In 1796, Jefferson wrote a letter he considered private to Philip Mazzei. Mazzei was an Italian doctor who corresponded frequently with Jefferson because of Jefferson's lifelong goal to produce a high-quality Virginia wine.[263] Also in this letter, Jefferson wrote that "the aspect of our politics has wonderfully changed since you left us. In place of that noble love of liberty & republican government which carried us triumphantly thro' the war, an Anglican monarchical & aristocratical party has sprung up. . . . whose avowed object is to draw over us the substance as they have already done the forms of the British government."[264] The word "wonderfully" was sarcastic, and the party referenced was Washington's Federalist party.

Jefferson was accusing George Washington and his assembled government of being tyrants or aspiring to be such—and not just any tyrants, but the same ones that Washington lost men trying to beat. Jefferson identified the tyrants as "all the officers of the government, all who want to be officers, all timid men who prefer the calm of despotism to the boisterous sea of liberty."[265] Jefferson did not stop there, though. He continued, "it would give you fever were I to name to you the apostates who have gone over to their heresies, men who were Samsons in the field & Solomones in the council, but who have had their heads shorn by the harlot of England." Mazzei published the letter in an Italian newspaper—for obvious reasons: it is brilliant writing. A French newspaper then had the letter translated and published in France and, eventually, it was reprinted in an English newspaper. It was not long before the letter's contents got back to Washington. Jefferson's political enemies called the letter a slur on Washington and it was seen as a betrayal of America's father. This breach in loyalty ended Jefferson's relationship with Washington— the two never corresponded after the affair.

People expect loyalty. So be loyal. A good friend is not likely to lie with your wife. A good colleague is not likely to bash you to others, and is especially not likely to bash you publicly. Neither standard asks much, so try to meet them. There may not be real, tangible rewards for not sleeping with your friend's wife or for not bashing a colleague, but no reward is assuredly better than actual, negative consequences. This lesson isn't hard to learn, but it too often proves hard to follow for those in power, used to getting their way, Thomas Jefferson included.

PETTY AND NARCISSISTIC

Jefferson was a master of language, but he was also careless with it at times. When talking about the Union he had worked so hard to build, he stated, cavalierly, that the states should secede rather than submit to the federal government over the issue of slavery.[266] One has to wonder if he would have felt the same way if he had known that the institution of slavery would become even uglier after his death or that 620,000 Americans would fall in the "secession" he proposed. In addition to being, at times, careless with his words, he also had a side to him that was spiteful and vain.

PETTY

Throughout his career, Jefferson showed that he could be petty. The instances could be small. For example, when Jefferson's friend and a hero of the American Revolution, Thaddeus Kosciusko, died in 1817, Jefferson was named the executor of his estate. Kosciusko left his money to establish a fund to purchase the freedom of slaves and educate them. Thomas Jefferson refused to execute his friend's will, believing that deportation was a better "solution" for the American slave problem.

At other times, Jefferson's pettiness had enormous consequences. In 1786, when he and John Adams were meeting with King George in London, he was treated with discourtesy by those he described as "the ulcerations in the narrow mind of that mulish being." For the next 20 years, he carried deep rancor for British diplomats. As President, he exacted his revenge. When British Ambassador Anthony Merry and his wife arrived in Washington D.C., he frustrated their ability to find suitable housing.[267] When he was to officially receive the Ambassador to inspect his credentials, he took every opportunity to snub the Ambassador, even coming to the meeting in slippers. While these acts did not lead directly to the War of 1812, they certainly did not make relations with Great Britain, the most powerful nation in the world, any more amicable. When Aaron Burr went looking for allies for his scheme to make a new nation on the doorstep of the United States, he found a friendly ear in Ambassador Merry.

Jefferson took political attacks personally and would build intricate plans to impose his will on his political enemies, wanting not just to beat them but to crush them.[268] Jefferson felt some need for historical vindication. This, along with his recurring petty "tantrums" and careless pen, were the source of many complications and conflicts that he might otherwise have easily avoided. It is this author's opinion that saying something you don't mean in a conversation is easy. It comes out quickly and is, often, quickly forgiven because of that.

There is much less of an excuse for carelessness in writing, though. Jefferson would write bitter retorts to affronts and perceived affronts to his person, his politics, and his principled arguments. Mail was slow, then, so he usually had time to reflect upon his letters before the postman came. He thus had the opportunity to tone down his attacks or tear up the letter entirely. Apparently, however, he rarely used that time to make a rational, reasoned decision.

Today, communications are instantaneous and perhaps too convenient. In this environment, it is even more important that we learn to "count to ten" before blasting out that scathing message. **Don't hit send until you have actually considered the possible ramifications of the message going out.** Remember, even if you send a private message, that message is copied, transferred, and translated too quickly to retract once "send" is hit. Friends are too precious to lose for want of a few minutes reflection.

Jefferson's vindictive attitude was even focused at his friends at times. Because he was not involved with the Constitutional Convention as he was serving in France, he sought to undermine the ratification process (to his good friend James Madison's embarrassment).[269] A man he once admired, Patrick Henry, became the target of his criticism because he was jealous of his public speaking abilities. Jefferson accused him of focusing too much on his "style over substance."[270] Jefferson was also critical of Henry's impulsive nature—this criticism was leveled despite the fact that Jefferson himself was impetuous at times.[271]

Jefferson's stubbornness actually prevented him from talking with John Adams, a great friend at one point, for a decade because of political fights that were long over. Eventually, the two did reconnect when their mutual friend, Dr. Rush, distressed at the estrangement, effected the reconciliation in 1812. One has to think, these two men helped defeat the most powerful nation in the world and establish a new nation that became the beacon of freedom to the world. What could they have accomplished if they had only put away their petty swords? It seems, however, that Jefferson's tendency toward pettiness stemmed from another character flaw we will next explore in Jefferson, and one that most great men and women of history have carried: vanity.

In short, **Don't be petty.** Put aside your pride when deciding upon any course of action. There is a lot to be said to be the "bigger man" who rises above petty differences. The moderate—being, by definition, toward the middle of the spectrum—after all, is in the best position to persuade both sides toward the middle.

NARCISSISM

Jefferson was an expert at covering up his narcissistic propensities. Even John Adams, at the height of his competition with Jefferson, said, "never can be an hour in this man's company without something of the marvelous."[272] Yet looking at the whole of the historical record on Jefferson and his own writings, we can see but a sliver of what is best described as an indifference to others. When Shays' Rebellion ended with the death of half a dozen of his fellow Americans, Jefferson wrote, "What signify a few lives lost in a generation or two?" Are those lives lost not sons, fathers, husbands, and Americans? On one hand, Jefferson loved to protest against Aristocratic affinities, but with statements such as these, you have to wonder if he truly cared about the life of his "plebeians."[273] Other historians have noted Jefferson's tendency to be dismissive or even ruthless when writing about "the casualties inflicted by those of whom he approved."[274] True, this is a characteristic often seen in leaders, one we can always expect to be used against them in the hindsight of history. It seems that Jefferson, on some level, reveled in it.

Jefferson was also narcissistic about his writings. When his original draft of the Declaration of Independence was edited—because he had gone too far in his critiques; the new government did not want to cut all ties with England— Jefferson fumed. He sent copies of the original to his friends and made sure that a copy got leaked to the press. He refused to admit that the edited copy was superior to his own, though he did accept that this was the political reality. Moreover, many of the complaints Jefferson made in the original draft were factually untrue (his claim of the King forcing slavery on the colonies was discussed earlier), making some of the edits he fumed over necessary.[275]

Confidence is attractive; vanity is not. Many of us—perhaps even myself— are a little vain. The key is to come off as confident in your abilities, but also as able to take criticism and use it constructively. To make the best argument, editing is necessary. Remember, "the first draft of anything is shit."

To those who study American history, Jefferson is a complex case study. He was clearly brilliant: his writing abilities and his ability to inspire a vision for the future enabled him to motivate men at a crucial moment in our nation's history. The many contradictions the man embodied, though, leave those of us who revere but study the man, grasping for explanations. Those contradictions, without clear explanation, affect the people of this nation still today.[276] His imprint is just too large not to be affected by his persuasive arguments against the institution of slavery *and* his ownership of slaves; his passionate pleas for an equality of all men to pursue the rights bestowed upon each of us by our Creator *and* his insistence that the Haitians and Native Americans fit where the whites in power wanted them to fit; his confirmed place in American popular historiography *and* the many flaws of character we see upon close examination of the elevated, though still human, man.

What can we learn from Jefferson's mistakes? That is a difficult question to answer. In the big picture, we learn lessons like "Don't be a racist," "Don't be misogynistic," and "Don't own slaves and advocate genocide." But those aren't—this author hopes—useful tips to the reader. Rather, we look to the causes of Jefferson's mistakes and draw lessons from those flaws of character that gave rise to these mistakes.

What can we learn from Jefferson's flaws, from his many contradictions, then? When I was young, I heard an axiom that seems instructive, here: **a stupid man never learns from his mistakes, an average man will learn from his mistakes, a smart man will learn from other's mistakes, and a genius will anticipate a mistake before it happens and adapt.** What did Jefferson learn from all this? How did he grow as a person and an intellect? These are questions that those studying the history of any number of disciplines that Jefferson touched will never stop asking.

Lessons Learned
- Do not be swayed by popular opinion or the needs of today when you know you are right.
- Don't open yourself up to attacks, personally or professionally.
- Stay focused on the future and work consistently toward it.
- Follow basic precepts: if everyone else does it out of tradition or a sense of being polite, do that, too.
- People expect loyalty. So be loyal.
- Don't be petty.
- Confidence is attractive; vanity is not.
- A stupid man never learns from his mistakes, an average man will learn from his mistakes, a smart man will learn from other's mistakes, and a genius will anticipate a mistake before it happens and adapt.

7

JEFFERSON'S OPENING STATEMENT TO AMERICA

The inspiration for this book began with the Gettysburg Address, so it seems fitting to begin with Mr. Lincoln. In 1863, when Lincoln was drafting the Gettysburg Address, he was pondering the ultimate question—Was it worth it? Could the United States, "so conceived and so dedicated," pass the great test of the Civil War and "long endure."[277] To Lincoln it was more than just a speech to rally the troops, congratulate the generals on the victory, or reiterate his belief that the Union must survive. Indeed, Lincoln was considering American ideology itself, wondering whether the American experiment could survive through and beyond the horrors of the Civil War, horrors that were ubiquitously evident by the time Lincoln gave his speech. Thomas Jefferson considered and helped to shape our unique American ideology when he declared it to be "self-evident" that the people are the masters of their own destiny, that we are endowed by our Creator with "certain unalienable Rights."

Lincoln understood the power of the Declaration of Independence. Lincoln also knew that, to best connect with his audience at Gettysburg and across the nation, he needed to link his words and his message to a greater theme— something that would resonate powerfully with Americans of the North and the South alike. Lincoln knew that he needed his audience to hear his own words in the context of ideals of permanence, in the context of principles beyond reproach in the minds of all those that heard and read the speech.

Trial attorneys use this same skill when delivering closing arguments. An attorney ties the words he uses in closing together with a theme he has laid out, first, in his opening.[278] In that opening, a good attorney will announce what the trial is really about by suggesting a theme larger than the particular facts of the case itself. The trial, then, is not about some guy dishonoring a seemingly minor provision in a contract in order to get a more favorable interest rate on a different deal. Rather, the case becomes something more: a case about a man breaking his word, a bond that used to mean something in this country.

Both the North and South considered themselves true to the original, foundational principles upon which the United States were founded. Lincoln carefully chose his words to link his message concerning the particular events leading up to and flowing from November 19, 1863, to the most foundational principles of the United States. Lincoln found those principles in the Declaration of Independence—and he knew his audience would, too. Lincoln thus used the Declaration to set his theme for the Gettysburg Address.

Lincoln saw that the Declaration of Independence offered not only a moral justification for the revolution against Great Britain, but also a legal one. To his credit, Jefferson argued that the legal basis of the Declaration was rooted in English constitutional precedence, using Great Britain's own laws against them. As Thomas Jefferson cited English precedent to argue his points, so too did Lincoln cite American precedent to argue his. To Jefferson, the Declaration was an opportunity to change the condition of mankind on a global scale. To Lincoln, the Declaration was a promise to the nation.

It was the promise of the Declaration that laid the foundation for Lincoln's articulation of our "new nation, conceived in liberty, and dedicated to the proposition that all men are created equal." When Jefferson said that all men were created equal, he meant it—in his own way: excluded from Jefferson's interpretation, however, were women, African-Americans, Native Americans, and other minorities. Despite Jefferson's limited view on who should inherit the "divine freedom" that served as the underpinning of his Declaration, his words were much bigger than himself; his words invoked grand principles to which people could only dream to aspire at the time.

A common trait we see among those considered great—Jefferson and Lincoln, included—is that they thought and acted "big," with "big" things resulting. One important aspect of thinking in terms of grand principles and seemingly unattainable dreams is that it allows you to persuade others by giving them hope for something greater than what currently is. The power to inspire hope is a powerful tool for any persuader. **Think big, act big, and, with hard work and some luck, big things will follow.** This lesson is evidenced by the history of this nation: by reading words written toward one end in 1776 in a much broader, much "bigger," way, we have expanded upon Jefferson's unjust definition of "man" and are, very gradually, securing true freedom under the law for all.

Lincoln and Americans, generally, have reshaped the words and thoughts of Jefferson's Declaration into a truer meaning of equality. Lincoln himself held the Declaration in the highest regard, once saying, "I have never had a feeling, politically, that did not spring from the sentiments embodied in the Declaration of Independence."[279] When Lincoln said that "all men are created equal," he was, in effect, equating the bloodshed of his Civil War with that of Jefferson's War of Independence. In this reference to the Declaration, he boldly asserted that the Civil War was about equality and that the nation was hemorrhaging human lives to uphold what the Declaration of Independence truly stood for—and, therefore, what America truly stood for. After the Address, the "crowd departed with a new thing on its ideological luggage, that new constitution Lincoln had substituted for the one they brought with them. They walked off, from [the battlefield] under a changed sky, into a different America."[280] By his words, Lincoln had revolutionized the Revolutionary War, "giving people a new past to live with that would change their future indefinitely."[281]

Lincoln, it seems, gleaned a great deal from Jefferson's Declaration of Independence, enabling him to effectively persuade an embattled America that his was the correct course. Lincoln's gleaning of the Declaration led him to effect radical and positive change. It seems, therefore, worth our time to examine this great work for the lessons it has to teach.

DRAFTING AND PERFECTING THE DECLARATION

In June 1776, Richard Henry Lee, a delegate of Virginia, was instructed by the Virginia Convention to present a resolution calling for independence from the British Empire. The resolution, which was seconded by John Adams, moved that the United Colonies should be "absolved from all allegiance to the British Crown, and that all political connection between them and the state of Great Britain is, and ought to be, totally dissolved," a line drafted into the Declaration. For months, the Congress had debated how it would proceed. With the proposal of this resolution, the motion that would change everything was finally on the table. No longer would the Colonies be seen as belligerent children that needed to be scolded and spanked back into the British fold. The men in Philadelphia knew that the resolution would mean war. And, while people had already died in the controversy brewing between Britain and her colonies, this was something altogether different.

As is typical with legislative bodies, before drafting the actual document called for by the resolution, Congress needed to debate the need to have a debate about whether to sever ties with the King in the first place. Today, we look at this event through the lens of history; we must keep in mind that at that time, however, the delegates were not concerned with building a Great American Empire or spreading Freedom throughout the known world. Rather, the chatter that dominated the conversation was domestic politics; international relations were only really discussed as those relations concerned trade.[282]

In addition, many of the delegates were concerned that a document that no longer pretended to believe that negotiated reconciliation was the answer or even possible would alienate those colonies with the heaviest concentration of loyalists (and the greatest economic interest in maintaining the relationship with Britain): Pennsylvania, Maryland, Delaware, and New York. In New York, for example, the tenant farmers were heavy supporters of the Crown, as were the Dutch settlers in New Jersey. The German settlers in Pennsylvania were not particularly loyal to the King, but they did view war as bad for business, preferring to cling to familiar ties. Also in Pennsylvania, the Quakers, though sympathetic to the colonists' complaints, were opposed to war of any type. Further, the leaders of the movement to dissolve their current government understood that if the colonies were not united, they would fall. That Ben Franklin knew this has been famously memorialized in American history by his quote made at the signing of the Declaration that, once they had signed, "We must all hang together, or assuredly we shall all hang separately." Jefferson commented that if there was not domestic unity, "foreign powers would either refuse to join themselves to our fortunes, or having us so much in their power ... they would insist on terms proportionately more hard and prejudicial."

When Lee made his motion for independence, the majority of the 13 colonies favored that action. Yet, as Jefferson noted, "it was thought most prudent to wait a while" and, because New York, New Jersey, Pennsylvania, Maryland, and South Carolina needed more time, it was better to wait than to force the issue and risk not having unanimity.[283]

The lesson here is powerful and familiar: **Compromising and winning is better than standing stubbornly resolute and losing.** It does not matter how persuasive your sales proposal is if your customer is just not ready to buy. When that is the case, she is simply not ready. We have all been in a store looking over some new item when a pushy clerk comes up too close and too often, making us want to leave the store just to get away from the clerk. Pushing persuasion on someone who is absolutely not in the market to be persuaded will only alienate that individual, driving them away from you and your cause. That, obviously, is not what we want from our attempts at persuasion.

A vote on the motion to declare independence was postponed for three weeks until the first week in July of 1776, giving the five states who were still debating the issue of independence internally time to so debate.

In today's climate, political bodies often take years to address issues and even longer to actually accomplish anything. Moreover, delay is often used as a weapon to thwart some action or to bargain for concessions. It is important to remember, though, that prudence suggests that you **wait to push your agenda until you have built a consensus**, especially when drafting something requiring the approval of a committee or some other multimember body. This is as true today as it was in 1776 and surely as true as it will be long into the future.

In the interim, Jefferson and the other founding fathers who supported the revolution wasted no time. One committee was appointed to draft a declaration of independence, another to make plans for a new federal government, and a third to prepare for treating with foreign governments. The question that remained was, just who was going to draft the declaration?

John Adams thought that Jefferson should author the declaration. This "decision" by Adams involved, in reality, some scheming "with roots in a secret conversation that had taken place two years before." On the eve of the First Continental Congress in 1774, Benjamin Rush and a few other delegates met with John Adams and the Massachusetts contingent on the outskirts of Philadelphia.[284] The delegates, two years before the signing of the Declaration, agreed that independence was a likely conclusion to the conflict with Great Britain but knew that caution must be exercised until they were prepared. Adams reported as to the advice he received,

> [Y]ou must not utter the word independence, nor give the least hint or insinuation of the idea, either in Congress or any private conversation; if you do, you are undone; for the idea of independence is as unpopular in Pennsylvania, and in all the Middle and Southern States, as the Stamp Act itself. No man dares to speak of it. Moreover, you are the representatives of the suffering State. Boston and Massachusetts are under a rod of iron. British fleets and armies are tyrannizing over you; you yourselves are personally obnoxious to them and all the friends of government; you have been long persecuted by them all; your feelings have been hurt, your passions excited; you are thought to be too warm, too zealous, too sanguine. You must be, therefore, very cautious; you must not come forward with any bold measures, you must not pretend to take the lead.

Rush knew, and Adams agreed, that any proposals to come out of Massachusetts would be thought too incendiary, too passionate, and not representative of the colonists' best interests elsewhere. Adams was then advised to choose the right mouthpiece for his own true beliefs:

> You know Virginia is the most populous State in the Union. They are very proud of their ancient dominion, as they call it; they think they have a right to take the lead, and the Southern States, and Middle States too, are too much disposed to yield it to them.[285]

As Jon Meacham noted in his Pulitzer Prize winning book on Jefferson, "Adams appreciated the straight talk."[286] In 1822, when asked by Timothy Pickering just why Adams had supported Jefferson to head the committee and draft the Declaration, Adams was frank: "You inquire why so young a man as Mr. Jefferson was placed at the head of the committee for preparing a Declaration of Independence? I answer . . . to place a Virginian at the head of everything."[287] Adams went on to note that there were three committees to work concurrently, "one for the Declaration of Independence, another for preparing articles of confederation, and another for preparing a treaty to be proposed to France."[288] Richard Lee, who made the motion for independence and who also was a Virginian, was selected to head the Committee of Confederation. This is not to say that Adams was only a schemer, placing consensus above all. Adams knew that each of those men, and Jefferson in particular, had true gifts that the revolutionary cause should exploit. Jefferson, according to Adams, "came into Congress in June, 1775, and brought with him a reputation for literature, science, and a happy talent of composition. Writings of his were handed about, remarkable for the peculiar felicity of expression." Adams also knew that Jefferson was not a boisterous member of Congress, rather it was Jefferson's silence in large crowds that gave him a peculiar reputation as one who was "frank, explicit, and decisive upon committees and in conversation—not even Samuel Adams was more so." Adams further related that those attributes of Jefferson "soon seized upon my heart; and upon this occasion I gave him my vote, and did all in my power to procure the votes of others."

Apparently, Jefferson was surprised at his selection, assuming Adams himself would be the author. As Adams remembered their conversation about drafting the Declaration, Jefferson had even suggested that Adams write the draft, Jefferson needing prodding to take responsibility for such a momentous task:[289]

Jefferson: "Why will you not? You ought to do it."
Adams: "I will not."
Jefferson: " Why?"
Adams: "Reasons enough."
Jefferson: "What can be your reasons?"
Adams: "Reason first, you are a Virginian, and a Virginian ought to appear at the head of this business. Reason second, I am obnoxious, suspected, and unpopular. You are very much otherwise. Reason third, you can write ten times better than I can."
Jefferson: "Well, if you are decided, I will do as well as I can."[290]

Adams, who also viewed drafting the Declaration as too taxing on his own time, pushed others to have Jefferson selected. "I think he had one more vote than any other, and that placed him at the head of the committee. I had the next highest number, and that placed me the second. The committee met, discussed the subject, and then appointed Mr. Jefferson and me to make the draft, I suppose because we were the two first on the list."[291]

Three distinct lessons can be drawn from the circumstances resulting in Jefferson's selection to head the committee to draft the Declaration. First, **the long game matters**. Adams was thinking about who should draft the declaration two years before it needed to be done and when most people would have thought independence was insanity. Adams knew that, by thinking toward this end for so long, he would be better able to prepare an overall strategy, as well as be better able to stay on goal. Too often persuasive writers and speakers do not keep the end game in mind when they plan the message for today, this minute in the here and now. Rather, persuasive writers and speakers should use their talents to guide today's audience toward accepting the bigger argument to come a week, month, or even years later. **Write for today so that today's audience will be in the right position to say yes when you are ready to unleash your real endgame on that audience tomorrow.** By thinking about who would be best able, and best politically, to draft a declaration two years in advance, when the time finally came, Adams had set the stage to maneuver Jefferson into the position.

Second, **recognize the strengths of those around you and utilize them**. This is a lesson we should be familiar with, but Adams's actions here give us a prime example. Adams must have recognized that the drafter of the Declaration would live in fame, or infamy, and fame and recognition were things Adams longed for over the course of his career. But he understood that, although Jefferson was not a persuasive speaker, he was a very powerfully persuasive writer. This acknowledgment freed Adams to engage in business that was in line with his strengths: here, maneuvering delegates and giving speeches to build up support for independence. The bottom line is something you have read before: as long as there are no ethical concerns, **place your mission first and your ego second**.

This leads us to our third lesson: **it is critical to understand the political environment when drafting a persuasive document.** This is similar to the lesson to "know your audience," but can be even more damning to your argument if not paid attention to. You can draft the most appealing argument in the world to a like-minded audience, but if it is delivered when the political winds are blowing against you, then those same winds are blowing against your audience, making their support of your argument unlikely at best. **If it seems like political suicide to make your point at a given time, then it's likely political suicide to accept or support your point, too.** This is true outside of politics proper, too. If you are pitching a sale, mind the economic and social landscape to know if your pitch will land. Here, Adams understood that Virginia held a special place in the soon-to-be created Confederation, and by having Jefferson lead the way, he would not only secure Virginia's support but also add to his own credibility.

In approaching the drafting of the Declaration, Jefferson's goals were to be both poetic and logical, to plainly define the facts and basis upon which the Revolution was justified for the American people.[292] Jefferson needed to create "sympathy for the larger cause while condemning Britain in compelling terms."[293] He explained his purpose in a letter to Henry Lee in 1825:

> [W]ith respect to our rights, and the acts of the British government contravening those rights, there was but one opinion on this side of the water. All American whigs thought alike on these subjects.
>
> When forced, therefore, to resort to arms for redress, an appeal to the tribunal of the world was deemed proper for our justification. This was the object of the Declaration of Independence. Not to find out new principles, or new arguments, never before thought of, not merely to say things which had never been said before; but to place before mankind the common sense of the subject, in terms so plain and firm as to command their assent, and to justify ourselves in the independent stand we are compelled to take. Neither aiming at originality of principle or sentiment, nor yet copied from any particular and previous writing, it was intended to be an expression of the American mind, and to give to that expression the proper tone and spirit called for by the occasion.

All its authority rests then on the harmonizing sentiments of the day, whether expressed in conversation, in letters, printed essays, or in the elementary books of public right, as Aristotle, Cicero, Locke . . . .[294]

"As he sat to write the Declaration at Jacob Graff's house—he slept in one room and wrote in a private parlor across the stairs—Jefferson knew what had to be done, he knew how to do it."[295] He intended to express the "proper tone and spirit called for by the occasion,"[296] he knew how to do it, he had the tools to do it, and he did it.

In due course, Jefferson completed his masterpiece and on June 28, 1776, Jefferson's Declaration was introduced to the Congress. The debate to adopt the document began on July 1, 2014. In total, nearly 50 alterations were made to the document.

Jefferson hated being edited, especially by a committee. Franklin noted that Jefferson seemed to feel that every edit was not a suggestion to improve the document but an attack on his person. Despite the cuts, when the final document was sewed together, "it was still [Jefferson's] voice at the core of the enterprise. And the author of the document saw his words as sacred."[297] In his autobiography, Jefferson wrote about some of those changes that affected him most:

> The pusillanimous idea that we had friends in England worth keeping terms with, still haunted the minds of many. For this reason those passages which conveyed censures on the people of England were struck out, lest they should give them offence. The clause too, reprobating the enslaving the inhabitants of Africa, was struck out in complaisance to South Carolina and Georgia, who had never attempted to restrain the importation of slaves, and who on the contrary still wished to continue it. Our northern brethren also I believe felt a little tender under those censures; for tho' their people have very few slaves themselves yet they had been pretty considerable carriers of them to others."

Thus, there were definitely substantive edits that needed to be made for political reasons. Jefferson still saw the cuts as affronts to his own abilities, but saw in the end that the real import of his words remained.

Ernest Hemingway summed up this lesson eloquently and, in Hemingway's fashion, succinctly: "the first draft of anything is shit." **Edit.** Editing is the process of perfecting your work. It **ensures that your words are the right words, that your order is the right order, and that your message carries through in a clear, concise, and persuasive way.** Although Jefferson was not a fan of having others edit his work, he understood that editing was a necessary part of the persuasive process. Often it is at this point that the author ensures her argument is hitting the critical points. This is especially true in legal writing, where the editing process involves not only a determination that they have addressed the legal question at hand but also that they have double checked that they have countered their opponent's claims. A gifted writer not only counters arguments his opponent is making, but also anticipates and blocks (or weakens) arguments that they might expect to make in the future. The purpose is also to persuade people who are not "opponents," but who may not be convinced to see your side in a situation. So when editing, **make sure you have given the reader clear reasons to accept your argument and to refute the other side's position, and to do so for reasons the reader will think are just and proper.** It's all in how you draft, redraft, and edit your argument.

A further point needs addressed, here. **Typos are deadly to your ability to persuade.** They distract a reader and highlight for the reader that the author's argument is not perfect. In fact, a reader is most often less likely to *look for* holes in your work if there are not overt errors that jump out. But a reader who encounters typos, formatting, or other nonsubstantive mistakes early on may be a harsher critic of substantive matters, too. In this way, the author's credibility is on the line. Therefore, **an author must make the time to clean any writing of typographical errors.** Treat editing as the powerful tool it is and not as a chore to be avoided or given short shrift. It is also tremendously useful just to look at your work with "cold eyes," after having let your work sit for a few days or, better, to get another set of eyes on your work. Time or a new perspective can help you catch those errors so simple to fix but so damning if passed along to a reader you are attempting to persuade.

This, admittedly, is not my strong suit. My students and likely my readers often find typos in my work—it is something I constantly work on. In working on this, I'm driven by a quote of the late, great Vince Lombardi: "Perfection is not attainable, but if we chase perfection we can catch excellence."

On July 2, 1776, Congress adopted Lee's Resolution for Independence. Two days later, they ratified the Declaration of Independence. The Declaration went into print on July 6th and was publicly read for the first time on July 8, 1776, to a crowd cheering, "God bless the free states of North America!"

The significance of the Declaration was apparent from the moment it came into existence. With a pen, Jefferson changed the world. He articulated a new form of government that had not existed, in any meaningful way, for almost 2,000 years. He articulated a government that was to be *of* and *for* the people, and in which all men were created equal in the eyes of that government.

THE DECLARATION OF INDEPENDENCE.

IT'S CALLED "CLASSIC" FOR A REASON

Aristotle taught persuaders over 2,300 years ago that the goal of argumentative writing was to convince your audience that your ideas are legitimate—or, at least, more legitimate than your opponent's arguments. Aristotle divided his means of persuasion into the three categories discussed in detail in Chapter 1: *ethos, pathos,* and *logos.* This section aims to use our understanding of these terms developed in Chapter 1 to examine Jefferson's use of each in his drafting of the Declaration of Independence. Jefferson, in writing the Declaration, understood Aristotle's analysis of rhetoric and adopted it fully.

The lesson here is simple: **when you know a method works—use it**.

ETHOS

Ethos, Greek for character, is the appeal based on the credibility of the persuader. It is focused on how trustworthy the writer is and is conveyed via tone, style, and an author's reputation in the community. This last is important, because the writer's reputation, as it relates to her *ethos,* can be independent from the particular message. For example, your rabbi's advice on religious or moral matters carries weight; your rabbi's advice on which car to buy may not carry so much weight. An author's expertise in a given field also informs this reputation in the community. For example, where a doctor that you don't know gives you advice on what to eat, that likely will make an impression on you; where a subordinate who has always told the truth despite having the opportunity to lie to their benefit tells you something, you're likely to listen. In essence, you can persuade others based on your character. This is often referred to as an argument's "ethical appeal." It hardly seems surprising, of course, that we tend to believe people we respect.

The key here is that **you, as a persuasive writer, should strive to internalize this trait, and project the impression that your writing is not only worth reading but is also worth believing**. Jefferson understood this need, so made himself appear to be an authority by demonstrating a mastery of the facts, correctness in the law, and that moral and philosophical authority were on his side.

One simple, practical lesson to increase your perceived ethos is to **pay attention to your wardrobe**. When I teach larger classes, I wear a suit. I do that not only because I believe in the philosophy of "dress like a lawyer, think like a lawyer" (or in my case, "dress like a law professor, think like a law professor"), but also because I want to increase my students' perceived *ethos* of me. I already start from a place of authority, but that would quickly be eroded if I were to come to class dressed in shorts and flip-flops.

Another lesson of which we should all be cognizant is the need to **carefully consider your mode of delivery, the tone of your writing, and your audience when attempting to increase your *ethos***. For instance, sending a formal letter for settlement on firm letterhead conveys a seriousness that an e-mail, or even less so, a text can convey. **Ensure that you strike the correct tone with your audience**. This is another lesson that I, personally, struggle with: I am often too familiar in tone, which can devalue my message. Lastly, as in all things, **know your audience**. This is critical in ensuring that you are maximizing your *ethos* and can be as simple as not using words that a particular generation would not understand. An example: "yolo," apparently, is the new slang for "cool" and an acronym for "you only live once." Recently, a student asked me for a letter of recommendation. When I agreed, she told me, "that is yolo." I was not only unimpressed, confused, and reconsidering my recommendation, but then embarrassed that I had no idea what she was talking about, which slowly turned into shame when I spent ten precious minutes looking it up.

It is clear from reading the Declaration of Independence that Jefferson understood the importance of prestige and community standing as it relates to persuasiveness. Indeed, the opening sentence states that what follows is the "the unanimous Declaration of the thirteen United States of America." It thus started from a position of power, representing that a single voice was speaking for a united people. And the first substantive passage draws on the highest authorities to say that this united people, speaking with one voice, have both God and nature on their side:

> When in the Course of human events, it becomes necessary for one people to dissolve the political bands which have connected them with another, and to assume among the powers of the earth, the separate and equal station to which the Laws of Nature and of Nature's God entitle them, a decent respect to the opinions of mankind requires that they should declare the causes which impel them to the separation.

Jefferson, here, along with appealing to emotion (*pathos*), was establishing that he and his colleagues were of ethical standing, rational, and of moral character. Later, Jefferson ensures that he is clear—that they are prudent men who are cautious and reasonable, men of experience and maturity. He lets his readers know that this is not some simple mob of individuals, merely unhappy with the tax structure between Britain and the Colonies. "Prudence," he says, "indeed, will dictate that Governments long established should not be changed for light and transient causes; and accordingly all experience hath shewn, that mankind are more disposed to suffer, while evils are sufferable, than to right themselves by abolishing the forms to which they are accustomed."

Jefferson declared to the King, Parliament, the British, and the world that, as prudent men, they had petitioned for redress and had been rebuffed: "In every stage of these Oppressions We have Petitioned for Redress in the most humble terms: Our repeated Petitions have been answered only by repeated injury." The Declaration not only proffered that they were reasonable men but also cited to facts. Specifically, Jefferson noted that the Colonies had engaged the government and people of Britain and "have appealed to their native justice . . . and we have conjured them by the ties of our common kindred to disavow these usurpations, which, would inevitably interrupt our connections and correspondence."The reader thus realizes, on his own though by Jefferson's guidance, that because the colonists' pleas for help went ignored, independence was sought as their only real remedy left: "They too have been deaf to the voice of justice and of consanguinity. We must, therefore, acquiesce in the necessity, which denounces our Separation, and hold them, as we hold the rest of mankind, Enemies in War, in Peace Friends."

In concluding, the Declaration made its most dramatic and effective *ethos*-focused argument. First, Jefferson drew in the Supreme authority to establish the Colonies' credibility. Where once the colonists pleaded with the King to no avail, the colonists were now "appealing to the Supreme Judge of the world for the rectitude of our intentions." Further, Jefferson reiterated that this Declaration spoke with one voice for all the people of all the Colonies, that it was submitted "in the Name, and by the Authority of the good People of these Colonies."

Three critical lessons can be gathered from Jefferson's use of *ethos* in drafting the Declaration. First, **when you are writing on behalf of someone with a higher level of credibility than you, ensure people know it.** Jefferson does not make a personal argument for independence; he rather makes an argument on behalf of everyone currently living under the yoke of British rule. He specifically cites to the independent persons, the governments of each colony (elected representatives), and God as his sources of authority— Jefferson was merely their mouthpiece, their pen.

Second, as mentioned, a key trait of *ethos* is the appeal to moral authority. **If you have the moral high ground, let the reader know it.** That said, don't dwell on that one point, but mention it as one of many points on which you win your argument. Jefferson not only decried Britain's treatment of the colonies, as will be discussed next, but he also ensured that the people of America had the moral high ground. Jefferson made this point perhaps more strongly than any other. Specifically, Jefferson makes clear that the Declaration was a reaction to Britain's mistreatment of the Colonies and that independence was a measure of last resort after so many failed appeals to King and what used to be country. He was unequivocal that the Declaration was necessary to prevent "an absolute Tyranny over these States."

Lastly, as mentioned, **tone and an understanding of one's audience is important when constructing an argument's** *ethos*. Here, Jefferson struck the perfect tone between the indignation many colonists wanted to hear and the humility expected of respectable gentlemen when discussing grievances. To the masses, Jefferson wrote that his people are entitled by God to "decent respect" and that the "history of the present King of Great Britain is a history of repeated injuries and usurpations." To those who cared about the gentleman's code, King and Parliament included, he wrote that the colonies had appealed to the King's and Parliament's "magnanimity" and sovereignty, but were only repressed further.

These seemingly competing messages struck a balance that allowed the Declaration to resonate with distinct audiences. It let two audiences know, in their own languages, that the Colonies were starting a war with the most powerful nation in the world. By not antagonizing Great Britain beyond what was necessary to make their case, they strengthened their argument. Next, we examine the effectiveness of passion. **If over-the-top, passion can be a distraction or may turn off even otherwise interested readers.** By using passion sparingly in a piece that seems, for the most part, moderate, you make your whole piece seem calm, intelligent, and only more persuasive for its perceived moderation.

PATHOS

Pathos refers to a persuader's ability to appeal to a reader through emotion. Jefferson was a master at appealing to sentiment and passion. An appeal to *pathos* does not attempt to achieve only an emotional response, but also seeks to have the readers sympathize and empathize with the author's argument— to feel the writer's passion as their own. Indeed, the word *pathos* is rooted in the Greek *pascho*, which means to suffer. *Pascho* is used 39 times in the New Testament, mostly referring to Jesus's suffering for the sins of man. Hence, in some sense, *pathos* seeks to draw the reader in to the point of suffering with the writer. A common way of expressing an emotional appeal is through a story, where esoteric concepts of logic can be described in tangible terms.[298] "The values, beliefs, and understandings of the writer are implicit in the story and conveyed imaginatively to the reader."[299] *Pathos* thus is both a plea to the emotions and the imagination of the reader.[300]

Jefferson understood that engaging *pathos* means more than just writing a tearjerker—he knew that **you must ensure that the evocative language you do choose to use advances your argument**. For instance, when I teach on the subject of sexual crimes, I use the word "rape" in my student handouts and lectures. There is a tendency in the legal academy to try and soft-pedal some of the harshness that inevitably comes with the territory. Some, when teaching this sensitive subject, call the crime "sexual assault," which, while that is a legally accurate description in many jurisdictions, does not carry the real impact that the word "rape" carries. "Rape" is powerful; it incites anger, fear, and sadness. "Sexual assault," on the other hand, sounds almost clinical and invites an explanation of the circumstances. I don't use "rape" purely to elicit these emotions, but rather to pull my students into the world of the victim, to experience some of what they feel—obviously not the worst of what they feel—and to face the facts as the victim or defendant preserve them. Did the defendant have a reason to think there was consent? Would a reasonable person think consent was given?

When I worked at the US Department of Justice as a federal prosecutor, I was careful in how I described victims, witnesses, and defendants. For example, when working on national security cases arising out of the war in Afghanistan, I rebuffed the office's policy to call our targets "unauthorized combatants." Instead, I called them what they were. I called them the term that would evoke the feelings I needed the jury to feel. I called them, simply, terrorists, Al-Qaeda, Mujahideen (those engaged in Jihad), or Taliban.

Another practical lesson to take from a discussion of pathos is to **offer emotionally charged reasoning through the presentation of visuals**. In my class on sexual crimes, I have found that putting a face on this particular crime is powerful. When I begin this class, I give students a handout and put up a PowerPoint with a picture of Cherice Morales. The handout is a single page and lists some very basic facts about Cherice. It lists that at the age of 14, she was raped by her 49-year-old high school teacher who received a 1-month prison sentence after the judge in the case suspended his 15-year sentence because the victim was "older than her chronological age." It says that Cherice killed herself at the age of 16, soon after the sentencing. I wrote the handout dispassionately so that the students would see the stark contrast between the horrific crime and the ridiculous sentence and reasoning handed down. The students read the facts of the case while Cherice's face hangs on the screen. The point of the exercise is to take the crime of rape out of a vacuum and explore it for what it is—a crime against people, real people, not historical figures on the pages of casebooks.

This, however, brings up another lesson: there is a fine line between offering an emotionally charged argument that implores the reader to follow you and manipulating a reader into siding with you. **Do not attempt to intellectually pickpocket your reader by using emotion. The real goal is to present your argument so the reader sees your points through the lens you set out, not to break down the reader's will by overpowering them with emotional arguments.** By doing the latter, you lose credibility, build resentment toward you and your argument, and, ultimately, either make yourself unpersuasive or actively persuade the reader to be adverse to your position.

The Declaration has a strong *pathos* theme that runs throughout. Indeed, it seems that Jefferson chose each word to be as realistically descriptive as it could be, avoiding hyperbolic phrasing so as not to lose credibility and persuasiveness. He chose his words to best appeal to the world to see the King's wrongs. A nonexhaustive list includes the following:

- "a right inestimable to them and formidable to tyrants only";
- "invasions on the rights of the people";
- "dangers of invasions from without, and convulsions within";
- "swarms of [soldiers] to harass our people";
- "murders . . . they commit . . . on these [people]";
- "establishing therein an arbitrary government . . . [of] absolute rule";
- "[the King] has abdicated [our] government"; and
- "waging war against us."

The Declaration was moderate on some levels, but it was also the instrument to tell the story of the Colonies' struggle against a tyrant to the world. So it needed to tell the real story, without glossing over the important details that would influence readers' perceptions of these Americans and their cause. The Declaration was not a debate. It was not a negotiation. Jefferson had one chance to write to the world and convince them of the justness of the revolutionary cause. In short, he needed more than just evocative language. He needed to tell the world what was happening and why the drastic measure of independence was the only remedy the people had left to them. Toward the end of Jefferson's list of grievances, he inserted the blunt and powerful language,

> [the King] has plundered our seas, ravaged our Coasts, burnt our towns, and destroyed the lives of our people. He is at this time transporting large Armies of foreign Mercenaries to compleat the works of death, desolation and tyranny, already begun with circumstances of Cruelty & perfidy scarcely paralleled in the most barbarous ages, and totally unworthy the Head of a civilized nation. He has constrained our fellow Citizens taken Captive on the high Seas to bear Arms against their Country, to become the executioners of their friends and Brethren, or to fall themselves by their Hands.

Because of these travesties, Jefferson declared, a "Prince whose character is thus marked by every act which may define a Tyrant, is unfit to be the ruler of a free people."

The Declaration, by its nature, is a document invoking pathos. It is an emotional plea for justice. But its emotion is strategic—even the particulars on the list of the King's wrongs toward the colonists were chosen with purpose. For instance, the Declaration criticized the King for "cutting off our Trade with all parts of the world." This was a call to other European nations, telling them that if the Colonies became independent, then business would be good. A complaint with a deeper meaning in the Declaration is the accusation that the King hired Mercenaries to fight against the Colonies. At the time the Declaration was written, a significant portion of "Americans" actually considered themselves British and either totally rejected independence or only supported the efforts of the Continental Congress as far as addressing particular grievances with the King, not leaving the Empire. But the notion of sending non-British soldiers, many of whom were hessians (German auxiliaries), to kill British citizens in America was considered very abhorrent and turned the opinion of many of those who were on the fence toward the independence movement.

Many in Jefferson's intended audience remembered that during England's own civil war, King Charles I lost the support of his subjects when he was seen to hire mercenaries to fight against English citizens (he actually deployed Scots, Welsh, and Irish, who were his own subjects and technically not mercenaries—but tell that to a mid-1600s Englishman). In that same war, the Parliament also lost considerable support from the populace for employing mercenaries (mostly Germans) who were seen as using brutal tactics, often directed at the civilians caught in the middle. As a result of this history, and despite the English civil war occurring over 100 years before Jefferson wrote the Declaration, there was a deep suspicion of using mercenaries by the common British citizen, especially against other Brits.

Jefferson understood this history lesson, as we should, too. **Often, you are not just trying to persuade the target of your writing; rather, by understanding who could potentially be reading your writing, you can design your message carefully and pick the right words and the right emotions to capture the hearts and minds of a larger audience.** Jefferson was not trying to persuade the King of anything—he most certainly had made up his mind years before. Instead, Jefferson sought to persuade other Americans, British citizens, and the nations of the world.

LOGOS

Logos—simply the Greek for "word"—refers to the consistency, clarity, and rational conclusion of the argument. Many simply say that the *logos* of an argument is the sense of logic in an argument. *Logos* also refers to the supporting evidence the writer uses to legitimize their message.

There are two separate, related but distinct, types of logic: deductive and inductive. Deductive reasoning—also known as top-down logic—is the process of forming a conclusion from several statements that flow into one another. The epitome of a classic deductive argument is the series attributed to Socrates:

1. All humans are mortal.
2. Socrates is human.
3. Therefore, Socrates is mortal.

Inductive reasoning, on the other hand, gives the reader examples and draws propositions and conclusions from them. Inductive reasoning is the way that most people think and more easily permits incorrect conclusions to be drawn. For example,

1. All life we know of is carbon based.
2. Therefore, if we find a new life-form, it will be carbon based.

This is not certain, however, because we don't know of all life forms, just the ones we already know of—the fallacy is highlighted by writing this out. In truth, there could be a silicone-based life form somewhere that we simply do not yet know of.

There are several key lessons we can take away from the idea of *logos*. First, **be sure to provide your reader with evidence.** Related opinions of other experts, empirical data, and physical evidence all add to your ability to persuade. The more evidence and authority you use in your argument, it can be said, the more legs it has to stand on. Don't just say, "my client lived too far away to commit the murder" if the medical examiner gives a time of death and several witnesses saw him at another location at that time. Instead, explain to your reader the distance, how long it would take to travel that distance, and the impossibility of your client being in two places at the time the murder took place. And **don't stop there, tell your reader how you know these facts: give your sources.** This is also a place where you can bring in some *ethos*. In fact, none of these aspects of Aristotle's elements of rhetoric are meant to exist in a vacuum without the other two. Be sure to cite to someone who is a subject matter expert or who has a strong character for trustworthiness—and **ride the proverbial coattails of another's** *ethos*.

Second, **avoid logical fallacies.** Formal fallacies are arguments that are always wrong because of their structure and can be deductive or inductive. For example, a deductive fallacy is presented below:

1. If Seattle is the capital of Washington State, then it must be in Washington State.

2. Seattle is in Washington State.
3. Seattle is the capital of Washington State.

This seems to flow, but is of course untrue. Although Seattle is in Washington State, Olympia is the capital. The "if" beginning the series leads to this false result.

An inductive fallacy may track the following pattern:

1. I have been to every zoo in the United States and every tiger is black and orange.
2. Therefore, all tigers are black and orange.

We know this is not true because we know white tigers exist. Yet the flow of the words makes sense without further thought.

Be precise in your premises and conclusions. This is especially true for writing oral arguments where we are more forgiving of mistakes. It is important to understand that **an entire argument can be unraveled with one disproven line of reasoning.** Some people believe that because jet fuel burns at a maximum temperature of 1,500 degrees and because steel melts at 2,750 degrees, the 9/11 World Trade towers' collapse must have been due to explosives planted by the CIA or by Israeli operatives or by (insert conspiracy theory here). However, experts know that such temperatures can weaken steel to the point that it becomes ineffective as support material for a skyscraper. An entire series of conspiracy theories falls apart because of similar fallacies. Note that this does not prove that there was no conspiracy, but Occam's razor suggests that, when two theories can explain an event, the simpler theory is the more likely option. Occam's razor thus impels us to accept the most straightforward explanation, that airliners crashing into the buildings caused their collapse.

Lastly, **be consistent.** There is power in consistency. Being consistent in your arguments not only adds to your credibility but also denies your opponents the opportunity to use your own words against you. Chapter 6 discussed Jefferson's own inconsistencies, which most definitely affected his ability to persuade in his own time (with some audiences) and affects his lasting legacy today.

A famous example of this can be seen in the Lincoln/Douglas debates where Lincoln and Douglas ran for the same Senate seat. Lincoln cornered Douglas between his own catch phrase of "popular sovereignty" (a notion that allows states to decide whether they will be a free or slave state) and his support of the Dred Scott decision (a decision preventing the government from interfering with owners' rights over slaves). By pointing out this contradiction to the audience, Lincoln put Douglas in a position where he had to either abandon his position of popular sovereignty, admit that the Dred Scott case helped the spread of slavery even into states that did not want it (a concept that directly contradicts popular sovereignty), or confess that the Dred Scott decision was bad law. All three options were impossible choices for Douglas, and Lincoln knew it.

Throughout the debates, Lincoln repeatedly attempted to force Douglas to take a stand and declare his interpretation of Dred Scott, a dilemma that Douglas could not escape. If he renounced the decision, he would lose the support of the South and tear the Democratic Party apart. On the other hand, if he tried to appease the slave powers and support the decision, his Illinois constituents would turn on him. Douglas did the only thing he could, given Lincoln's persistence. He pacified his voters, endorsing his political theory of popular sovereignty and saving his Senate seat. By appeasing his constituents on this point, however, he started a chain of events that would eventually lead to the divide of the Southern and Northern Democrats and, thus, to his loss to Lincoln in the presidential race. Douglas's lack of consistency lost him the White House, but gained the nation a great deal by Lincoln's election.

Jefferson's reasoning in writing the Declaration of Independence followed from his belief that the primary role of a government is to ensure the well-being of its citizens. Thus, when a government is no longer able to ensure their well-being, the people have a right, endowed by their Creator, to change that government. Jefferson also made the logical argument that, because the King had usurped the rights of the colonists, who were loyal British citizens, the people then had the right to throw off their chains and create a government that would uphold that social contract (a sacrosanct contract, according to Jefferson). In making this argument, Jefferson stated,

> We hold these truths to be self-evident, that all men are created equal, that they are endowed by their Creator with certain unalienable Rights,

that among these are Life, Liberty and the pursuit of Happiness. –That to secure these rights, Governments are instituted among Men, deriving their just powers from the consent of the governed, –That whenever any Form of Government becomes destructive of these ends, it is the Right of the People to alter or to abolish it, and to institute new Government, laying its foundation on such principles and organizing its powers in such form, as to them shall seem most likely to effect their Safety and Happiness.

The Declaration goes on to argue that logical reasoning drove the people of the colonies to conclude that, when they made every attempt to be subordinate to their sovereign, the King, but were still forced to give up their basic human rights, they had no choice but to create their own government:

> But when a long train of abuses and usurpations, pursuing invariably the same Object evinces a design to reduce them under absolute Despotism, it is their right, it is their duty, to throw off such Government, and to provide new Guards for their future security.--Such has been the patient sufferance of these Colonies; and such is now the necessity which constrains them to alter their former Systems of Government.

Jefferson knew that he had to provide more than just a series of abuses to persuade his diverse readers of the need for independence. He knew that **without the "why," a writing is nothing more than a story.** He knew that he had to provide the connection for the reader between the facts and the end sought. Jefferson did not just describe the plight of the American people, he told the world that *because* of this plight and *because* of the refusal of the King to provide redress or even listen, there was no alternative but independence.

A writing from a highly respected individual who is not only an expert in the subject upon which they are pontificating, but also one who has a reputation for trustworthiness, is not persuasive in and of itself. Neither is an emotional description of a factual event, even if its author is that same well-respected author. Moreover, while a writing that explains the logic of the argument may be somewhat persuasive, we know that not all-persuasive writing is created equal. Therefore, as Jefferson listed in detail exactly what the King did or failed to do in such an eloquent manner, **so too must you provide evidence to your reader**.

Think of a very clever criminal prosecutor who is about to conduct a murder trial. She has a brilliant theme for her case, she has practiced her opening statement and she not only has a spectacular delivery, but has ensured her tone is perfect and has conducted her jury research to understand her audience—her *ethos* is solid. This prosecutor does not stop there, this is an emotional case and she is prepared to deliver the case in a way that places the jurors in the shoes of not only the victim but also the cop and defendant at times—her *pathos* is solid. Lastly, the prosecutor has a logical road map of what she thinks happened: all As are Bs, all Bs are Cs; therefore, all As are Cs—so she has some logos. But does she win? No. A great story from a respectable person with a logical argument, more often than not, will lose without credible evidence to back it all up. One lesson we learned earlier is that **brevity is a key element in persuading.** While that is assuredly true, **brevity cannot make up for a lack of thoroughness in evidence and thoroughness cannot replace brevity**. It's the master persuader that finds the balance between the two.

BORROW FROM THE BEST

While history knows Jefferson as the "author" of the declaration, in reality, he was the chair of the committee to draft the document. A previous lesson gleaned from Jefferson's works was to stay open-minded to the input from others for edits, especially. Jefferson did seek the advice of his colleagues in perfecting the Declaration. The phrase, "self-evident," for example, came from Benjamin Franklin. Jefferson sent a draft to Franklin's home (Franklin was confined to his residence for medical reasons) with a note reading "will Doctor Franklin be so good as to suggest such alterations as his more enlarged view of the subject will dictate." It was a good alteration: that Jefferson was open to edits proved invaluable.

Jefferson had other influences in drafting the Declaration of Independence, beyond those who offered editing suggestions. Two such influences were Thomas Paine's *Common Sense* and John Locke's entire body of work.

There are few documents that have impacted modern history, and certainly American history, more than Thomas Paine's *Common Sense*. This incredible pamphlet, written in 1775, was originally signed simply, "Written by an Englishman." Only 48 pages long, it was the most important text yet to openly talk about independence. Paine reported that the pamphlet sold 120,000 copies in three months. He seems to have exaggerated a bit; but even a more credible estimate of 75,000 copies in a few weeks was a staggering number in colonial times. In *Common Sense*, Paine called to action the people living in the American Colonies and challenged the authority of the British Government. It was the first such document to use plain language to openly ask for independence. Jefferson's works often took on the tone of an affable intellectual because he largely wrote his works based from the works of eminent philosophers and toward those circles that had historically held power, the educated elite. Paine's tone, though, made his works more approachable to Americans of more humble origins. George Washington, in fact, had the pamphlet read to his troops in the field. Paine's *Common Sense* is widely hailed as a major contribution to the independence cause.

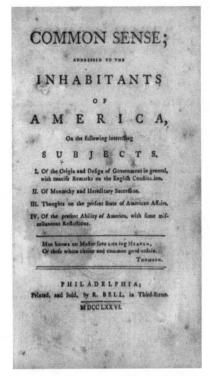

Jefferson had obviously read *Common Sense*—he read everything. He was immediately impressed by the bold ideas it presented so clearly. Reading the Declaration and *Common Sense* side-by-side, it is easy to spot many differences, but it is clear that Jefferson was influenced greatly by many of Paine's ideas. In fact, he very likely borrowed many ideas directly from Paine. Both documents directly attacked the King as a tyrant and openly called for independence. Paine, too, followed Aristotle's guide to persuasion, using *ethos*, *pathos*, and *logos* to provide the right foundation and flow for his argument. Perhaps the most striking similarity between Paine's *Common Sense* and Jefferson's Declaration of Independence is not what they share with each other but what they share with a third party, John Locke.

Pablo Picasso once said, "good artists copy, great artists steal." This is an easy lesson: **Don't plagiarize; do borrow from the best**. Often, the greatest writings are persuasive because they took something that was already good, already persuasive, and made it even better.

Locke's fingerprints are clear throughout both Paine's and Jefferson's works. In both, the authors contend that the people had a right and perhaps even a duty to rebel when oppressed. Paine and Jefferson applied that concept to the American situation, asserting that the ultimate obligation of a King was to safeguard the "natural rights" of his subjects. Both asserted that when he fails to do so, he should be removed.

In *Common Sense*, Paine declared that "Mankind being originally equals in the order of creation, the equality could only be destroyed by some subsequent circumstance, the distinctions of rich, and poor, may in a great measure be accounted for, and that without having recourse to the harsh, ill-sounding names of oppression and avarice." Paine's *commonsensical* (pun intended) approach in his piece demonstrates these philosophies to his reader plainly and uses them to justify and argue for American independence from Great Britain.

Jefferson similarly states in the Declaration that "All men are created equal, that they are endowed by their Creator with certain unalienable rights, that among these are life, liberty, and the pursuit of happiness. That to secure these rights, governments are instituted among men, deriving their just powers from the consent of the governed."

To arrive at those conclusions, both authors borrowed from Locke, who nearly 100 years earlier wrote in *The Second Treatise on Government*,

> A state also of equality, wherein all the power and jurisdiction is reciprocal, no one having more than another; there being nothing more evident, than that creatures of the same species and rank, promiscuously born to all the same advantages of nature, and the use of the same faculties, should also be equal one amongst another without subordination or subjection . . . .
>
> But though this be a state of liberty, yet it is not a state of licence: though man in that state have an uncontroulable liberty to dispose of his person or possessions, yet he has not liberty to destroy himself, or so much as any creature in his possession, but where some nobler use than

its bare preservation calls for it. The state of nature has a law of nature to govern it, which obliges every one: and reason, which is that law, teaches all mankind, who will but consult it, that being all equal and independent, no one ought to harm another in his life, health, liberty, or possessions: for men being all the workmanship of one omnipotent, and infinitely wise maker; all the servants of one sovereign master, sent into the world by his order, and about his business; they are his property, whose workmanship they are, made to last during his, not one another's pleasure: and being furnished with like faculties, sharing all in one community of nature, there cannot be supposed any such subordination among us, that may authorize us to destroy one another, as if we were made for one another's uses, as the inferior ranks of creatures are for our's. Every one, as he is bound to preserve himself, and not to quit his station wilfully, so by the like reason, when his own preservation comes not in competition, ought he, as much as he can, to preserve the rest of mankind, and may not, unless it be to do justice on an offender, take away, or impair the life, or what tends to the preservation of the life, the liberty, health, limb, or goods of another.

Jefferson was inspired by Locke even more than Paine had been. Perhaps the most famous line from the Declaration is, "all men are created equal, that they are endowed by their Creator with certain unalienable Rights, that among these are Life, Liberty and the pursuit of Happiness." This sentiment is echoed in the Fifth Amendment to the US Constitution, as well: "No person shall be . . . deprived of life, liberty, or property, without due process of law . . . ." Locke wrote on this topic in his *Second Treatise on Government*, stating that the nature of man was his being born "with a title to perfect freedom." Locke goes on define that this freedom means man should have "uncontrolled enjoyment of all the rights and privileges of the law of nature, equally with any other man, or number of men in the world, hath by nature a power, not only to preserve his property, that is, his life, liberty and estate, against the injuries and attempts of other[s.]" Jefferson took Locke's teachings to heart, and inserted these high philosophical notions into this nation's foundational documents.

THE TRIAD

Few writings have evoked such passion and the drive to change one's destiny as the Declaration of Independence. But the question still remains, Why was it so powerful? One reason is that the Declaration's structure uses the rule of three, also called the triad.

The lesson of the triad is that you should **address just three points, and address them well, rather than delving into the minutia.** This is a clear-cut rule, developed and tested over the course of history: a persuasive writer should convey exactly three points—not one, not two. This is not to say you need to create two more arguments if ever you intend to persuade. Rather, you should break your one argument into three parts, thinking through how best to do that to make each a solid leg for your argument to stand upon.

This rule is embedded deep in our culture and history. Three is an important number throughout antiquity. The Ancient Greek philosopher Pythagoras, who is often described as the first pure mathematician, believed three was one of the most important numbers, even a divine number. This is supported by the Greek belief that three Gods created the world. The divinity of three is seen in other cultures as well. Three things are prized above all in the ancient religion of Taoism: gentleness, frugality, and humility. The Hindu Trimurti, also called the Hindu trinity, consists of Brahma, Vishnu, and Shiva. The Christian belief in the Holy Trinity states that God exists in three separate bodies that are ultimately one: the Father, the Son, and the Holy Spirit. Even our form of government is divided into three equal branches: executive, legislative, and judicial.

This is not pure coincidence. The tripartite structure has been used by history's most effective communicators, all masters of the triad. General Douglas MacArthur successfully used the triad when he said, "Duty—Honor—Country, those three hallowed words reverently dictate **what you ought to be, what you can be,** and **what you will be.**" It just sounds powerful. Other individuals who have used the triad with seeming ease and perfection were Sir Winston Churchill, Dr. Martin Lutheran King, and, most recently, President Barack Obama. In one of his many speeches during World War II, Churchill stated that "[n]ever in the field of human conflict was so much owed by so many to so few." Even more famous was his address to citizens of England during the Battle of Britain. On the radio, while the battle was raging, he stated, "[w]e **shall fight them on the beaches, we shall fight them in the streets, we shall fight them in our homes,** we shall **never, never, never** surrender." This address had the desired effect: the British steeled their backbones, prevailing through the Battle of Britain and the war.

An especially persuasive written document was a letter written to fellow clergymen by Dr. King on April 16, 1963 while he was in the Birmingham jail. There, Dr. King wrote that "[t]he Negro has many pent-up resentments and latent frustrations, and he must release them. So **let him** march; **let him** make prayer pilgrimages to the city hall; **let him** go on freedom rides and try to understand why he must do so." Even more celebrated is his "I Have a Dream" speech, given on August 28, 1963, on the steps of the Lincoln Memorial. There, he delivered his most effective triad and one that still sends shivers down the spines of many: "**Free at last! Free at last!** Thank God Almighty, we are **free at last!**"

President Obama used the triad to perfection in his 2008 campaign. Indeed, his campaign slogan was in and of itself a triad—"yes we can"—and he used this simple triad with mastery. On January 27, 2008, when he lost the New Hampshire primary, he gave the following speech:

> For when we have faced down impossible odds, when we've been told we're not ready or that we shouldn't try or that we can't, generations of Americans have responded with a simple creed that sums up the spirit of a people: **Yes, we can. Yes, we can. Yes, we can.**
>
> It was a creed written into the founding documents that declared the destiny of a nation: **Yes, we can.**
>
> It was whispered by slaves and abolitionists as they blazed a trail towards freedom through the darkest of nights: **Yes, we can.**
>
> It was sung by immigrants as they struck out from distant shores and pioneers who pushed westward against an unforgiving wilderness: **Yes, we can.**

One, two, three; one, two, three; one, two, three. The structure allows for anticipation to build without making the reader wait so long that he loses interest or has time to wander.

The Triad has not only been used by and for the good of mankind, though. Hitler, too, was a master of the rule. During a speech of note he made while in Munich on February 21, 1941, the Fuhrer, addressing the English and American hope of an internal German coup, stated,

> **Then they said**: "Winter, General Winter is coming, and he will force Germany to her knees." But, unfortunately, the German people are 'winter-proof.' German history has passed through I do not know how many tens of thousands of winters. We will get through this one, too.
>
> **Then they say**: "Starvation will come." We are prepared against this, too. We know the humanitarian sentiments of our British opponents and so have made our preparations. I believe that starvation will reach them before it reaches us.
>
> **Then they said**: "Time is on our side." But time is only on the side of those who work. No one has been harder at work than we. Of that I can assure them. In fact, all these vague hopes which they are building up are absolutely childish and ridiculous.

In this author's opinion, one of the greatest examples of the rule of three is presented by Lincoln's Gettysburg Address. In a nearly 300-word speech, Lincoln employed this tool three times, in three paragraphs, in three minutes.

In the first instance,

1. "**we can not** dedicate";
2. "**we can not** consecrate";
3. "**we can not** hallow—this ground . . . ."

In the second, "[i]t is rather for us to be here dedicated to the great task remaining before us,"

1. **that** from these honored dead we take increased devotion to that cause for which they gave the last full measure of devotion";

2. "**that** we here highly resolve that these dead shall not have died in vain";
3. "**that** this nation, under God shall have a new birth of freedom . . . ."

In the third, Lincoln uses the rule most adroitly, expressing his hope that this

1. "government of the **people**";
2. "by the **people**";
3. "for the **people**, shall not perish from the earth."

Likewise, Jefferson was also a master of the rule of three. Jefferson understood the power and simplicity, and thus clarity, that resulted by his delivering words persuasively, rhythmically, and memorably. One reason that this method of delivery is so effective is because the brain is most proficient at processing, understanding, and recalling three items of information at a time. Jefferson used the triad on three occasions in the Declaration alone.

Of course, the most famous instance is his declaration that we each are entitled to "**life, liberty** and **the pursuit of happiness.**" Second, in the list of grievances against Great Britain, Jefferson accused the King of hiring mercenaries to complete the works of **death, desolation, and tyranny**" against the American people. Lastly, Jefferson concludes, "[a]nd for the support of this Declaration, with a firm reliance on the protection of divine Providence, we mutually pledge to each other our **Lives, our Fortunes, and our sacred Honor.**" Jefferson clearly understood the lyricism that came from this structure. When added to the many other elements at which he was master, his words take on such power as to make them evoke profound emotions still today.

REPETITION AND PARALLEL STRUCTURE

The great law professor Irving Younger said that only a true maestro of cross examination can break its basic rules. One such rule is that, "if the jury hears a fact once they may believe it, hears it twice they will believe it, and if heard a third time Jesus Christ himself will have to tell them otherwise."

The lesson here is that **we remember things we hear or read more than once; they just seem more important.** In fact, if we are not careful, we may believe things without any other evidence if we hear them more than once.

In drafting the Declaration, Jefferson ensured that his key points were repetitive. The first example of this is when, in speaking to the King's abuses, he wrote, "He has refused . . . He has Forbidden . . . He has refused . . . He has," etc. Here "He" was King George III, and by repeating his abuses the list appears longer—it seems like a never-ending list of abuses and struggles the Colonies face. Though not in threes, the repetition does aggrandize Jefferson's point. The repetition not only makes the complaints look more acute but also explains the frustrations felt by the colonists. Such a listing explains their lack of hope that the King would ever address their concerns. And it ensured that the world knew that the British Colonies in America tried to heal the rift but to no avail: "We have warned them . . . We have reminded them . . . We have appealed . . . We have conjured them by the ties of our common kindred to disavow these usurpations . . . ." The repetition makes it clear that this is not an exhaustive list, but simply a sample of the abuses of the Crown.

In addition to using repetition to ensure a reader is exposed to key points and highlighting key points in an argument, a persuasive writer should understand the principle of parallel structure (also called parallel form). Parallel structure is in the same family of persuasive stylistic qualities as repetition and refers to using a pattern of words to demonstrate two or more ideas are of equal importance. This is done to help the reader grasp a deeper meaning behind individual phrases.

It is easiest to understand this principle by seeing what it is not: Take, for example, "Gabriel was considered an outstanding employee because he was never tardy, he was also motivated and showed initiative." That is not an example of parallel structure and thus seems to lie flat. Compare that sentence with the following, "Gabriel was considered an outstanding employee because he was never tardy, he was motivated, and he showed initiative." The second sentence not only flows better, but the aspects of Gabriel's excellence as an employee build upon each other, exemplifying the greater message—that Gabriel is an outstanding employee.

Parallel structure is common in great writings. Take the Holy Bible: In Deuteronomy, 5:6-21 (the Ten Commandments), it is written that "Thou shalt not commit adultery, thou shalt not steal, thou shalt not bear false witness against thy neighbor," etc. In Matthew, 5:3-11, the Beatitudes (Jesus's Sermon on the Mount), it is written, "Blessed are the poor . . . . Blessed are they that mourn . . . . Blessed are the meek . . . . " Again, in Matthew, 6:9-13, the last sentence in the Lord's Prayer reads, "For thine is the kingdom, and the power, and the glory, forever. Amen."

Shakespeare, too, understood the power of this principle to make a common sentence appear poetic—sound knowledge, no doubt, for a poet to possess. In *Richard II*, scene III, King Richard laments his unfortunate position:

> "I'll give my jewels for a set of beads,
> My gorgeous palace for a hermitage,
> My gay apparel for an almsman's gown,
> My figured goblets for a dish of wood."

The Declaration of Independence, too, is filled with parallel structured arguments. Once such example is found in the list of the King's abuses:

> For cutting off our Trade with all parts of the world:
> For imposing Taxes on us without our Consent:
> For depriving us in many cases, of the benefits of Trial by Jury
> For transporting us beyond Seas to be tried for pretended offences
> For abolishing the free System of English Laws . . . .

For this, for that, for the other. The parallel structure helps Jefferson's argument that the abuses go on and on. The reader is constantly reminded by simple word choice and clause structure that this, and that, and the other are of the same type and seem to never end.

The Declaration's list of abuses, again, was intended to show the world the many harms the Colonies suffered under British rule. By structuring the complaint as such, it appeared longer and the suffering seemed harsher.

Structure your words, your clauses within sentences, your sentences, your paragraphs, and your section headings to make use of this principle. If you write things the same way, the reader knows they are related. So, if you want your position to seem consistent and strong, use parallel structure. Likewise, if you want your opponent's position to seem less so, vary the structures of the arguments you attribute to him. In this way, you continue to frame his best arguments on your own terms. Making your arguments stronger by using these principles can make all the difference in persuading your readers. Using the principle of parallel structure allows a writer to better define her points and insinuate that even more is going on, while keeping the language of the document concise.

IN THE NAME OF GOD

Jefferson's ability to use words and symbolism to entice his listener to see a case or issue through the perspective he desired was unmatched, and a primary method by which he achieved that was by invoking the name of God Almighty.

Christians strive to be "Christ-like," and 1700s America was a strongly Christian society. Jefferson used this to his advantage in drafting the Declaration; the deeply religious country made God an obvious point of reference for his audience. If God agrees with you, how can any lesser figure disagree?

Lincoln was also a master at invoking the Creator's name for his gain. In a debate with Stephen Douglas, Lincoln trapped Douglas between his words and the Word of God.

> [The Judge] has read from my speech in Springfield in which I say "that a house divided against itself cannot stand," [(Douglas had criticized this phrase during his opening remarks)]. Does the Judge say it can stand? I don't know whether he does or not. The Judge does not seem to be attending to me just now, but I would like to know is it his opinion that a house divided against itself can stand. If he does, then there is a question of veracity, not between him and me, but between the Judge and an authority of a somewhat higher character.

Lincoln cornered Douglas with this loaded question. Further, by only alluding to what "authority of a somewhat higher character" he meant, the audience had to come to the conclusion on their own, making it only more likely they would be persuaded as they realized it themselves. Douglas either had to admit he misspoke or admit Lincoln's slogan was correct. Douglas knew enough to recognize that he had stepped into a trap. He knew that his "house divided" phrasing was not just a slogan, it was a quote from Mathew, 12:25, when Jesus Christ stated "every kingdom divided against itself will be ruined, and every city or household divided against itself will not stand." Douglas had to insult himself or God—Lincoln was lawyering at its best.

The Declaration has several biblical allusions, two being most prominent. The first is in the introduction, when Jefferson states that the entire backing of the decree from the American people is a decree from God: "it becomes necessary for one people to dissolve the political bands which have connected them with another, and to assume among the powers of the earth, the separate and equal station to which the Laws of Nature and of Nature's God entitle them . . . ." The second allusion is in Jefferson's concluding paragraph where he "appeal[s] to the Supreme Judge of the world" for justice and moral authority.

To the right audience, speaking in the name of "God" can be extremely powerful and persuasive. It not only increases your *ethos* but also, for many, it gives your message more resonance. Specifically, it allows you to argue that you were not only wronged but also that your offender, by implication, wronged God. It should be reiterated that your audience and the circumstances must be just right to do this. In Jefferson's time, this could almost have been a universal truth, an authority recognized by all. Today, however, invoking the name of God must be done occasionally and with good reason in order to have the intended effect. In some environments, religious references and appeals to God may be seen as cheap and hollow attempts to elevate your argument.

In the end, the Declaration is remembered not only because it sparked a Revolution that, at its end, saw the most powerful nation in the world reeling and the birth of a future superpower but also because it was shocking, it was emotional, and it was persuasive. It is fixed in American history as one of her founding documents. Indeed, the father of the Constitution, James Madison, when debating the passage of the Bill of Rights, suggested that the Constitution needed a better preamble—one that solidified that America was a land of the people, for the people, by the people. He recommended the Declaration of Independence be copied into the preamble. In support of his modification, that ultimately failed, he said on June 18, 1789,

> First. That there be prefixed to the Constitution a declaration, that all power is originally vested in, and consequently derived from, the people. That Government is instituted and ought to be exercised for the benefit of the people; which consists in the enjoyment of life and liberty, with the right of acquiring and using property, and generally of pursuing and obtaining happiness and safety. That the people have an indubitable, unalienable, and indefeasible right to reform or change their Government, whenever it be found adverse or inadequate to the purposes of its institution.

The Declaration, itself, may not have made it into the Constitution, but the principles enunciated therein by Jefferson left their mark on the Constitution and on America's political thought and social trajectory through today.

Lessons Learned

- Think big, act big, and, with hard work and some luck, big things will follow.
- Compromising and winning is better than standing stubbornly resolute and losing.
- Timing can make all the difference. Wait to push your agenda until you have built a consensus.
- Write for today so that today's audience will be in the right position to say yes when you are ready to unleash your real endgame on that audience tomorrow.
- Know when your friends can help—and when they can't. If it seems like political suicide to make your point at a given time, then it's likely political suicide to accept or support your point, too.

- Edit. It ensures that your words are the right words, that your order is the right order, and that your message carries through in a clear, concise, and persuasive way.
- Draft, redraft, and edit your argument. It only gets stronger through time and effort.
- Pay attention to your wardrobe. It seems shallow, but flip-flops and a pressed suit create very different impressions.
- Present your argument so the reader sees your points through the lens you set out; do not just break down the reader's will by overpowering them with emotional arguments.
- Be precise in your premises and conclusions. An entire argument can be unraveled with one disproven line of reasoning.
- Don't plagiarize; do borrow from the best.
- Address just three points, and address them well, rather than delving into the minutia.
- Employ the Triad: Structure your words, your clauses within sentences, your sentences, your paragraphs, and your section headings to make use of the Triad: one, two three; one, two, three; one, two, three.

8

OTHER MASTERPIECES

Thomas Jefferson's Declaration of Independence is the undisputed magnum opus of his fame, demonstrating his great persuasive writing prowess. However, the Declaration was not the first and was not the last of Jefferson's works. Indeed, it was through his early writings that he gained the reputation of being a passionate, effective, and persuasive pamphleteer that opened up so many doors later in his career. This reputation would lead to his election to the Second Continental Congress as a delegate from Virginia and eventually to his appointment as the chair of the Declaration committee.

Jefferson was a writer, first and foremost, and a prolific one at that. Here, we will only be exploring a small sampling of his other works, including *A Summary View of the Rights of British Americans*, *Virginia's Statute for Religious Freedom*, and a selection of his letters. We will delve into these works to learn not only how Jefferson mastered the writing of words, but also how he persuaded others through them.[301]

A SUMMARY VIEW OF THE RIGHTS OF BRITISH AMERICANS (1774)

In his mid-twenties, Jefferson was profoundly curious, particularly with regard to the ongoing debates between the various colonies as to their proper relationship with the British Crown and Parliament. In the late 18th century, the game of politics was the equivalent of today's Hollywood movies, the NFL, and pop culture all rolled into one. Like many young intellectuals, Jefferson was seduced by the drama, action, and influence that politics provided. As previously discussed, Jefferson was appointed to the Virginia House of Burgesses in 1768. Because of his prominent family and their wealth, it was expected that he would be among the ruling elite in Virginia. However, there were many political giants active throughout the colonies, and his ambition was likely to be constrained by such notable personalities as Patrick Henry, Thomas Paine, John Hanson, John Hancock, and George Washington, to mention only the most famous in American history textbooks. He knew he couldn't compete with the accomplished orators of his time, but he could, and did, distinguish himself with his writing skills. Jefferson made his first major contribution to the dialogue of American politics, and the world for that matter, in 1774 when he authored *A Summary View of the Rights of British America* (the "*Summary*"). At the time it was published, the *Summary* was one of the most radical documents ever published in the English-speaking world. It was so radical precisely because the *Summary* directly challenged the King when most documents at the time found a way to skirt the issue to honor and maintain British sensibilities (and one's freedom from prison). In it, Jefferson declared that the legislative body in Virginia was equal to the Parliament in England.

The *Summary* was one of Jefferson's earliest works to be printed and widely distributed. It truly is a forceful and explosive reiteration of the Constitutional rights of the British citizens living in the colonies.[302] According to Jefferson, though, *Summary* was never meant to be published; rather, it was a "draught [he] prepared for a petition to the King."[303] Because he became ill while traveling, he sent the letter on to be reviewed and signed by other colonial leaders. "It was read generally by other members, approved by many, and thought too bold for the state of affairs at the time."[304]

The lesson here is to **always do your best. You never know who will read what you've written and, for that matter, which of your works will jump-start or define your career.**

When I was a federal prosecutor working for the U.S. Attorney's Office for the Southern District of California, I handled many felony cases. However, the case that gained me the most notoriety was a misdemeanor, "Stolen Valor" case, where no jail time was even sought by the government. San Diego, being a military-heavy community was very interested in a man claiming to be a retired Major General in the Marines who had earned a Purple Heart. I was ambushed twice for interviews and my pleadings were quoted in almost every area newspaper, even on some national news. I remember having two distinct thoughts: (1) why were the reporters not interested in the felony drug cases or the major human trafficking case I was working on with another prosecutor, cases in which we were actually breaking new legal ground and putting away truly evil people, and (2) I was so happy that I had taken the pleadings in this case seriously, ensuring they were complete and persuasive—even edited—a lesson I will never forget.

In the rearview mirror of our own history, we can see that the *Summary* was a strategic document: not only was it the forerunner to the Declaration of Independence, but it was also a test to determine how other colonial leaders, the King, Parliament, and the world would react to an aggressive assertion of American power.[305] The argument in the *Summary* was "dazzlingly drawn"[306] to lay out the credentials of the American people who had earned a place in the British Empire—not as vassals but as coequals:

> the lives, the labours, and the fortunes, of individual adventurers, was by these princes, at several times, parted out and distributed among the favourites and followers of their fortunes, and, by an assumed right of

the crown alone, were erected into distinct and independent governments; a measure which it is believed his majesty's prudence and understanding would prevent him from imitating at this day, as no exercise of
such a power, of dividing and dismembering a country, has ever occurred in his majesty's realm of England, though now of very antient
standing; nor could it be justified or acquiesced under there, or in any
other part of his majesty's empire.

The *Summary* presented a logical argument. It stated that Americans were
British citizens who freely settled in the colonies. As such, they were exercis-
ing their natural rights to explore the world—an "eat what you kill" argument,
if you will.[307]

In Jefferson's eyes, the New World was conquered and the settlements were
built and established "at the expence of individuals, and not of the British
public. Their own blood was spilt in acquiring lands for their settlement, their
own fortunes expended in making that settlement effectual; for themselves
they fought, for themselves they conquered, and for themselves alone they
have right to hold." Borrowing from ancient principles, Jefferson fervently
insisted that the lands in North America were blood-soaked and paid for by
the labor of its settlers who died sowing their farms, and by the efforts of its
warriors who died in defense of what they built. (The historic significance, and
irony, of this claim is not unnoticed by this author. Much of this nation was
built on the backs of enslaved people and the "conquered" of whom Jefferson
spoke were those Native Americans who have faced innumerable atrocities in
the name of freedom, Manifest Destiny, and American Empire.)

To Jefferson, the math was simple: The colonists' sacrifices of their fortunes
and blood superseded the traditional and moral claims of the King.[308]
Jefferson based his theory in law, but also upon his analysis that America had
forged a new nation, distinct from but parallel to the Motherland. As time
passed, the new bloodline was diverging further from that of their kinsmen in
Britain.[309]

Instead of addressing the King's claim that the colonies were merely an
extension of Britain, Jefferson metaphorically transformed the continent into
a separate frontier nation—formed by the righteous, conquering, hardwork-
ing labors of a distinct people.[310]

A key lesson can be learned here. **Precedent is powerful. If you can relate your argument to historical events, you can find persuasive power. What is even more powerful, though, is when you can use an opponent's own history against him.**

In his *Summary*, Jefferson embarked upon a history lesson of feudal and allodial land tenure.[311] He asserted that William the Conqueror, who he referred to as William the Norman, introduced the proposition that all land belonged to the Crown. Under English law, before William the Conqueror conquered, it was the land possessor who enjoyed title to the property above all claims. Moreover, while William sailed across the English Channel, he never sailed the Atlantic. Therefore, according to Jefferson's *Summary*, the lands in America were never conquered "nor surrendered to him, or any of his successors." Jefferson went on to argue that Americans "who migrated hither, were farmers, not lawyers. The fictitious principle that all lands belong originally to the king, they were early persuaded to believe real; and accordingly took grants of their own lands from the crown." Jefferson also used then-current British law to demonstrate how the King's inequitable treatment of the Americans favored the colonists' position.

There is an adage popular with trial attorneys that should be learned by all: **If the law is on your side, argue the law—If the facts are on yours side, argue the facts—If neither are on your side, pound your fist on the table and argue fairness.** In the *Summary*, Jefferson made a legal argument and argued the facts through the knowing lens of history, and by understanding that **equity can be just as effective an argument as either law or facts**, he argued that the unfairness of the King's actions had not weakened the colonists' case, but instead strengthened it.

Specifically, Jefferson cited the presence of British troops without the consent of the colonial legislative body. He stated in support of his argument the fact that if the King possessed the right to deploy troops without legislative consent, he could "swallow up all our other rights whenever he should think proper. But his majesty has no right to land a single armed man on our shores, and those whom he sends here are liable to our laws . . . ." Jefferson understood that a fundamental principle of English liberty and British law as recognized in the *English Bill of Rights* was that standing armies were void without the consent of a legislative body, Parliament in the case of Great Britain.[312]

By pointing out that if one fact can't be true without the other, then the decision maker has to either assume that either both facts exist or neither does. Jefferson's argument concerning the troops is more nuanced than one would perceive at first glance. Essentially, if "British Americans" are in fact British citizens and subject to the sovereignty of the Crown, then they should receive all the rights associated with that citizenship, to include no taxation without representation and the prevention of quartering of troops in private homes. On the other hand, if they are not full British citizens, then they are a separate people and just as sovereign as the Empire itself.

The shot across the bow from the *Summary* could not be mistaken, and was not mistaken by its readers. Jefferson's *Summary* asserted that the people of the colonies had "freedom of language and sentiment which become a free people" and that the King was a "servant[], not the proprietors of the people," a sentiment he expressed two years later in the Declaration. "[T]o secure these rights," he later wrote, "Governments are instituted among Men, deriving their just powers from the consent of the governed."

Again, **don't reinvent the wheel.** If something works, use it again. Even in this book, I have drawn on ideas expressed in other writings. As my Drill Sergeant would say, **"work smarter, not harder."**

The last lesson from the *Summary* comes from the very last paragraph and contains one of Jefferson's best one-liners:

> "Let those flatter who fear; it is not an American art."

Was this the first step in the rise of the American cowboy? Regardless, Jefferson was teaching us, and the King, that toadying is not the American way. **While there is a place for ingratiating yourself to your audience in some persuasive pieces, so too is there a time to be frank in others. There is a time when only to-the-point arguments will win over your crowd.**

STATUTE OF VIRGINIA FOR RELIGIOUS FREEDOM (1777)

When asked "What is Thomas Jefferson's legacy?" most of us focus on his role as a Founding Father (including his writing the Declaration of Independence) and his official offices (including as the third President of the United States). But perhaps a better question is, What did Jefferson want his legacy to be? What did he want to teach the world? In my case, when I die, I would like my tombstone to read:

HERE LIES

ARTHUR LAVERNE RIZER III

FATHER

TEACHER

SOLDIER

This is how I want my children and my children's children to remember me.

A BILL *for establishing* RELIGIOUS FREEDOM,
printed for the consideration of the PEOPLE.

WELL aware that the opinions and belief of men depend not on their own will, but follow involuntarily the evidence proposed to their minds; that Almighty God hath created the mind free, and manifested his Supreme will that free it shall remain, by making it altogether insusceptible of restraint: That all attempts to influence it by temporal punishments or burthens, or by civil incapacitations, tend only to beget habits of hypocrisy and meanness, and are a departure from the plan of the holy author of our religion, who being Lord both of body and mind, yet chose not to propagate it by coercions on either, as was in his Almighty power to do, but to extend it by its influence on reason alone: That the impious presumption of legislators and rulers, civil as well as ecclesiastical, who, being themselves but fallible and uninspired men, have assumed dominion over the faith of others, setting up their own opinions and modes of thinking, as the only true and infallible, and as such, endeavouring to impose them on others, hath established and maintained false religions over the greatest part of the world, and through all time: That to compel a man to furnish contributions of money for the propagation of opinions which he disbelieves and abhors, is sinful and tyrannical: That even the forcing him to support this or that teacher of his own religious persuasion, is depriving him of the comfortable liberty of giving his contributions to the particular pastor whose morals he would make his pattern, and whose powers he feels most persuasive to righteousness, and is withdrawing from the Ministry those temporal rewards which, proceeding from an approbation of their personal conduct, are an additional incitement to earnest and unremitting labour for the instruction of mankind: That our civil rights have no dependance on our religious opinions, any more than on our opinions in physicks or geometry: That therefore the proscribing any citizen as unworthy the publick confidence, by laying upon him an incapacity of being called to offices of trust and emolument, unless he profess or renounce this or that religious opinion, is depriving him injuriously of those privileges and advantages to which, in common with his fellow citizens he has a natural right: That it tends also to corrupt the principles of that very religion it is meant to encourage, by bribing with a monopoly of wordly honours and emoluments, those who will externally profess and conform to it: That though indeed these are criminal who do not withstand such temptation, yet neither are those innocent who lay the bait in their way: That the opinions of men are not the object of civil government, nor under its jurisdiction: That to suffer the civil Magistrate to intrude his powers into the field of opinion, and to restrain the profession or propagation of principles on supposition of their ill tendency, is a dangerous fallacy, which at once destroys all religious liberty; because he being of course Judge of that tendency will make his own opinions the rule of judgment, and approve or condemn the sentiments of others only as they shall square with, or differ from his own: That it is time enough for the rightful purposes of civil government for its officers to interfere when principles break out into overt acts against peace and good order: And finally, that truth is great and will prevail if left to herself; that she is the proper and sufficient antagonist to error, and has nothing to fear from the conflict, unless by human interposition, disarmed of her natural weapons, free argument and debate; errours ceasing to be dangerous when it is permitted freely to contradict them.

WE the General Assembly of *Virginia* do enact, that no man shall be compelled to frequent or support any religous Worship place or Ministry whatsoever, nor shall be enforced, restrained, molested, or burthened in his body or goods, nor shall otherwise suffer on account of his religious opinions or belief, but that all men shall be free to profess, and by argument to maintain their opinions in matters of religion, and that the same shall in no wise diminish, enlarge, or affect their civil capacities.

AND though we well know that this Assembly, elected by the people for the ordinary purposes of legislation only, have no power to restrain the acts of succeeding Assemblies, constituted with powers equal to our own, and that therefore to declare this act irrevocable would be of no effect in law; yet we are free to declare, and do declare, that the rights hereby asserted are of the natural rights of mankind, and that if any act shall be hereafter passed to repeal the present, or to narrow its operation, such act will be an infringement of natural right.

Jefferson's reads,

> HERE WAS BURIED
> THOMAS JEFFERSON
> AUTHOR OF THE
> DECLARATION
> OF
> AMERICAN INDEPENDENCE
> OF THE
> STATUTE OF VIRGINIA
> FOR
> RELIGIOUS FREEDOM
> AND FATHER OF THE
> UNIVERSITY OF VIRGINIA

The first thing to note about Jefferson's headstone is what isn't there. It does not mention his tenure as President, that he was a Founding Father, or that he was an accomplished Statesman. Jefferson wanted the world to remember him as a writer. Indeed, two of the three accomplishments he wished listed were his authorships; the third was for his role in creating a University to teach others how to write and to appreciate learning, among other disciplines. This was no accident. Jefferson designed his own headstone, giving explicit instructions as to its design as well as to the epitaph.

It is odd to think that we can learn something from a headstone, yet here we are. Even the oddities have teachable elements. Here, Jefferson's devotion to the profession of writing comes through. **Identifying yourself in a particular way is often the key to becoming that person. We often**

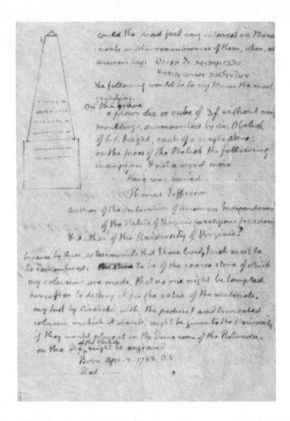

hear stories of athletes, artists, and even politicians that "will themselves to greatness." Sure, there is a lot to say for natural talent and learned skills, but often the axiom "fake it 'til you make it" is the key to success. Jefferson identified himself as a writer—it was who he was and how he wanted the world to remember him. He didn't have to fake it to make it; his self-identification and hard work to realize that identity made him.

We have already discussed the Declaration. We now shift our focus to the second entry on Jefferson's tombstone, the *Statute of Virginia for Religious Freedom* (the "*Statute*"). Jefferson drafted the *Statute* in 1777. It was introduced as a bill to the Virginia General Assembly in 1779, then sat in the Assembly until 1786. The reason for the long delay was the fierce opposition among members of the Church of England. Before the Revolution, the

Church of England was the established Church of colonial Virginia. Various laws required the colonists to attend service and support the Church through public taxes. In 1784, a resolution was proposed to enact a tax to support all Christian denominations. This tax bill, as all tax bills, caused great political excitement. Jefferson and his ally, James Madison, reintroduced the Religious Freedom Bill, which was enacted on January 16, 1786.

The lesson for persuasive writers is to **be persistent**. Just because you lose initially does not mean that the battle is over. If you are not persuasive enough the first time around, or if the timing or political winds just aren't yet right, simply **wait and plan for another opportunity to argue your case.** Some of the world's greatest triumphs in the progression of humanity have resulted from persistent persuaders. Every Scot schoolchild learns the story of Robert the Bruce and the spider. Inspired by seeing a small spider fail six times to make a web only to succeed on his seventh attempt, Robert the Bruce was able to persuade his small, discouraged army to try a seventh and final time to achieve victory against the British who had taken the first six. Persistence in the face of failure is a quality of leadership that only helps you persuade in the future. If you can point to, or if people know of, past instances when you were eventually proven right or successful, they will be that much more willing to follow you through present difficulties.

The *Statute* serves as one of the great pillars of religious freedom and as one of the models for and forerunners of the First Amendment to the US Constitution, which provides that "Congress shall make no law respecting an establishment of religion, or prohibiting the free exercise thereof." In his autobiography, Jefferson wrote about drafting the *Statute*:

> The bill for establishing religious freedom, the principles of which had, to a certain degree, been enacted before, I had drawn in all the latitude of reason and right. It still met with opposition; but, with some mutilations in the preamble, it was finally passed; and a singular

proposition proved that its protection of opinion was meant to be universal. Where the preamble declares, that coercion is a departure from the plan of the holy author of our religion, an amendment was proposed, by inserting the word "Jesus Christ," so that it should read, "a departure from the plan of Jesus Christ, the holy author of our religion;" the insertion was rejected by a great majority, in proof that they meant to comprehend, within the mantle of its protection, the Jew and the Gentile, the Christian and Mahometan, the Hindoo, and Infidel of every denomination.

The Statute secured the rights of Virginians to follow the faith of their choosing, without fear of coercion or retribution. Jefferson acknowledged that, as a statute, future legislative bodies could change the law later, but he warned that to do so would be "an infringement of a natural right."

Here, Jefferson **teaches us a very useful trick of persuasion: preemptive public shaming. Call your opponent out on his argument, but on your terms.** Specifically, by laying out potential consequences of your opponent's argument, you essentially persuade him against making the argument in the first place. A preemptive argument does not always have to shame your opponent to be effective. Take, for example, a situation where you are arguing with an individual who supports softening the drug laws in the United States, particularly for medical purposes. An opening salvo for your position could be that "methamphetamine is one of the most deadly and addictive drugs in the world: ninety percent of those who try it become addicted, the drug has little medicinal value, and it is a major funder in the Mexican cartel drug war." With this opening, there is a strong chance your opponent will be persuaded to avoid even arguing for a softening of laws regarding methamphetamine. The more realistic arguments for softening marijuana laws, though, may be harder to preemptively counter.

Jefferson was bold in drafting the *Statute*, pulling no punches. He outlined the ugly history in the western world of the oppression of man in the name of

God, which was thinly veiled religious slavery. He characterized the subjection by the religious elite, for their own benefit, as follows:

> the impious presumption of legislators and rulers, civil as well as ecclesiastical, who being themselves but fallible and uninspired men, have assumed dominion over the faith of others, setting up their own opinions and modes of thinking as the only true and infallible, and as such endeavouring to impose them on others, hath established and maintained false religions over the greatest part of the world, and through all time; that to compel a man to furnish contributions of money for the propagation of opinions which he disbelieves, is sinful and tyrannical . . . .

Jefferson understood the potency of religion and further understood how despots could and had used religion for their own tyrannical purposes throughout history. His *Statute* was a bulwark against that oppression.

The lesson here is one that extends well past persuasive writing. **Cut your opponents off from their source of power. That is a great first step toward victory.** By preventing future American dictators from using God to dominate, Jefferson stripped away one of the most frequently abused tools used by tyrants throughout history. This lesson extends past mere persuasion. Freedom of religion is so integral to our way of life that we hardly think about it, today. But the same can't be said of Jefferson's time. Despite that, Jefferson codified this freedom, and was accused of being an atheist as a result. That "new" ideology, to protect the people's freedom to practice any or no religion, gave birth to an idea that protects us today, so much so that we too often take it for granted.

The words of the *Statute* are profound and commanding—making it one of my favorite Jefferson writings. Jefferson wrote, "Almighty God hath created the mind free." The sentiment is that your mind is free to choose a religion of your own. Of course, it must be admitted that by basing his Statute on the presumption that "a" God exists, it can be seen as repressive to atheists and agnostics. However, Jefferson's declaration that "our civil rights have no dependence on our religious opinions, any more than our opinions in physics or geometry" made it clear that religious affiliation or lack thereof was separate from a citizen's civil rights.

The Statute is short. It only spans three paragraphs. Today, persuasive writing demands succinctness because there is so much competing noise for our readers' attention. Thus, "brevity is next to Godliness" becomes an even truer proverb. In the late 1700s, when paper was expensive and printers used every trick to make use of fewer characters, brevity was also quite important.

The key is that a persuasive writer must not fall into the trap of believing the misconception that length equals rigor or the trap of confusing quantity with quality. Persuasion comes from many aspects. Sheer length is not one of them. As Nobel Prize laureate Sir Peter Medawar noted, "**Good writing upon a subject is almost always shorter than bad writing on the same subject.**"

Jefferson not only would have understood today's concept of "sound bites" but also the concept of "talking points." He had themes in all of his work, including in the language of the *Statute*. Specifically, he would continually circle back to language from the Declaration of Independence. The Declaration and the ideals it professed were incredibly popular at the time, and Jefferson freely used its fame in his arguments. As discussed, Jefferson had argued in the Declaration that the "laws of nature" and of God entitle man to be free from a tyrannical King. Jefferson's *Statute* echoes this, citing that the "Holy author . . . chose not to propagate [religion] by coercion . . . ." Therefore, God entitled man to also be free from tyrannical clergy. Jefferson teaches us that **citing back to a popular work—a work that has already proven to be persuasive—is not lazy; it's smart.**

The persuasiveness of the *Statute* speaks for itself. Because it is the official law in Virginia, it is no surprise that it was cited by the Supreme Court of Virginia in *Perry v. Commonwealth* (1846), holding that the *Statute* declared, to the Christian and the Mahometan, the Jew and the Gentile, the Epicurean and the Platonist (if any such there be amongst us), that so long as they keep within its pale, all are equally objects of its protection; securing safety to the people, safety to the government, safety to religion; and . . . securing purity of faith and practice far more effectually than by clothing the ministers of religion with exclusive temporal privileges . . . .

Yet the Supreme Court of the United States, which has no obligation toward Virginia's statutory enactments or judicial precedent, also recognized the persuasiveness of the *Statute* as persuasive authority in the 1878 case, *Reynolds v. United States*. It again cited to the *Statute* in 1947 in *Emerson v. Board of Education*, holding that First Amendment protections for religious freedom "had the same objective and were intended to provide the same protection against governmental intrusion on religious liberty as the Virginia statute." Even on an international level, the *Statute* had enormous influence in emboldening those who sought religious freedom. "Almost immediately upon its adoption, Jefferson had copies published in Europe."[313] Edwin Gaustad, a scholar on America's religious history, noted that "[f]rom the perspective of more than two centuries later, it is possible to add that the Jeffersonian law set Western Civilization and democratic republics everywhere upon a dramatically different path." Thanks in part to Jefferson and his *Statute*, democratic governments across the world began to recognize that religious toleration was not enough to secure freedom. Democratic governments were forced to recognize that religious liberty could not be a mere privilege arrogantly and condescendingly bestowed upon the masses, but rather as Jefferson's *Statute* proffered, it was a human and natural right to be zealously cherished and preserved.[314]

LETTERS TO LEARN

A great source of political power tapped by Jefferson was his ability to write persuasive letters to family, allies, and enemies. There are literally hundreds of letters drafted by Jefferson ranging on topics from his disappointment over the amount of vegetables his farm produced in a given year to correspondence with then-President George Washington detailing his understanding of how the new federal government was supposed to work. Here, we explore three of his letters. We explore, first, his letter to William Smith, often called the "Tree of Liberty" letter. We then look to a letter from his exchange with the Danbury Baptists, in which we first see the phrase "separation between church and state." Finally, we examine a letter to Samuel Kercheval, written after Jefferson left the presidency and in which Jefferson sums up his views on the flourishing experiment in democracy.

LETTER TO WILLIAM STEPHENS SMITH (1787)

On November 13, 1787, Jefferson wrote to William Smith, a diplomatic official in London, commenting on Shays' Rebellion. The Rebellion was an armed uprising in Massachusetts that was put down by the organized state militia. Jefferson wrote, "God forbid we should ever be 20 years without such a rebellion ... the tree of liberty must be refreshed from time to time with the blood of patriots and tyrants. It is natural manure."

In that letter, Jefferson also asserted that the rebels were, in their own way, protecting American freedoms by ensuring the people had the right to keep the government honest—by force if necessary. He also accused the rebellion of being "founded in ignorance" and worried that the Constitutional Convention was excessively influenced by the rebellion. "[O]ur Convention has been too much impressed by the insurrection of Massachusetts: and in the spur of the moment they are setting up a kite to keep the hen yard in order."[315]

Jefferson was not a casual or what we would call a folksy writer. However, we can see from his "setting up a kite to keep the hen yard in order" comment that he understood that simple, unpretentious, friendly words often make concepts easier to understand. In a sense, and to these readers, Jefferson was just a storyteller—conveying ideas through anecdotes. Being able to be a good storyteller and plain spoken is extremely helpful, if not essential, to being a successful persuasive writer. The storyteller, after all, is the narrator of events and gets to choose what information gets told where. In short, the narrator has the ability to tell or withhold certain facts in certain ways to make his case appear more favorable or the other side's case less so.

Moreover, readers generally appreciate "plain speak" over the more overindulgent writers' self-important "ten dollar words." People appreciate folksy writers—those writers come across as familiar, as one of our own.

Developing the ability to write in a folksy style provides you with many advantages. By and large, people tend to believe writers who use this style over a more formal script. However, it is important not to overdo it. If you push the folksy style too far, you may come across not as the next-door neighbor but as simple-minded or, worse, fake. In either case, you will have lost your ability to persuade that audience. This lesson, then, appears again: **(1) figure out what works and, then, (2) use it.**

Turning back to Jefferson's letter to Smith, the fear that Jefferson expressed of the Constitutional Convention being overly influenced by the rebellion was not unfounded. The delegates had taken Shays' Rebellion seriously, blaming the lack of an institutional response on a systematically weak central government that was struggling to define and protect the liberties for which they had just fought.[316] The result was Congress authorizing an Army to, in part, "suppress insurrections."

Soon after he issued that letter, Jefferson wrote to James Madison, reinforcing his belief that the nation needed "a little rebellion now and then" and, again, sharing his view that the rebels in this particular uprising were "absolutely unjustifiable." Jefferson's almost flippant attitude toward rebellion and its potential to yield positive fruits tempered over time. Soon after the Constitution was finalized and sent for ratification, Jefferson declared, in a 1787 letter to a Dutch diplomat named Charles William Frederick Dumas, "Happy for us, that when we find our constitutions defective and insufficient to secure the happiness of our people, we . . . assemble with all the coolness of philosophers and set it to rights, while every other nation on earth must have recourse to arms to amend or to restore their constitutions." Here we should take a step back to view another Jeffersonian contradiction: his seeming approval of violent rebellion and his celebration of our unique bloodless transitions of power.

Jefferson recanted further after his election to the presidency in 1801. It was then that Jefferson's opinions that he outlined in the letter to Smith transformed. In stark contrast to his view that rebellions were a legitimate method for keeping the government in check (as opposed to elections), Jefferson proposed the formation and recruitment of a national military academy, West Point, to ensure the United States had a professionally trained officer corps.[317] This suggestion was in response to Aaron Burr's failed conspiracy to create an independent republic in the Southwest portion of the country.[318] Practical necessity, once again, gave Jefferson the opportunity to reverse his position. And once again, he took it.

In conclusion, the lessons from the Smith letter are more profound than discussed: **use humor to persuade, write with plain words,** and if appropriate **understand that "folksy" can be more persuasive than ultra-formal.** More specifically, though, the lesson that should be taken away is not something drawn directly from the letter, but from what happened after he wrote that letter—**practical necessity may dictate a change in an opinion** formerly held. **Be mindful,** though, **of your audience's perception of that changed opinion.** Even if correct, it will be fodder for opponents.

A major problem in some areas today, most notably in politics, is that you are rarely "allowed" to evolve your thinking and adopt new positions. A businessman who doesn't adapt will eventually find his buggy-whip business failing. A scientist who ignores advancing discoveries will spend his time dabbling with chemicals in an attempt to turn lead into gold. The politician, though, who doesn't change his mind risks the best interests of the country. But, of course, the politician who does change his mind is at risk of being labeled a flip-flopper. His opponents can apply one of the lessons identified herein against him; they can use his own statements against him. And in an age when everything is captured by a camera, a microphone, or on social media, many political figures are locked into positions that become ever more untenable because of this "trap." **Be able to articulate the difference between a core principle and an opinion or mere hypothesis,** something mutable with changing circumstances, understandings, or facts. **Be willing to adjust your position to best deal with new information.** As this book is written, the nation's attitude toward marijuana usage is changing, yet some resist the tide. The late Senator Byrd (West Virginia) was able to reverse the perception of his early racist past (he had been a member of the Ku Klux Klan), but at a continuing cost that frightened other politicians who observed his struggles. The country would be better off if we "permitted" our leaders to grow, to abandon mistakes they made in their younger years. Unfortunately, "the system" does not seem to offer an easy way to accomplish this.

A valuable lesson that any writer can learn is that **what is true today may not be true tomorrow.** The ability to grow is an absolute necessity for developing the ability to persuade. **It is *critical* for a persuasive writer to be able to admit when she is wrong and move on.** Despite how important this skill is, it is the one most often ignored and is the most difficult to recognize. This ability is essential for several reasons. First, it allows you to develop a more effective argument. If your ego is so completely enveloped in the opinions you hold, you will never be able to see your own blunders, and you will never be able to dump your bad arguments for better ones borrowed from others.

Moreover, you can lose credibility when you are seen as never admitting when you are wrong. As discussed, you should stay true to your principles and values. There are limits to that, however. When new information surfaces and you learn that your position is clearly wrong, sticking to your position may be seen as pure stubbornness, not as principled.

LETTER TO DANBURY BAPTISTS (1802)

The Danbury Baptists' exchange was a series of letters written between Thomas Jefferson and the Danbury Baptist Association of Connecticut. The correspondence started with the Association writing to Jefferson, who was then President of the United States, on October 7, 1801, to protest what they considered infringements on Baptists' religious liberties by the Connecticut legislature. They said, "what religious privileges we enjoy (as a minor part of the State) we enjoy as favors granted, and not as inalienable rights: and these favors we receive at the expense of such degrading acknowledgments, as are inconsistent with the rights of freemen." The Association acknowledged that, as President, Jefferson did not have any direct power over the Connecticut legislature, saying, "we are sensible that the president of the United States is not the national legislator, and also sensible that the national government cannot destroy the laws of each state." Rather, they were appealing to the influence Jefferson had as the drafter of the Declaration of Independence, as a Founding Father, and as an advocate for religious freedom: "but our hopes are strong that the sentiments of our beloved president, which have had such genial effect already, like the radiant beams of the sun, will shine and prevail through all these states and all the world, till hierarchy and tyranny be destroyed from the earth." In short, they wanted Jefferson to use his bully pulpit to put pressure on the legislature and end its persecution.

Jefferson responded on January 1, 1802, with his "wall of separation" letter. Jefferson sympathized with the Baptists in their opposition to an established religion in Connecticut, saying, "[b]elieving with you that religion is a matter which lies solely between Man & his God, that he owes account to none other for his faith or his worship, that the legitimate powers of government reach actions only, [and] not opinions . . . ." Jefferson then expressed his veneration for the First Amendment, decreeing that Congress "make no law respecting an establishment of religion, or prohibiting the free exercise thereof." Jefferson, using his skills as a storyteller, then coined his now famous sound bite, "building a wall of separation between Church [and] State."

This leads us to the first lesson from the Danbury Baptists letter. In today's society of 15-second news clips, we are all aware of the benefit of having snappy quips. Though the public was more receptive to longer writings in Jefferson's time, Jefferson was well aware that short punch lines were easier to remember and imprint in the minds of his audience than pages of text, no matter how eloquently, passionately, and logically written.

Some of the most prevalent examples of sound bites in American history are Teddy Roosevelt's "walk softly and carry a big stick," Franklin D. Roosevelt's "the only thing to fear is fear itself," and John F. Kennedy's "ask not what your country can do for you, but what you can do for your country." My own favorite sound bite does not come from American history, but from Julius Caesar: "Veni, Vidi, Vici," which translates to "I came, I saw, I conquered."

Jefferson's career was filled with such pithy sound bites from his time as a lawyer, his presidency, and his retirement. Some of his most famous quotes are provided below and, in true writer's style, are sometimes borrowings from other greats:

- "Never put off tomorrow what you can do today";
- "Never trouble another for what you can do yourself";
- "Never spend your money before you have it";
- "Pride costs us more than hunger, thirst, and cold";
- "We never repent of having eaten too little";
- "Nothing is troublesome that we do willingly";
- "How much pain have cost us the evils which have never happened";
- "When angry, count ten, before you speak; if very angry, a hundred."

Try to develop a memorable sound bite when writing a persuasive document. Even for those readers accustomed to long text, a well-written, concisely phrased quip will be appreciated, or at least noticed. For instance, if you are writing to a doctor's office because you disagree with a bill, the phrase "this is not about what I am legally entitled to, it's about what I am entitled to as your patient" is a concise, powerful statement of your overall message. And when representing an auto accident victim who lost a leg, the sound bite "making my victim whole" is easily remembered and seems to play well to juries.

By providing a theme to your audience, you reduce the likelihood of your audience making up their own theme—possibly a theme that does not emphasize the point you'd like to make. And a short statement, conveying the most important information, is easy to remember and gives a lasting effect to your message for your reader.

Another lesson we can draw from Jefferson's response letter is, again, in what the letter did not say. The Danbury Baptist Association of Connecticut was attempting to elicit Jefferson into some type of action—to use his office to put political pressure on the Connecticut legislature. However, Jefferson decided that this was not a situation in which he wanted to become involved and expend his political capital, but his words of counsel and support of their principles won him goodwill with the Danbury Baptists, nonetheless, and with others who read the exchange of letters.

LETTER TO SAMUEL KERCHEVAL (1816)

Jefferson's letter to Samuel Kercheval, July 12, 1816, was written 40 years after the Declaration of Independence was drafted and signed, after Jefferson served two terms as President, and after his beloved Monticello was completed (at least after one of his "drafts" of Monticello was completed—he made plans for his home until he died). Jefferson was 73 and had turned his attention to the last item listed on his tombstone—the founding of the University of Virginia. This letter is particularly poignant as it serves to give us insight into Jefferson's view of the American experiment after we ratified our Constitution, added five states to the Union, and survived not one, but two wars against the British.

One of the themes in Kercheval's letter is a concern of the massing of power in Virginia's executive and a call to give more power to the people. Jefferson was blunt concerning Virginia's Constitution:

> judges ... of law when they choose it, are not selected by the people, nor amenable to them. They are chosen by an officer named by the court

and executive. Chosen, did I say? Picked up by the sheriff from the loungings of the court yard, after everything respectable has retired from it. Where then is our republicanism to be found? Not in our constitution certainly, but merely in the spirit of our people.

Jefferson then systematically suggested amendments to the Virginia Constitution to make it more in line with what he thought a constitution should look like in a liberal democracy. Some, though not all, of Jefferson's suggestions are presented below:

1. General suffrage (for all men, still not women or slaves);
2. Executive chosen by the people and not the legislature (Jefferson was appointed Governor of Virginia in 1779 by the legislature); and
3. Judges elected or removable (they were neither in 1816).

The lesson, here, is two-fold. **Never be unwilling to try to make a writing better**. Jefferson was immensely proud of his home state, but was willing to criticize its founding and governing document. Jefferson himself sent notes to be incorporated into the original Virginia Constitution (although they arrived too late from Philadelphia to be used). Jefferson was not only willing to suggest changes inspired by his experience to date to the Virginia Constitution, but was also willing to suggest improvements to the written documents that governed the American experiment as a whole, including the US Constitution. On this point, Jefferson stated, "[s]ome men look at constitutions with sanctimonious reverence, and deem them like the arc of the covenant, too sacred to be touched. They ascribe to the men of the preceding age a wisdom more than human, and suppose what they did to be beyond amendment."

Jefferson, however, knew that in order for a democracy to flourish, it had to be willing to change with the times. Likewise, in order for an author to truly flourish, he must **learn to adapt his writing to the times.** Indeed, there is no doubt that Shakespeare's words are still beautiful, but any writer writing in Shakespearian English today would be playing to a small crowd, indeed, and even then would not be terribly well-received or persuasive—rather, it would seem bizarre. Jefferson was frank on this point—the dead should not rule us today by their understanding of the needs of yesterday; only we truly understand the needs of today. Speaking on the men who drafted the Virginia Constitution and their time, Jefferson wrote, "I knew that age well; I belonged to it, and labored with it. It deserved well of its country. It was very like the present, but without the experience of the present; and forty years of experience in government is worth a century of book-reading . . . ." Jefferson went so far as to say that his fellow founders of Virginia and the United States would echo his sentiment: "and this they would say themselves, were they to rise from the dead."

Jefferson was convinced that *bellum omnium in omnia* ("war of all against all")—which Jefferson interpreted as the "abusive state of man"—is set in motion by allowing one departure from principle to exist, explaining that one departure from principle "becomes a precedent for a second; that second for a third; and so on, till the bulk of the society is reduced to be mere automatons of misery, and to have no sensibilities left but for sinning and suffering."

Eventually, Virginia heeded Jefferson's pleas to improve his state's governing document. In 1851, through a Constitutional Convention, property ownership was eliminated as a requirement from voting, giving full suffrage to all white Virginian males—a marked improvement, though not yet ideal. The 1851 Constitution also changed the method by which the Governor was elected from election by the state legislature to a popular vote. In 1864, when the Civil War was nearing its bloody end, Virginia abolished slavery. A Constitutional Convention in 1870 gave full suffrage to all male citizens of Virginia, including blacks. This victory in human rights was short lived due to a series of Jim Crow laws passed between 1890 and 1902. It was not until the Civil Rights movement and the *Brown v. Board of Education* decision was handed down, over 50 years later, that blacks regained their full voting rights.

Lessons Learned
- Always do your best. You never know who will read what you've written and, for that matter, which of your works will jumpstart or define your career.
- If the law is on your side, argue the law—If the facts are on your side, argue the facts—If neither are on your side, pound your fist on the table and argue fairness. Equity can be just as effective an argument as either law or facts.

- Don't reinvent the wheel. Use what you know works.
- Remember that there are times when only a to-the-point argument will win over your crowd.
- Identifying yourself in a particular way is often the key to becoming that person. We often hear stories of athletes, artists, and even politicians who "will themselves to greatness." Sure, there is a lot to say for natural talent and learned skills, but often the axiom "fake it 'til you make it" is the key to success.
- Be concise: "Good writing upon a subject is almost always shorter than bad writing on the same subject."
- Use humor to persuade, write with plain words, and, if appropriate, understand that "folksy" can be more persuasive than ultra-formal.
- Be willing to adjust your position to best deal with new information.
- What is true today may not be true tomorrow. It is *critical* for a persuasive writer to be able to admit when she is wrong and move on.
- Try to develop a memorable sound bite when writing a persuasive document.
- Read! Keep learning! But, most importantly, write! There's just no substitute for actually doing the thing you're trying to do better.

CONCLUSION

America's history is filled with a great many larger-than-life personalities. Each dominated the political scene for a time, some made dramatic changes to our systems, and, often, they left the country in a better condition than they found it. Thomas Jefferson is a personality of a different sort, however. He was not so dominant because of a larger-than-life personality; rather, he dominated because of his profound, innate ability to communicate. Where many of our American greats have been tremendous oralists, Jefferson was a writer. He defined his place in our history books, our hearts, and our minds by his writings that so fundamentally changed how people all over the globe perceived their realities. The principles he founded the Declaration of Independence upon still inspire Americans and people all over the world to fight for the rights that are justly theirs. The human rights movement, it can be said, really began with Jefferson's declaration of rights under natural law, inherent rights bestowed upon each of us by our mere existence.

That, obviously, raises the man's most profound contradiction: Jefferson wrote of grand principles, but lived with the grimy realities all around him. Slavery, the Haitian revolution, misogynistic tendencies, pettiness, vanity, etc.: Jefferson was a man who definitely knew what hypocrisy truly meant. Though in his letters, he seems to argue for some justifications for his mistakes like those just above, the force of those arguments never quite lands. For a man who made such effective use of *ethos, pathos,* and *logos* in his Great works, that his justifying arguments for slavery do not succeed may be somewhat surprising. Upon examination, the most likely reason for this failure to truly persuade is that this brilliant man did, in fact, know right from wrong, and so found it difficult to mount an argument with logic, passion, and ethics. No, it is most likely that the reality Jefferson faced as a member of the Virginia gentry in the 1700s and 1800s was just convenient. It afforded him a certain lifestyle.

Surely, the man was a hypocrite. Surely, the man had the potential to contradict himself three and four times over. Surely, too, the man did more for this country and for the rights of everyday folk around the world than most others over the entire course of history.

Jefferson's persuasive writing abilities, more than anything else, established him from a young age as a leading citizen of the colonies. His brilliance, dedication to learning and understanding, and ability to see the outer edges of what was possible made him the perfect vessel for the revolutionary American ideals to be disseminated around the world. Jefferson's understanding of the diverse audiences to whom he needed to communicate and his ability to simultaneously cater to their disparate interests stand as lessons for all aspiring persuasive writers. His vision, perhaps more than anything, remains a part of the American psyche—it guides us even today toward greatness.

Where other greats left the scene to retirement so another worthy could step in, Jefferson's departure from the American scene stands apart. His departure left a vacuum still filled to this day by his words memorialized in our foundational documents. He is often compared to the philosopher warrior kings of old: he studied legal and moral philosophy, he was a revolutionary who risked assuredly hanging together with Franklin, and he was the Third President of the United States. Jefferson, Washington, Lincoln: all three of these men have left their distinct indelible marks upon America. Without Washington's leadership, Jefferson's accomplishments would have come to naught. Without Jefferson's Declaration, Lincoln's Gettysburg Address would not have resonated so profoundly for all Americans. Without Lincoln's considerable contributions, Jefferson's statement that "all men are created equal" would not stand for the thing its plain words would suggest.

The War for Independence, the writing of the Declaration and the Constitution, and the writing of and constant reexamination of the rights guaranteed to us under the Bill of Rights have each highlighted the grave contradictions between who we said we were and what we have been in truth. Yet the gradual suffrage of those who were originally excluded has brought to life Jefferson's powerful and persuasive declaration "that all men are created equal." Ultimately, the American Revolution is history's only revolution that still inspires. And Thomas Jefferson was its guiding scribe.

APPENDIX A
Excerpts from John Locke's The Second Treatise on Government Sec. 4, 6-8, 87-89, 95, 123, 131 (1690)

John Locke's writings inspired or first enunciated many of the themes that Jefferson used across his works, including the notion of the "equality of men" by nature. Below are portions of one of two treaties Locke wrote on civil government and in which we see the same natural rights language we see throughout Jefferson's own most esteemed writings.

SECTIONS 4–6, AND 8

Sect. 4. TO understand political power right, and derive it from its original, we must consider, what state all men are naturally in, and that is, a state of perfect freedom to order their actions, and dispose of their possessions and persons, as they think fit, within the bounds of the law of nature, without asking leave, or depending upon the will of any other man. A state also of wherin all the power and jurisdiction is reciprocal, no one having more than another; there being nothing more evident, than that the creatures of the same species and rank, promiscuously born to all the same advantages of nature, and the use of the same faculties, should also be equal one amongst another without subordination or subjection, unless the lord and master of them all should, by any manifest declaration of his will, set one above another, and confer on him, by an evident and clear appointment, an undoubted right to dominion and sovereignty.

Sect. 5. This equality of men by nature, the judicious Hooker looks upon as so evident in itself, and beyond all question, that he makes it the foundation of that obligation to mutual love amongst men, on which he builds the duties they owe one another, and from whence he derives the great maxims of justice and charity. His words are,

> The like natural inducement hath brought men to know that it is no less their duty, to love others than themselves; for seeing those things which are equal, must needs all have one measure; if I cannot but wish to receive good, even as much at every man's hands, as any man can wish unto his own soul, how should I look to have any part of my desire herein satisfied, unless myself be careful to satisfy the like desire, which is undoubtedly in other men, being of one and the same nature? To have any thing offered them repugnant to this desire, must needs in all respects grieve them as much as me; so that if I do harm, I must look to suffer, there being no reason that others should shew greater measure of love to me, than they have by me shewed unto them: my desire therefore to be loved of my equals in nature as much as possible may be, imposeth upon me a natural duty of bearing to them-ward fully the like affection; from which relation of equality between ourselves and them that are as ourselves, what several rules and canons natural reason hath drawn, for direction of life, no man is ignorant .Eccl. Pol. Lib. 1.

Sect. 6. But though this be a state of liberty, yet it is not a state of licence: though man in that state have an uncontroulable liberty to dispose of his person or possessions, yet he has not liberty to destroy himself, or so much as any creature in his possession, but where some nobler use than its bare preservation calls for it. The state of nature has a law of nature to govern it, which obliges every one: and reason, which is that law, teaches all mankind, who will but consult it, that being all equal and independent, no one ought to harm another in his life, health, liberty, or possessions: for men being all the workmanship of one omnipotent, and infinitely wise maker; all the servants of one sovereign master, sent into the world by his order, and about his business; they are his property, whose workmanship they are, made to last during his, not one another's pleasure: and being furnished with like faculties, sharing all in one community of nature, there cannot be supposed any such subordination amongus, that may authorize us to destroy one another, as if we were made for one another's uses, as the inferior ranks of creatures are for our's. Every one, as he is bound to preserve himself, and not to quit his station wilfully, so by the like reason, when his own preservation comes not in competition, ought he, as much as he can, to preserve the rest of mankind, and may not, unless it be to do justice on an offender, take away, or impair the life, or what tends to the preservation of the life, the liberty, health, limb, or goods of another.

Sect. 8. And thus, in the state of nature, one man comes by a power over another; but yet no absolute or arbitrary power, to use a criminal, when he has got him in his hands, according to the passionate heats, or boundless extravagancy of his own will; but only to retribute to him, so far as calm reason and conscience dictate, what is proportionate to his transgression, which is so much as may serve for reparation and restraint: for these two are the only reasons, why one man may lawfully do harm to another, which is that we call punishment. In transgressing the law of nature, the offender declares himself to live by another rule than that of reason and common equity, which is that measure God has set to the actions of men, for their mutual security; and so he becomes dangerous to mankind, the tye, which is to secure them from injury and violence, being slighted and broken by him. Which being a trespass against the whole species, and the peace and safety of it, provided for by the law of nature, every man upon this score, by the right he hath to preserve mankind in general, may restrain, or where it is necessary, destroy things noxious to them, and so may bring such evil on any one, who hath transgressed that law, as may make him repent the doing of it, and thereby deter him, and by his example others, from doing the like mischief. And in the case, and upon this ground, every man hath a right to punish the offender, and be executioner of the law of nature.

SECTIONS 87–89

Sect. 87. Man being born, as has been proved, with a title to perfect freedom, and an uncontrouled enjoyment of all the rights and privileges of the law of nature, equally with any other man, or number of men in the world, hath by nature a power, not only to preserve his property, that is, his life, liberty and estate, against the injuries and attempts of other men; but to judge of, and punish the breaches of that law in others, as he is persuaded the offence deserves, even with death itself, in crimes where the heinousness of the fact, in his opinion, requires it. But because no political society can be, nor subsist, without having in itself the power to preserve the property, and in order thereunto, punish the offences of all those of that society; there, and there only is political society, where every one of the members hath quitted this natural power, resigned it up into the hands of the community in all cases that exclude him not from appealing for protection to the law established by it. And thus all private judgment of every particular member being excluded, the community comes to be umpire, by settled standing rules, indifferent, and the same to all parties; and by men having authority from the community, for the execution of those rules, decides all the differences that may happen between any members of that society concerning any matter of right; and punishes those offences which any member hath committed against the society, with such penalties as the law has established: whereby it is easy to discern, who are, and who are not, in political society together. Those who are united into one body, and have a common established law and judicature to appeal to, with authority to decide controversies between them, and punish offenders, are in civil society one with another: but those who have no such common appeal, I mean on earth, are still in the state of nature, each being, where there is no other, judge for himself, and executioner; which is, as I have before shewed it, the perfect state of nature.

Sect. 88. And thus the common-wealth comes by a power to set down what punishment shall belong to the several transgressions which they think worthy of it, committed amongst the members of that society, (which is the power of making laws) as well as it has the power to punish any injury done unto any of its members, by any one that is not of it, (which is the power of war and peace;) and all this for the preservation of the property of all the members of that society, as far as is possible. But though every man who has entered into civil society, and is become a member of any commonwealth, has thereby quitted his power to punish offences, against the law of nature, in prosecution of his own private judgment, yet with the judgment of offences, which he has given up to the legislative in all cases, where he can appeal to the magistrate, he has given a right to the common-wealth to employ his force, for the execution of the judgments of the common-wealth, whenever he shall be called to it; which indeed are his own judgments, they being made by himself, or his representative. And herein we have the original of the legislative and executive power of civil society, which is to judge by standing laws, how far offences are to be punished, when committed within the common-wealth; and also to determine, by occasional judgments founded on the present circumstances of the fact, how far injuries from without are to be vindicated; and in both these to employ all the force of all the members, when there shall be need.

SECTION 123

IF man in the state of nature be so free, as has been said; if he be absolute lord of his own person and possessions, equal to the greatest, and subject to no body, why will he part with his freedom? why will he give up this empire, and subject himself to the dominion and controul of any other power? To which it is obvious to answer, that though in the state of nature he hath such a right, yet the enjoyment of it is very uncertain, and constantly exposed to the invasion of others: for all being kings as much as he, every man his equal, and the greater part no strict observers of equity and justice, the enjoyment of the property he has in this state is very unsafe, very unsecure. This makes him willing to quit a condition, which, however free, is full of fears and continual dangers: and it is not without reason, that he seeks out, and is willing to join in society with others, who are already united, or have a mind to unite, for the mutual preservation of their lives, liberties and estates, which I call by the general name, property.

SECTION 131

But though men, when they enter into society, give up the equality, liberty, and executive power they had in the state of nature, into the hands of the society, to be so far disposed of by the legislative, as the good of the society shall require; yet it being only with an intention in every one the better to preserve himself, his liberty and property; (for no rational creature can be supposed to change his condition with an intention to be worse) the power of the society, or legislative constituted by them, can never be supposed to extend farther, than the common good; but is obliged to secure every one's property, by providing against those three defects above mentioned, that made the state of nature so unsafe and uneasy. And so whoever has the legislative or supreme power of any common-wealth, is bound to govern by established standing laws, promulgated and known to the people, and not by extemporary decrees; by indifferent and upright judges, who are to decide controversies by those laws; and to employ the force of the community at home, only in the execution of such laws, or abroad to prevent or redress foreign injuries, and secure the community from inroads and invasion. And all this to be directed to no other end, but the peace, safety, and public good of the people.

APPENDIX B
Transcription from Howell v. Netherland (1770)

Five years before the Declaration of Independence, Jefferson wrote a hyper-technical memorandum of law for the court, maintaining that because there was no positive law dictating his client's status as a slave, there was no legal means to continue his slavery. Jefferson's pro bono advocacy for this slave gave him an early reputation at the court for the strength and clarity of his persuasive writing in a cause for which he, as a slave owner, could easily have been biased against.

On behalf of the plaintiff it was insisted, 1st, that if he could be detained in servitude by his first master, he could not be aliened. But 2nd, that he could not be detained in servitude.

1. It was observed that the purpose of the act was to punish and deter women from that confusion of species, which the legislature seems to have considered as an evil, and not to oppress their innocent offspring. That accordingly it had made cautious provision for the welfare of the child, by leaving it to the discretion of the church wardens to choose out a proper master; and by directing, that that master should provide for it sufficient food, clothing, and lodging, and should not give immoderate correction. For these purposes the master enters into covenants with the church wardens; and to admit he had a power after this to sell his ward, would be to admit him a power of discharging himself of his covenants. Nor is this objection answered by saying that the covenants of the first master are transferred to the alienee, because he may be insolvent of the damages which should be recovered against him, and indeed they might be of such a nature as could not be atoned

199

for, either to the servant or to society; such, for instance, would be a corruption of morals either by the wicked precept or example of the master, or of his family. The truth is, the master is bound to the servant for food, raiment, and protection and is not at liberty, by aliening his charge, to put it out of his own power to afford them when wanting. The servant may as well set up a right of withdrawing from his master those personal services which he, in return, is bound to yield him. Again, the same trust which is created by express compact in favor of the first mulatto, is extended by the law to her issue. The legislature confiding that the choice of a master for the first mulatto, by the church wardens, would be prudent, vest the issue in him also without further act to be done; and the master, at the time he takes the mother, knowing that her issue also is to be under her servitude on the same conditions, does by accepting her, tacitly undertake to comply with those conditions raised by the law in their favor. These servants bear greater resemblance to apprentices than to slaves. Thus, on the death of the first master, they go to his executor as an apprentice would, and not to his heir as a slave. The master is chosen, in both cases, from an opinion of his peculiar propriety for that charge, and the performances of his duty in both cases is secured by mutual covenants. Now it is well known that an apprentice can not be aliened; and that, not from any particular provision of the legislature, but from the general nature of the connection and engagements between them: there being, as was before observed, a trust reposed in the diligence and discretion of the master; and a trust by our law cannot be assigned. It adheres to the person as closely as does his integrity, and he can no more transfer the one than the other to a purchaser. But,

2. It was insisted, that the plaintiff, being a mulatto of the third generation, would not be detained in servitude under any law whatever: the grand position now to be proved being that one law had reduced to servitude the first mulatto only, the immediate offspring of a white woman by a negro or mulatto man; that a second law had extended it to the "children" of that mulatto; but that no law had yet extended it to her grandchildren, or other issue more remote than this. To prove this, a general statement of these laws was premised. Act of 1705, c. 49 s. 18. "If any woman servant shall have a bastard child, by a negro or mulatto, or if a free Christian white woman shall have such bastard child by a negro or mulatto; in both the said cases the churchwardens shall bind the said child to be a servant until it shall be of thirty one years of age." In other parts of the act, it is declared who shall be slaves, and

what a manumission of them; from sect. 34 to 39. are regulations solely relative to slaves, among which is sect. 36. "Baptism of slaves doth not exempt them from bondage; and all children shall be bond or free according to the condition of their mothers and the particular directions of this act."

Act. 1723. c. 4. s. 22. "Where any female mulatto or Indian, by law obliged to serve till the age of thirty or thirty one years shall, during the time of her servitude, have any child born of her body, every such child shall serve the master or mistress of such mulatto or Indian, until it shall attain the same age, the mother of such child was obliged, by law, to serve unto."

In 1748, the Assembly revising and digesting the whole body of our acts of Assembly, in act 14. s. 4. incorporate the clauses before cited, without any addition or alteration. And in 1753, c. 2. s. 4. 13., the law of 1748, is re-enacted with some new matter which does not effect the present question.

Now it is plain the plaintiff does not come within the description of the act of 1705, s. 18.; that only reducing to servitude "the child of a white woman by a negro or mulatto man." This was the predicament of the plaintiff's grandmother. I suppose it will not be pretended that the mother being a servant, the child would be a servant also under the law of nature, without any particular provision in the act. Under the law of nature, all men are born free, every one comes into the world with a right to his own person, which includes the liberty of moving and using it at his own will. This is what is called personal liberty, and is given him by the author of nature, because necessary for his own sustenance. The reducing the mother to servitude was a violation of the law of nature: surely then the same law cannot prescribe a continuance of the violation to her issue, and that too without end, for if it extends to any, it must to every degree of descendants. Puff. b. 6. c. 3. s. 4. 9. supports this doctrine. For having proved that servitude to be rightful, must be founded on either compact, or capture in war, he proceeds to shew that the children of the latter only follow the condition of the mother: for which he gives this reason, that the person and labor of the mother in a condition of perfect slavery, (as he supposes to be that of the captive in war) being the property of the master, it is impossible she should maintain it but with her master's goods; by which he supposes a debt contracted from the infant to the master. But he says in cases of servitude founded on contract, "The food of the future issue is contained or implied in their own maintenance, which their master owes them as a just debt; and consequently their children are not involved in a necessity of slavery." This is the nature of the servitude introduced by the act of 1705, the master deriving his title to the service of the mother, entirely from the contract entered into with the churchwardens. That the bondage of the mother does not under the law of nature, infer that of her issue, as included in her, is further obvious from this consideration, that by the same reason, the bondage of the father would infer that of his issue; for he may with equal, and some anatomists say with greater reason, be said to include all his posterity. But this very law admits there is no such descent of condition from father to child, when it imposes servitude on the child of a slave, which would have been unnecessary, if the condition had descended of course. Again, if it be a law of nature that the child shall follow the condition of the parent, it would introduce a very perplexing dilemma; as where the one parent is free and the other a slave. Here the child is to be a slave says this this law by inheritance of the father's bondage: but it is also to be free, says the same law by inheritance of its mother's freedom. This contradiction proves it to be no law of nature.

But the 36th section of the act will perhaps be cited as the entailing condition of the mother on the child, where it says, that "children shall be bond or free according to the condition of the mother, and the particular direction of this act." Now that the word "bond" in this clause relates to "slaves" only, I am justified in asserting, not only from common parlance but also from its sense in other parts of this very act. And that on the other hand it considers those who were to be free after a temporary servitude, as described under the word "free." In this very section 36, it says, "baptism of slaves does not exempt them from bondage." Here then in the very sentence now under consideration, the word bondage is used to express perpetual slavery; and we cannot conceive they meant to use it in two different senses in the same sentence. So in clause nineteen of the same act, it says, "to prevent that abominable mixture of white men or women with negroes or mulattoes, whatever white man or woman being free, shall intermarry with a negro or mulatto, &c. shall be committed to prison, &c." Now unless the act means to include white servants and apprentices under the denomination of "freemen," then a white servant or apprentice may intermarry with a negro or mulatto. But this is making the act miss of its purpose, which was "to prevent the abominable mixture of white men or women with negroes or mulattoes." But to put it out of dispute, the next clause (twenty) says that "if any minister shall, notwithstanding, presume to marry a white man or woman with a negro or mulatto," he shall incur such a penalty. Here then the prohibition is extended to whites in general, without saying "free whites" as the former clause did. But these two clauses are plainly co-extensive; and consequently the word "free" in the nineteenth, was intended to include the temporary white servants taken in by the twentieth clause, under the general appellation of "white men or women." So that this act where it speaks of bondmen, means those who are "perpetual slaves," and where of "freemen," those who are to be free after a temporary servitude, as well as those who are so now. Indeed to suppose, where the act says, "the children of a bondwoman shall be bond," that it means "the children of a temporary servant shall be temporary servants," would infer too much: for it would make temporary servants of the children of white servant women, or of white apprentice women, which yet was never pretended. The conclusion I draw from this, is, that since the temporary service of a white woman does not take from her the appellation of a freewoman, in the sense of this act, and her children under this very clause are free, as being the children of a free woman, neither does the temporary servitude of a mulatto exclude her from the same appellation, and her children also shall be free under this clause, as the children of a free woman. So that the meaning of this clause is, that children shall be slaves, where slavery was the condition of the mother; and free, where freedom either immediate or remote, was her condition: excepting only the instance of the mulatto bastard, which this act makes a servant, though the mother was free. This is the case alluded to by the last words of the clause, "according to the particular direction of this act." Because in this case, the act had made a temporary servant of the child, though the mother was not so.

Then comes the act of 1723, directing that where any female mulatto or Indian, by law obliged to serve till thirty or thirty one, shall have a child during her servitude, such child shall serve the same master to the same age. This act does itself prove that the child was not obliged to serve under the former law of 1705, which had imposed servitude on the mother; and consequently that the clause "children shall be bond or free, according to the condition of the mother," affected the children of slaves only. For wherefore else was this law made? If the children of a mulatto held in temporary servitude were to follow the condition of the mother, and be temporary servants under the law of 1705, that of 1723 was wholly unnecessary. But on the contrary, when we find an Assembly within 18 years after the law of 1705, had been passed, the one half or whom would probably be the same members who had passed that law, when we see these people I say, enacting expressly that the children should be temporary servants, it is a strong proof the makers of the first law had not intended they should be so. Expositio contemporanea est optima, is a maxim in our law, because such exposition is supposed to be taken from the makers of the law themselves, who best knew their own intention; and it is doubly conclusive, where the makers themselves pass a new act to testify their intention. So that I hold it certain, the act of 1705, did not extend to the children of the first mulatto, or that of 1723, would not have been made.

That the act of 1723, did not extend to the plaintiff, is apparent from its words. "Where any female mulatto by law obliged to serve till thirty one (that is, the plaintiff's grandmother) shall during the time of her servitude, have a child born of her body (that is, the plaintiff's mother) such a child shall serve till thirty one." This act describes the plaintiff's mother then as the subject on which to operate. The common sense of mankind would surely spare me the trouble of proving the word "child" does not include the grandchild, great-grandchild, great-great-grandchild, &c. in infinitum. Or if that would not, the act itself precludes me, by declaring it meant only a "child born of her body." So that as the law of 1705, has made a servant of the first mulatto, that of 1723, extends it to her children.

The act of 1748, is the next in course. At this time all our acts were revised and digested, and sent in one volume to receive his Majesty's approbation. These two laws being found to be on the same subject, were then incorporated without any alteration. This however, could not affect their meaning, which is still to be sought after by considering the component acts in their separate state. At any rate it cannot affect the condition of the plaintiff, who was born in 1742, which was six years before it was made. The same may be said of the law of 1753, which is copied from 1748, with only the addition of some new matter, foreign to the present question. So that on the laws of 1705, and 1723, alone, it is to be determined; with respect to which I have endeavored to shew;

That the first of them subjected to servitude, the first mulatto only.

That this did not, under the law of nature, affect the liberty of the children. Because, under that law we are all born free.

Because, the servitude of the mother was founded on compact, which implies maintenance of her children, so as to have them under no obligation to the master.

And because, this descent of condition from parent to child, would introduce a contradiction where the one parent is free, and the other in servitude.

That as little are they affected by the words of the act, "children shall be bond or free, according to the condition of the mother."

Because that act uses the word "bond," so as to shew it means thereby those only who are perpetual slaves, and by the word "free" those who are entitled to freedom in præsenti or infuturo; and consequently calling the mother "free," says her children shall be "free."

Because it would make servants of the children of white servants or apprentices, which nobody will say is right.

And because the passing the act of 1723, to subject the child to servitude, shews it was not subject to that state under the old law.

And lastly, that the act of 1723, affects only "children of such mulattoes," as when that law was made were obliged to serve till thirty-one; which takes in the plaintiff's mother who was of the second generation, but does not extend to himself who is of the third.

So that the position at first laid down is now proven, that the act of 1705, makes servants of the first mulatto, that of 1723, extends it to her children, but that it remains for some future legislature, if any shall be found wicked enough, to extend it to the grandchildren and other issue more remote, to the "nati natorum et qui nascentur ab illis."

APPENDIX C
A Summary View of the Rights of British Americans (1774)

The Summary *was a combative publication, meant as a last ditch effort to warn the King that his American subjects' patience was at its end. It was distributed throughout the colonies and in Britain, making "Thomas Jefferson" a household name on both sides of the Atlantic.*

Resolved, that it be an instruction to the said deputies, when assembled in general congress with the deputies from the other states of British America, to propose to the said congress that an humble and dutiful address be presented to his majesty, begging leave to lay before him, as chief magistrate of the British empire, the united complaints of his majesty's subjects in America; complaints which are excited by many unwarrantable encroachments and usurpations, attempted to be made by the legislature of one part of the empire, upon those rights which God and the laws have given equally and independently to all. To represent to his majesty that these his states have often individually made humble application to his imperial throne to obtain, through its intervention, some redress of their injured rights, to none of which was ever even an answer condescended; humbly to hope that this their joint address, penned in the language of truth, and divested of those expressions of servility which would persuade his majesty that we are asking favours, and not rights, shall obtain from his majesty a more respectful acceptance. And this his majesty will think we have reason to expect when he reflects that he is no more than the chief officer of the people, appointed by the laws, and circumscribed with definite powers, to assist in working the great machine of government, erected for their use, and consequently subject to their superintendance. And in order that these our rights, as well as the invasions of them, may be laid more fully before his majesty, to take a view of them from the origin and first settlement of these countries.

To remind him that our ancestors, before their emigration to America, were the free inhabitants of the British dominions in Europe, and possessed a right which nature has given to all men, of departing from the country in which chance, not choice, has placed them, of going in quest of new habitations, and of there establishing new societies, under such laws and regulations as to them shall seem most likely to promote public happiness. That their Saxon ancestors had, under this universal law, in like manner left their native wilds and woods in the north of Europe, had possessed themselves of the island of Britain, then less charged with inhabitants, and had established there that system of laws which has so long been the glory and protection of that country. Nor was ever any claim of superiority or dependence asserted over them by that mother country from which they had migrated; and were such a claim made, it is believed that his majesty's subjects in Great Britain have too firm a feeling of the rights derived to them from their ancestors, to bow down the sovereignty of their state before such visionary pretensions. And it is thought that no circumstance has occurred to distinguish materially the British from the Saxon emigration. America was conquered, and her settlements made, and firmly established, at the expence of individuals, and not of the British public. Their own blood was spilt in acquiring lands for their settlement, their own fortunes expended in making that settlement effectual; for themselves they fought, for themselves they conquered, and for themselves alone they have right to hold. Not a shilling was ever issued from the public treasures of his majesty, or his ancestors, for their assistance, till of very late times, after the colonies had become established on a firm and permanent footing. That then, indeed, having become valuable to Great Britain for her commercial purposes, his parliament was pleased to lend them assistance against an enemy, who would fain have drawn to herself the benefits of their commerce, to the great aggrandizement of herself, and danger of Great Britain. Such assistance, and in such circumstances, they had often before given to Portugal, and other allied states, with whom they carry on a commercial intercourse; yet these states never supposed, that by calling in her aid, they thereby submitted themselves to her sovereignty. Had such terms been proposed, they would have rejected them with disdain, and trusted for better to the moderation of their enemies, or to a vigorous exertion of their own force. We do not, however, mean to under-rate those aids, which to us were doubtless valuable, on whatever principles granted; but we would shew that they cannot give a title to that authority which the British parliament would arrogate over us, and that they may amply be repaid by our giving to the inhabitants of Great Britain such exclusive privileges in trade as may be advantageous to them, and at the same time not too restrictive to ourselves. That settlements having been thus effected in the wilds of America, the emigrants thought proper to adopt that system of laws under which they had hitherto lived in the mother country, and to continue their union with her by submitting themselves to the same common sovereign, who was thereby made the central link connecting the several parts of the empire thus newly multiplied.

But that not long were they permitted, however far they thought themselves removed from the hand of oppression, to hold undisturbed the rights thus acquired, at the hazard of their lives, and loss of their fortunes. A family of princes was then on the British throne, whose treasonable crimes against their people brought on them afterwards the exertion of those sacred and sovereign rights of punishment reserved in the hands of the people for cases of extreme necessity, and judged by the constitution unsafe to be delegated to any other judicature. While every day brought forth some new and unjustifiable exertion of power over their subjects on that side the water, it was not to be expected that those here, much less able at that time to oppose the designs of despotism, should be exempted from injury.

Accordingly that country, which had been acquired by the lives, the labours, and the fortunes, of individual adventurers, was by these princes, at several times, parted out and distributed among the favourites and (1) followers of their fortunes, and, by an assumed right of the crown alone, were erected into distinct and independent governments; a measure which it is believed his majesty's prudence and understanding would prevent him from imitating at this day, as no exercise of such a power, of dividing and dismembering a country, has ever occurred in his majesty's realm of England, though now of very antient standing; nor could it be justified or acquiesced under there, or in any other part of his majesty's empire.

That the exercise of a free trade with all parts of the world, possessed by the American colonists, as of natural right, and which no law of their own had taken away or abridged, was next the object of unjust encroachment. Some of the colonies having thought proper to continue the administration of their government in the name and under the authority of his majesty king Charles the first, whom, notwithstanding his late deposition by the commonwealth of England, they continued in the sovereignty of their state; the parliament for the commonwealth took the same in high offence, and assumed upon themselves the power of prohibiting their trade with all other parts of the world, except the island of Great Britain. This arbitrary act, however, they soon recalled, and by solemn treaty, entered into on the 12th day of March, 1651, between the said commonwealth by their commissioners, and the colony of Virginia by their house of burgesses, it was expressly stipulated, by the 8th article of the said treaty, that they should have "free trade as the people of England do enjoy to all places and with all nations, according to the laws of that commonwealth." But that, upon the restoration of his majesty king Charles the second, their rights of free commerce fell once more a victim to arbitrary power; and by several acts (2) of his reign, as well as of some of his successors, the trade of the colonies was laid under such restrictions, as shew what hopes they might form from the justice of a British parliament, were its uncontrouled power admitted over these states. History has informed us that bodies of men, as well as individuals, are susceptible of the spirit of tyranny. A view of these acts of parliament for regulation, as it has been affectedly called, of the American trade, if all other evidence were removed out of the case, would undeniably evince the truth of this observation. Besides the duties they impose on our articles of export and import, they prohibit our going to any markets northward of Cape Finesterre, in the kingdom of Spain, for the sale of commodities which Great Britain will not take from us, and for the purchase of others, with which she cannot supply us, and that for no other than the arbitrary purposes of purchasing for themselves, by a sacrifice of our rights and interests, certain privileges in their commerce with an allied state, who in confidence that their exclusive trade with America will be continued, while the principles and power of the British parliament be the same, have indulged themselves in every exorbitance which their avarice could dictate, or our necessities extort; have raised their commodities, called for in America, to the double and treble of what they sold for before such exclusive privileges were given them, and of what better commodities of the same kind would cost us elsewhere, and at the same time give us much less for what we carry thither than might be had at more convenient ports. That these acts prohibit us from carrying in quest of other purchasers the surplus of our tobaccoes remaining after the consumption of Great Britain is supplied; so that we must leave them with the British merchant for whatever he will please to allow us, to be by him reshipped to foreign markets, where he will reap the benefits of making sale of them for full value. That to heighten still the idea of parliamentary justice, and to shew with what moderation they are like to exercise power, where themselves are to feel no part of its weight, we take leave to mention to his majesty certain other acts of British parliament, by which they would prohibit us from manufacturing for our own use the articles we raise on our own lands with our own labour. By an act (3) passed in the 5th Year of the reign of his late majesty king George the second, an American subject is forbidden to make a hat for himself of the fur which he has taken perhaps on his own soil; an instance of despotism to which no parallel can be produced in the most arbitrary ages of British history. By one other act (4) passed in the 23d year of the same reign, the iron which we make we are forbidden to manufacture, and heavy as that article is, and necessary in every branch of husbandry, besides commission and insurance, we are to pay freight for it to Great Britain, and freight for it back again, for the purpose of supporting not men, but machines, in the island of Great Britain. In the same spirit of equal and impartial legislation is to be viewed the act of parliament (5), passed in the 5th year of the same reign, by which American lands are made subject to the demands of British creditors, while their own lands were still continued unanswerable for their debts; from which one of these conclusions must necessarily follow, either that justice is not the same in America as in Britain, or else that the British parliament pay less regard to it here than there. But that we do not point out to his majesty the injustice of these acts, with intent to rest on that principle the cause of their nullity; but to shew that experience confirms the propriety of those political principles which exempt us from the jurisdiction of the British parliament. The true ground on which we declare these acts void is, that the British parliament has no right to exercise authority over us.

That these exercises of usurped power have not been confined to instances alone, in which themselves were interested, but they have also intermeddled with the regulation of the internal affairs of the colonies. The act of the 9th of

Anne for establishing a post office in America seems to have had little connection with British convenience, except that of accommodating his majesty's ministers and favourites with the sale of a lucrative and easy office.

That thus have we hastened through the reigns which preceded his majesty's, during which the violations of our right were less alarming, because repeated at more distant intervals than that rapid and bold succession of injuries which is likely to distinguish the present from all other periods of American story. Scarcely have our minds been able to emerge from the astonishment into which one stroke of parliamentary thunder has involved us, before another more heavy, and more alarming, is fallen on us. Single acts of tyranny may be ascribed to the accidental opinion of a day; but a series of oppressions, begun at a distinguished period, and pursued unalterably through every change of ministers, too plainly prove a deliberate and systematical plan of reducing us to slavery.

That the act (6) passed in the 4th year of his majesty's reign, intitled "An act for granting certain duties in the British colonies and plantations in America, &c."

One other act (7), passed in the 5th year of his reign, intitled "An act for granting and applying certain stamp duties and other duties in the British colonies and plantations in America, &c."

One other act (8), passed in the 6th year of his reign, intitled "An act for the better securing the dependency of his majesty's dominions in America upon the crown and parliament of Great Britain;" and one other act (9), passed in the 7th year of his reign, intitled "An act for granting duties on paper, tea, &c." form that connected chain of parliamentary usurpation, which has already been the subject of frequent applications to his majesty, and the houses of lords and commons of Great Britain; and no answers having yet been condescended to any of these, we shall not trouble his majesty with a repetition of the matters they contained.

But that one other act (10), passed in the same 7th year of the reign, having been a peculiar attempt, must ever require peculiar mention; it is intitled "An act for suspending the legislature of New York." One free and independent legislature hereby takes upon itself to suspend the powers of another, free and independent as itself; thus exhibiting a phoenomenon unknown in nature, the creator and creature of its own power. Not only the principles of common sense, but the common feelings of human nature, must be surrendered up before his majesty's subjects here can be persuaded to believe that they hold their political existence at the will of a British parliament. Shall these governments be dissolved, their property annihilated, and their people reduced to a state of nature, at the imperious breath of a body of men, whom they never saw, in whom they never confided, and over whom they have no powers of punishment or removal, let their crimes against the American public be ever so great? Can any one reason be assigned why 160,000 electors in the island of Great Britain should give law to four millions in the states of America, every individual of whom is equal to every individual of them, in virtue, in understanding, and in bodily strength? Were this to be admitted, instead of being a free people, as we have hitherto supposed, and mean to continue ourselves, we should suddenly be found the slaves, not of one, but of 160,000 tyrants, distinguished too from all others by this singular circumstance, that they are removed from the reach of fear, the only restraining motive which may hold the hand of a tyrant.

That by "an act (11) to discontinue in such manner and for such time as are therein mentioned the landing and discharging, lading or shipping, of goods, wares, and merchandize, at the town and within the harbour of Boston, in the province of Massachusetts Bay, in North America," which was passed at the last session of British parliament; a large and populous town, whose trade was their sole subsistence, was deprived of that trade, and involved in utter ruin. Let us for a while suppose the question of right suspended, in order to examine this act on principles of justice: An act of parliament had been passed imposing duties on teas, to be paid in America, against which act the Americans had protested as inauthoritative. The East India Company, who till that time had never sent a pound of tea to America on their own account, step forth on that occasion the assertors of parliamentary right, and send hither many ship loads of that obnoxious commodity. The masters of their several vessels, however, on their arrival in America, wisely attended to admonition, and returned with their cargoes. In the province of New England alone the remonstrances of the people were disregarded, and a compliance, after being many days waited for, was flatly refused. Whether in this the master of the vessel was governed by his obstinacy, or his instructions, let those who know, say. There are extraordinary situations which require extraordinary interposition. An exasperated people, who feel that they possess power, are not easily restrained within limits strictly regular. A number of them assembled in the town of Boston, threw the tea into the ocean, and dispersed without doing any other act of violence. If in this they did wrong, they were known and were amenable to the laws of the land, against which it could not be objected that they had ever, in any instance, been obstructed or diverted from their regular course in favour of popular offenders. They should therefore not have been distrusted on this occasion. But that ill fated colony had formerly been bold in their enmities against the house of Stuart, and were now devoted to ruin by that unseen hand which governs the momentous affairs of this great empire. On the partial representations of a few worthless ministerial dependents, whose constant office it has been to keep that government embroiled, and who, by their treacheries, hope to obtain the dignity of the British knighthood, without calling for a party accused, without asking a proof, without attempting a distinction between the guilty and the innocent, the whole of that antient and wealthy town is in a moment reduced from opulence to beggary. Men who had spent their lives in extending the British commerce, who had invested in that place the wealth their honest endeavours had merited, found themselves and their families thrown at once on the world for subsistence by its charities. Not the hundredth part of the inhabitants of that town had been concerned in the act complained of; many of them were in Great Britain and in other parts beyond sea; yet all were involved in one indiscriminate ruin, by a new executive power, unheard of till then, that of a British parliament. A property, of the value of many millions of money, was sacrificed to revenge, not repay, the loss of a few thousands. This is administering justice with a heavy hand indeed! and when is this tempest to be arrested in its course? Two wharfs are to be opened again when his majesty shall think proper. The residue which lined the extensive shores of the bay of Boston are forever interdicted the exercise of commerce. This little exception seems to have been thrown in for no other purpose than that of setting a precedent for investing his majesty with legislative powers. If the pulse of his people shall beat calmly under this experiment, another and another will be tried, till the measure of despotism be filled up. It would be an insult on common sense to pretend that this exception was made in order to restore its commerce to that great town. The trade which cannot be received at two wharfs alone must of necessity be transferred to some other place; to which it will soon be followed by that of the two wharfs. Considered in this light, it would be an insolent and cruel mockery at the annihilation of the town of Boston.

By the act (12) for the suppression of riots and tumults in the town of Boston, passed also in the last session of parliament, a murder committed there is, if the governor pleases, to be tried in the court of King's Bench, in the island of Great Britain, by a jury of Middlesex. The witnesses, too, on receipt of such a sum as the governor shall think it reasonable for them to expend, are to enter into recognizance to appear at the trial. This is, in other words, taxing them to the amount of their recognizance, and that amount may be whatever a governor pleases; for who does his majesty think can be prevailed on to cross the Atlantic for the sole purpose of bearing evidence to a fact? His expences are to be borne, indeed, as they shall be estimated by a governor; but who are to feed the wife and children whom he leaves behind, and who have had no other subsistence but his daily labour? Those epidemical disorders, too, so terrible in a foreign climate, is the cure of them to be estimated among the articles of expence, and their danger to be warded off by the almighty power of parliament? And the wretched criminal, if he happen to have offended on the American side, stripped of his privilege of trial by peers of his vicinage, removed from the place where alone full evidence could be obtained, without money, without counsel, without friends, without exculpatory proof, is tried before judges predetermined to condemn. The cowards who would suffer a countryman to be torn from the bowels of their society, in order to be thus offered a sacrifice to parliamentary tyranny, would merit that everlasting infamy now fixed on the authors of the act! A clause (13) for a similar purpose had been introduced into an act, passed in the 12th year of his majesty's reign, intitled "An act for the better securing and preserving his majesty's dockyards, magazines, ships, ammunition, and stores;" against which, as meriting the same censures, the several colonies have already protested.

That these are the acts of power, assumed by a body of men, foreign to our constitutions, and unacknowledged by our laws, against which we do, on behalf of the inhabitants of British America, enter this our solemn and determined protest; and we do earnestly entreat his majesty, as yet the only mediatory power between the several states of the British empire, to recommend to his parliament of Great Britain the total revocation of these acts, which, however nugatory they be, may yet prove the cause of further discontents and jealousies among us.

That we next proceed to consider the conduct of his majesty, as holding the executive powers of the laws of these states, and mark out his deviations from the line of duty: By the constitution of Great Britain, as well as of the several American states, his majesty possesses the power of refusing to pass into a law any bill which has already passed the other two branches of legislature. His majesty, however, and his ancestors, conscious of the impropriety of opposing their single opinion to the united wisdom of two houses of parliament, while their proceedings were unbiassed by interested principles, for several ages past have modestly declined the exercise of this power in that part of his empire called Great Britain. But by change of circumstances, other principles than those of justice simply have obtained an influence on their determinations; the addition of new states to the British Empire has produced an addition of new, and sometimes opposite interests. It is now, therefore, the great office of his majesty, to resume the exercise of his negative power, and to prevent the passage of laws by any one legislature of the empire, which might bear injuriously on the rights and interests of another. Yet this will not excuse the wanton exercise of this power which we have seen his majesty practise on the laws of the American legislatures. For the most trifling reasons, and sometimes for no conceivable reason at all, his majesty has rejected laws of the most salutary tendency. The abolition of domestic slavery is the great object of desire in those colonies, where it was unhappily introduced in their infant state. But previous to the enfranchisement of the slaves we have, it is necessary to exclude all further importations from Africa; yet our repeated attempts to effect this by prohibitions, and by imposing duties which might amount to a prohibition, have been hitherto defeated by his majesty's negative: Thus preferring the immediate advantages of a few African corsairs to the lasting interests of the American states, and to the rights of human nature, deeply wounded by this infamous practice. Nay, the single interposition of an interested individual against a law was scarcely ever known to fail of success, though in the opposite scale were placed the interests of a whole country. That this is so shameful an abuse of a power trusted with his majesty for other purposes, as if not reformed, would call for some legal restrictions.

With equal inattention to the necessities of his people here has his majesty permitted our laws to lie neglected in England for years, neither confirming them by his assent, nor annulling them by his negative; so that such of them as have no suspending clause we hold on the most precarious of all tenures, his majesty's will, and such of them as suspend themselves till his majesty's assent be obtained, we have feared, might be called into existence at some future and distant period, when time, and change of circumstances, shall have rendered them destructive to his people here. And to render this grievance still more oppressive, his majesty by his instructions has laid his governors under such restrictions that they can pass no law of any moment unless it have such suspending clause; so that, however immediate may be the call for legislative interposition, the law cannot be executed till it has twice crossed the Atlantic, by which time the evil may have spent its whole force.

But in what terms, reconcileable to majesty, and at the same time to truth, shall we speak of a late instruction to his majesty's governor of the colony of Virginia, by which he is forbidden to assent to any law for the division of a county, unless the new county will consent to have no representative in assembly? That colony has as yet fixed no boundary to the westward. Their western counties, therefore, are of indefinite extent; some of them are actually seated many hundred miles from their eastern limits. Is it possible, then, that his majesty can have bestowed a single thought on the situation of those people, who, in order to obtain justice for injuries, however great or small, must, by the laws of that colony, attend their county court, at such a distance, with all their witnesses, monthly, till their litigation be determined? Or does his majesty seriously wish, and publish it to the world, that his subjects should give up the glorious right of representation, with all the benefits derived from that, and submit themselves the absolute slaves of his sovereign will? Or is it rather meant to confine the legislative body to their present numbers, that they may be the cheaper bargain whenever they shall become worth a purchase.

One of the articles of impeachment against Tresilian, and the other judges of Westminister Hall, in the reign of Richard the second, for which they suffered death, as traitors to their country, was, that they had advised the king that he might dissolve his parliament at any time; and succeeding kings have adopted the opinion of these unjust judges. Since the establishment, however, of the British constitution, at the glorious revolution, on its free and antient principles, neither his majesty, nor his ancestors, have exercised such a power of dissolution in the island of Great Britain; and when his majesty was petitioned, by the united voice of his people there, to dissolve the present parliament, who had become obnoxious to them, his ministers were heard to declare, in open parliament, that his majesty possessed no such power by the constitution. But how different their language and his practice here! To declare, as their duty required, the known rights of their country, to oppose the usurpations of every foreign judicature, to disregard the imperious mandates of a minister or governor, have been the avowed causes of dissolving houses of representatives in America. But if such powers be really vested in his majesty, can he suppose they are there placed to awe the members from such purposes as these? When the representative body have lost the confidence of their constituents, when they have notoriously made sale of their most valuable rights, when they have assumed to themselves powers which the people never put into their hands, then indeed their continuing in office becomes dangerous to the state, and calls for an exercise of the power of dissolution. Such being the causes for which the representative body should, and should not, be dissolved, will it not appear strange to an unbiassed observer, that that of Great Britain was not dissolved, while those of the colonies have repeatedly incurred that sentence?

But your majesty, or your governors, have carried this power beyond every limit known, or provided for, by the laws: After dissolving one house of representatives, they have refused to call another, so that, for a great length of time, the legislature provided by the laws has been out of existence. From the nature of things, every society must at all times possess within itself the sovereign powers of legislation. The feelings of human nature revolt against the supposition of a state so situated as that it may not in any emergency provide against dangers which perhaps threaten immediate ruin. While those bodies are in existence to whom the people have delegated the powers of legislation, they alone possess and may exercise those powers; but when they are dissolved by the lopping off one or more of their branches, the power reverts to the people, who may exercise it to unlimited extent, either assembling together in person, sending deputies, or in any other way they may think proper. We forbear to trace consequences further; the dangers are conspicuous with which this practice is replete.

That we shall at this time also take notice of an error in the nature of our land holdings, which crept in at a very early period of our settlement. The introduction of the feudal tenures into the kingdom of England, though antient, is well enough understood to set this matter in a proper light. In the earlier ages of the Saxon settlement feudal holdings were certainly altogether unknown; and very few, if any, had been introduced at the time of the Norman conquest. Our Saxon ancestors held their lands, as they did their personal property, in absolute dominion, disencumbered with any superior, answering nearly to the nature of those possessions which the feudalists term allodial. William, the Norman, first introduced that system generally. The lands which had belonged to those who fell in the battle of Hastings, and in the subsequent insurrections of his reign, formed a considerable proportion of the lands of the whole kingdom. These he granted out, subject to feudal duties, as did he also those of a great number of his new subjects, who, by persuasions or threats, were induced to surrender them for that purpose. But still much was left in the hands of his Saxon subjects; held of no superior, and not subject to feudal conditions. These, therefore, by express laws, enacted to render uniform the system of military defence, were made liable to the same military duties as if they had been feuds; and the Norman lawyers soon found means to saddle them also with all the other feudal burthens. But still they had not been surrendered to the king, they were not derived from his grant, and therefore they were not holden of him. A general principle, indeed, was introduced, that "all lands in England were held either mediately or immediately of the crown," but this was borrowed from those holdings, which were truly feudal, and only applied to others for the purposes of illustration. Feudal holdings were therefore but exceptions out of the Saxon laws of possession, under which all lands were held in absolute right. These, therefore, still form the basis, or ground-work, of the common law, to prevail wheresoever the exceptions have not taken place. America was not conquered by William the Norman, nor its lands surrendered to him, or any of his successors. Possessions there are undoubtedly of the allodial nature. Our ancestors, however, who migrated hither, were farmers, not lawyers. The fictitious principle that all lands belong originally to the king, they were early persuaded to believe real; and accordingly took grants of their own lands from the crown. And while the crown continued to grant for small sums, and on reasonable rents; there was no inducement to arrest the error, and lay it open to public view. But his majesty has lately taken on him to advance the terms of purchase, and of holding to the double of what they were; by which means the acquisition of lands being rendered difficult, the population of our country is likely to be checked. It is time, therefore, for us to lay this matter before his majesty, and to declare that he has no right to grant lands of himself. From the nature and purpose of civil institutions, all the lands within the limits which any particular society has circumscribed around itself are assumed by that society, and subject to their allotment only. This may be done by themselves, assembled collectively, or by their legislature, to whom they may have delegated sovereign authority; and if they are alloted in neither of these ways, each individual of the society may appropriate to himself such lands as he finds vacant, and occupancy will give him title.

That in order to enforce the arbitrary measures before complained of, his majesty has from time to time sent among us large bodies of armed forces, not made up of the people here, nor raised by the authority of our laws: Did his majesty possess such a right as this, it might swallow up all our other rights whenever he should think proper. But his majesty has no right to land a single armed man on our shores, and those whom he sends here are liable to our laws made for the suppression and punishment of riots, routs, and unlawful assemblies; or are hostile bodies, invading us in defiance of law. When in the course of the late war it became expedient that a body of Hanoverian troops should be brought over for the defence of Great Britain, his majesty's grandfather, our late sovereign, did not pretend to introduce them under any authority he possessed. Such a measure would have given just alarm to his subjects in Great Britain, whose liberties would not be safe if armed men of another country, and of another spirit, might be brought into the realm at any time without the consent of their legislature. He therefore applied to parliament, who passed an act for that purpose, limiting the number to be brought in and the time they were to continue. In like manner is his majesty restrained in every part of the empire. He possesses, indeed, the executive power of the laws in every state; but they are the laws of the particular state which he is to administer within that state, and not those of any one within the limits of another. Every state must judge for itself the number of armed men which they may safely trust among them, of whom they are to consist, and under what restrictions they shall be laid.

To render these proceedings still more criminal against our laws, instead of subjecting the military to the civil powers, his majesty has expressly made the civil subordinate to the military. But can his majesty thus put down all law under his feet? Can he erect a power superior to that which erected himself? He has done it indeed by force; but let him remember that force cannot give right.

That these are our grievances which we have thus laid before his majesty, with that freedom of language and sentiment which becomes a free people claiming their rights, as derived from the laws of nature, and not as the gift of their chief magistrate: Let those flatter who fear; it is not an American art. To give praise which is not due might be well from the venal, but would ill beseem those who are asserting the rights of human nature. They know, and will therefore say, that kings are the servants, not the proprietors of the people. Open your breast, sire, to liberal and expanded thought. Let not the name of George the third be a blot in the page of history. You are surrounded by British counsellors, but remember that they are parties. You have no ministers for American affairs, because you have none taken from among us, nor amenable to the laws on which they are to give you advice. It behoves you, therefore, to think and to act for yourself and your people. The great principles of right and wrong are legible to every reader; to pursue them requires not the aid of many counsellors. The whole art of government consists in the art of being honest. Only aim to do your duty, and mankind will give you credit where you fail. No longer persevere in sacrificing the rights of one part of the empire to the inordinate desires of another; but deal out to all equal and impartial right. Let no act be passed by any one legislature which may infringe on the rights and liberties of another. This is the important post in which fortune has placed you, holding the balance of a great, if a well poised empire. This, sire, is the advice of your great American council, on the observance of which may perhaps depend your felicity and future fame, and the preservation of that harmony which alone can continue both to Great Britain and America the reciprocal advantages of their connection. It is neither our wish, nor our interest, to separate from her. We are willing, on our part, to sacrifice every thing which reason can ask to the restoration of that tranquillity for which all must wish. On their part, let them be ready to establish union and a generous plan. Let them name their terms, but let them be just. Accept of every commercial preference it is in our power to give for such things as we can raise for their use, or they make for ours. But let them not think to exclude us from going to other markets to dispose of those commodities which they cannot use, or to supply those wants which they cannot supply. Still less let it be proposed that our properties within our own territories shall be taxed or regulated by any power on earth but our own. The God who gave us life gave us liberty at the same time; the hand of force may destroy, but cannot disjoin them. This, sire, is our last, our determined resolution; and that you will be pleased to interpose with that efficacy which your earnest endeavours may ensure to procure redress of these our great grievances, to quiet the minds of your subjects in British America, against any apprehensions of future encroachment, to establish fraternal love and harmony through the whole empire, and that these may continue to the latest ages of time, is the fervent prayer of all British America!

APPENDIX D
Excerpt from Thomas Paine's Common Sense (1775–1776)

Thomas Paine's Common Sense *stands alongside Jefferson's Declaration of Independence as two of the foundational documents of American thought. Paine's language, too, was heavily influenced by Locke's works.*

MANKIND being originally equals in the order of creation, the equality could only be destroyed by some subsequent circumstance: the distinctions of rich and poor may in a great measure be accounted for, and that without having recourse to the harsh ill-sounding names of oppression and avarice. Oppression is often the CONSEQUENCE, but seldom or never the MEANS of riches; and tho' avarice will preserve a man from being necessitously poor, it generally makes him too timorous to be wealthy.

But there is another and great distinction for which no truly natural or religious reason can be assigned, and that is the distinction of men into KINGS and SUBJECTS. Male and female are the distinctions of nature, good and bad the distinctions of Heaven; but how a race of men came into the world so exalted above the rest, and distinguished like some new species, is worth inquiring into, and whether they are the means of happiness or of misery to mankind.

In the early ages of the world, according to the scripture chronology there were no kings; the consequence of which was, there were no wars; it is the pride of kings which throws mankind into confusion. Holland, without a king hath enjoyed more peace for this last century than any of the monarchical governments in Europe. Antiquity favours the same remark; for the quiet and rural lives of the first Patriarchs have a snappy something in them, which vanishes when we come to the history of Jewish royalty.

Government by kings was first introduced into the world by the Heathens, from whom the children of Israel copied the custom. It was the most prosperous invention the Devil ever set on foot for the promotion of idolatry. The Heathens paid divine honours to their deceased kings, and the Christian World hath improved on the plan by doing the same to their living ones. How impious is the title of sacred Majesty applied to a worm, who in the midst of his splendor is crumbling into dust!

As the exalting one man so greatly above the rest cannot be justified on the equal rights of nature, so neither can it be defended on the authority of scripture; for the will of the Almighty as declared by Gideon, and the prophet Samuel, expressly disapproves of government by Kings.

All anti-monarchical parts of scripture have been very smoothly glossed over in monarchical governments, but they undoubtedly merit the attention of countries which have their governments yet to form. "Render unto Cesar the things which are Cesar's" is the scripture doctrine of courts, yet it is no support of monarchical government, for the Jews at that time were without a king, and in a state of vassalage to the Romans.

Near three thousand years passed away, from the Mosaic account of the creation, till the Jews under a national delusion requested a king. Till then their form of government (except in extraordinary cases where the Almighty interposed) was a kind of Republic, administered by a judge and the elders of the tribes. Kings they had none, and it was held sinful to acknowledge any being under that title but the Lord of Hosts. And when a man seriously reflects on the idolatrous homage which is paid to the persons of kings, he need not wonder that the Almighty, ever jealous of his honour, should disapprove a form of government which so impiously invades the prerogative of Heaven.

Monarchy is ranked in scripture as one of the sins of the Jews, for which a curse in reserve is denounced against them. The history of that transaction is worth attending to.

The children of Israel being oppressed by the Midianites, Gideon marched against them with a small army, and victory thro' the divine interposition decided in his favour. The Jews, elate with success, and attributing it to the generalship of Gideon, proposed making him a king, saying, "Rule thou over us, thou and thy son, and thy son's son." Here was temptation in its fullest extent; not a kingdom only, but an hereditary one; but Gideon in the piety of his soul replied, "I will not rule over you, neither shall my son rule over you. THE LORD SHALL RULE OVER YOU." Words need not be more explicit: Gideon doth not decline the honour, but denieth their right to give it; neither doth he compliment them with invented declarations of his thanks, but in the positive style of a prophet charges them with disaffection to their proper Sovereign, the King of Heaven.

About one hundred and thirty years after this, they fell again into the same error. The hankering which the Jews had for the idolatrous customs of the Heathens, is something exceedingly unaccountable; but so it was, that laying hold of the misconduct of Samuel's two sons, who were intrusted with some secular concerns, they came in an abrupt and clamorous manner to Samuel, saying, "Behold thou art old, and they sons walk not in thy ways, now make us a king to judge us like all the other nations." And here we cannot observe but that their motives were bad, viz. that they might be LIKE unto other nations, i.e. the Heathens, whereas their true glory lay in being as much UNLIKE them as possible. "But the thing displeased Samuel when they said, give us a King to judge us; and Samuel prayed unto the Lord, and the Lord said unto Samuel, hearken unto the voice of the people in all that they say unto thee, for they have not rejected thee, but they have rejected me, THAT I SHOULD NOT REIGN OVER THEM. According to all the works which they have done since the day that I brought them up out of Egypt even unto this day, wherewith they have forsaken me, and served other Gods: so do they also unto thee. Now therefore hearken unto their voice, howbeit, protest solemnly unto them and show them the manner of the King that shall reign over them," i.e. not of any particular King, but the general manner of the Kings of the earth whom Israel was so eagerly copying after. And notwithstanding the great distance of time and difference of manners, the character is still in fashion. "And Samuel told all the words of the Lord unto the people, that asked of him a King. And he said, This shall be the manner of the King that shall reign over you. He will take your sons and appoint them for himself for his chariots and to be his horsemen, and some shall run before his chariots" (this description agrees with the present mode of impressing men) "and he will appoint him captains over thousands and captains over fifties, will set them to clear his ground and to reap his harvest, and to make his instruments of war, and instruments of his chariots, And he will take your daughters to be confectionaries, and to be cooks, and to be bakers" (this describes the expense and luxury as well as the oppression of Kings) "and he will take your fields and your vineyards, and your olive yards, even the best of them, and give them to his servants. And he will take the tenth of your seed, and of your vineyards, and give them to his officers and to his servants" (by which we see that bribery, corruption, and favouritism, are the standing vices of Kings) "and he will take the tenth of your men servants, and your maid servants, and your goodliest young men, and your asses, and put them to his work: and he will take the tenth of your sheep, and ye shall be his servants, and ye shall cry out in that day because of your king which ye shell have chosen, AND THE LORD WILL NOT HEAR YOU IN THAT DAY." This accounts for the continuation of Monarchy; neither do the characters of the few good kings which have lived since, either sanctify the title, or blot out the sinfulness of the origin; the high encomium of David takes no notice of him OFFICIALLY AS A KING, but only as a MAN after God's own heart. "Nevertheless the people refused to obey the voice of Samuel, and they said, Nay, but we will have a king over us, that we may be like all the nations, and that our king may judge us, and go out before us and fight our battles." Samuel continued to reason with them but to no purpose; he set before them their ingratitude, but all would not avail; and seeing them fully bent on their folly, he cried out, "I will call unto the Lord, and he shall send thunder and rain" (which was then a punishment, being in the time of wheat harvest) "that ye may perceive and see that your wickedness is great which ye have done in the sight of the Lord, IN ASKING YOU A KING. So Samuel called unto the Lord, and the Lord sent thunder and rain that day, and all the people greatly feared the Lord and Samuel. And all the people said unto Samuel, Pray for thy servants unto the Lord thy God that we die not, for WE HAVE ADDED UNTO OUR SINS THIS EVIL, TO ASK A KING." These portions of scripture are direct and positive. They admit of no equivocal construction. That the Almighty hath here entered his protest against monarchical government is true, or the scripture is false. And a man hath good reason to believe that there is as much of kingcraft as priestcraft in withholding the scripture from the public in popish countries. For monarchy in every instance is the popery of government.

To the evil of monarchy we have added that of hereditary succession; and as the first is a degradation and lessening of ourselves, so the second, claimed as a matter of right, is an insult and imposition on posterity. For all men being originally equals, no one by birth could have a right to set up his own family in perpetual preference to all others for ever, and tho' himself might deserve some decent degree of honours of his contemporaries, yet his descendants might be far too unworthy to inherit them. One of the strongest natural proofs of the folly of hereditary right in Kings, is that nature disapproves it, otherwise she would not so frequently turn it into ridicule, by giving mankind an ASS FOR A LION.

Secondly, as no man at first could possess any other public honors than were bestowed upon him, so the givers of those honors could have no power to give away the right of posterity, and though they might say "We choose you for our head," they could not without manifest injustice to their children say "that your children and your children's children shall reign over ours forever." Because such an unwise, unjust, unnatural compact might (perhaps) in the next succession put them under the government of a rogue or a fool. Most wise men in their private sentiments have ever treated hereditary right with contempt; yet it is one of those evils which when once established is not easily removed: many submit from fear, others from superstition, and the more powerful part shares with the king the plunder of the rest.

This is supposing the present race of kings in the world to have had an honorable origin: whereas it is more than probable, that, could we take off the dark covering of antiquity and trace them to their first rise, we should find the first of them nothing better than the principal ruffian of some restless gang, whose savage manners of pre-eminence in subtilty obtained him the title of chief among plunderers; and who by increasing in power and extending his depredations, overawed the quiet and defenseless to purchase their safety by frequent contributions. Yet his electors could have no idea of giving heredi-tary right to his descendants, because such a perpetual exclusion of them-selves was incompatible with the free and restrained principles they professed to live by. Wherefore, hereditary succession in the early ages of monarchy could not take place as a matter of claim, but as something casual or comple-mental; but as few or no records were extant in those days, the traditionary history stuff'd with fables, it was very easy, after the lapse of a few generations, to trump up some superstitious tale conveniently timed, Mahomet-like, to cram hereditary right down the throats of the vulgar. Perhaps the disorders which threatened, or seemed to threaten, on the decease of a leader and the choice of a new one (for elections among ruffians could not be very orderly) induced many at first to favour hereditary pretensions; by which means it happened, as it hath happened since, that what at first was submitted to as a convenience was afterwards claimed as a right.

APPENDIX E
Virginia's Statute for Religious Freedom (drafted in 1777; passed in 1786)

A model for and forerunner to the First Amendment, Virginia's Statute for Religious Freedom *secured the rights of Virginians to follow the faith of their choosing, without fear of coercion or retribution from their government.*

Well aware that the opinions and belief of men depend not on their own will, but follow involuntarily the evidence proposed to their minds; that Almighty God hath created the mind free, and manifested his supreme will that free it shall remain by making it altogether insusceptible of restraint; that all attempts to influence it by temporal punishments, or burthens, or by civil incapacitations, tend only to beget habits of hypocrisy and meanness, and are a departure from the plan of the holy author of our religion, who being lord both of body and mind, yet chose not to propagate it by coercions on either, as was in his Almighty power to do, but to extend it by its influence on reason alone; that the impious presumption of legislators and rulers, civil as well as ecclesiastical, who, being themselves but fallible and uninspired men, have assumed dominion over the faith of others, setting up their own opinions and modes of thinking as the only true and infallible, and as such endeavoring to impose them on others, hath established and maintained false religions over the greatest part of the world and through all time: That to compel a man to furnish contributions of money for the propagation of opinions which he disbelieves and abhors, is sinful and tyrannical; that even the forcing him to support this or that teacher of his own religious persuasion, is depriving him of the comfortable liberty of giving his contributions to the particular pastor whose morals he would make his pattern, and whose powers he feels most persuasive to righteousness; and is withdrawing from the ministry those temporary rewards, which proceeding from an approbation of their personal conduct, are an additional incitement to earnest and unremitting labours for the instruction of mankind; that our civil rights have no dependance on our religious opinions, any more than our opinions in physics or geometry; that therefore the proscribing any citizen as unworthy the public confidence by laying upon him an incapacity of being called to offices of trust and emolument, unless he profess or renounce this or that religious opinion, is depriving him injuriously of those privileges and advantages to which, in common with his fellow citizens, he has a natural right; that it tends also to corrupt the principles of that very religion it is meant to encourage, by bribing, with a monopoly of worldly honours and emoluments, those who will externally profess and conform to it; that though indeed these are criminal who do not withstand such temptation, yet neither are those innocent who lay the bait in their way; that the opinions of men are not the object of civil government, nor under its jurisdiction; that to suffer the civil magistrate to intrude his powers into the field of opinion and to restrain the profession or propagation of principles on supposition of their ill tendency is a dangerous falacy, which at once destroys all religious liberty, because he being of course judge of that tendency will make his opinions the rule of judgment, and approve or condemn the sentiments of others only as they shall square with or differ from his own; that it is time enough for the rightful purposes of civil government for its officers to interfere when principles break out into overt acts against peace and good order; and finally, that truth is great and will prevail if left to herself; that she is the proper and sufficient antagonist to error, and has nothing to fear from the conflict unless by human interposition disarmed of her natural weapons, free argument and debate; errors ceasing to be dangerous when it is permitted freely to contradict them.

We the General Assembly of Virginia do enact that no man shall be compelled to frequent or support any religious worship, place, or ministry whatsoever, nor shall be enforced, restrained, molested, or burthened in his body or goods, nor shall otherwise suffer, on account of his religious opinions or belief; but that all men shall be free to profess, and by argument to maintain, their opinions in matters of religion, and that the same shall in no wise diminish, enlarge, or affect their civil capacities.

And though we well know that this Assembly, elected by the people for the ordinary purposes of legislation only, have no power to restrain the acts of succeeding Assemblies, constituted with powers equal to our own, and that therefore to declare this act irrevocable would be of no effect in law; yet we are free to declare, and do declare, that the rights hereby asserted are of the natural rights of mankind, and that if any act shall be hereafter passed to repeal the present or to narrow its operation, such act will be an infringement of natural right.

APPENDIX F
Declaration of Independence (1776)

Although Jefferson's notoriety in his own time really began with his publica-
tion of the Summary View of the Rights of British Americans, *he is no*
doubt remembered best for his primary authorship of America's Declaration
of Independence. *Though a joint effort, his original draft was largely fol-*
lowed by the drafting committee and struck the tone of the document that still
evokes strong emotions in readers today.

When in the Course of human events, it becomes necessary for one people to
dissolve the political bands which have connected them with another, and
to assume among the powers of the earth, the separate and equal station to
which the Laws of Nature and of Nature's God entitle them, a decent respect
to the opinions of mankind requires that they should declare the causes which
impel them to the separation.

We hold these truths to be self-evident, that all men are created equal, that
they are endowed by their Creator with certain unalienable Rights, that
among these are Life, Liberty and the pursuit of Happiness.—That to secure
these rights, Governments are instituted among Men, deriving their just
powers from the consent of the governed,—That whenever any Form of Government becomes destructive of these ends, it is the Right of the People to
alter or to abolish it, and to institute new Government, laying its foundation
on such principles and organizing its powers in such form, as to them shall
seem most likely to effect their Safety and Happiness. Prudence, indeed,
will dictate that Governments long established should not be changed for
light and transient causes; and accordingly all experience hath shewn, that

mankind are more disposed to suffer, while evils are sufferable, than to right themselves by abolishing the forms to which they are accustomed. But when a long train of abuses and usurpations, pursuing invariably the same Object evinces a design to reduce them under absolute Despotism, it is their right, it is their duty, to throw off such Government, and to provide new Guards for their future security.—Such has been the patient sufferance of these Colonies; and such is now the necessity which constrains them to alter their former Systems of Government. The history of the present King of Great Britain is a history of repeated injuries and usurpations, all having in direct object the establishment of an absolute Tyranny over these States. To prove this, let Facts be submitted to a candid world.

He has refused his Assent to Laws, the most wholesome and necessary for the public good.

He has forbidden his Governors to pass Laws of immediate and pressing importance, unless suspended in their operation till his Assent should be obtained; and when so suspended, he has utterly neglected to attend to them.

He has refused to pass other Laws for the accommodation of large districts of people, unless those people would relinquish the right of Representation in the Legislature, a right inestimable to them and formidable to tyrants only.

He has called together legislative bodies at places unusual, uncomfortable, and distant from the depository of their public Records, for the sole purpose of fatiguing them into compliance with his measures.

He has dissolved Representative Houses repeatedly, for opposing with manly firmness his invasions on the rights of the people.

He has refused for a long time, after such dissolutions, to cause others to be elected; whereby the Legislative powers, incapable of Annihilation, have returned to the People at large for their exercise; the State remaining in the mean time exposed to all the dangers of invasion from without, and convulsions within.

He has endeavoured to prevent the population of these States; for that purpose obstructing the Laws for Naturalization of Foreigners; refusing to pass others to encourage their migrations hither, and raising the conditions of new Appropriations of Lands.

He has obstructed the Administration of Justice, by refusing his Assent to Laws for establishing Judiciary powers.

He has made Judges dependent on his Will alone, for the tenure of their offices, and the amount and payment of their salaries.

He has erected a multitude of New Offices, and sent hither swarms of Officers to harrass our people, and eat out their substance.

He has kept among us, in times of peace, Standing Armies without the Consent of our legislatures.

He has affected to render the Military independent of and superior to the Civil power.

He has combined with others to subject us to a jurisdiction foreign to our constitution, and unacknowledged by our laws; giving his Assent to their Acts of pretended Legislation:

For Quartering large bodies of armed troops among us:

For protecting them, by a mock Trial, from punishment for any Murders which they should commit on the Inhabitants of these States:

For cutting off our Trade with all parts of the world:

For imposing Taxes on us without our Consent:

For depriving us in many cases, of the benefits of Trial by Jury:

For transporting us beyond Seas to be tried for pretended offences

For abolishing the free System of English Laws in a neighbouring Province, establishing therein an Arbitrary government, and enlarging its Boundaries so as to render it at once an example and fit instrument for introducing the same absolute rule into these Colonies:

For taking away our Charters, abolishing our most valuable Laws, and altering fundamentally the Forms of our Governments:

For suspending our own Legislatures, and declaring themselves invested with power to legislate for us in all cases whatsoever.

He has abdicated Government here, by declaring us out of his Protection and waging War against us.

He has plundered our seas, ravaged our Coasts, burnt our towns, and destroyed the lives of our people.

He is at this time transporting large Armies of foreign Mercenaries to compleat the works of death, desolation and tyranny, already begun with circumstances of Cruelty & perfidy scarcely parallelled in the most barbarous ages, and totally unworthy the Head of a civilized nation.

He has constrained our fellow Citizens taken Captive on the high Seas to bear Arms against their Country, to become the executioners of their friends and Brethren, or to fall themselves by their Hands.

He has excited domestic insurrections amongst us, and has endeavoured to bring on the inhabitants of our frontiers, the merciless Indian Savages, whose known rule of warfare, is an undistinguished destruction of all ages, sexes and conditions.

In every stage of these Oppressions We have Petitioned for Redress in the most humble terms: Our repeated Petitions have been answered only by repeated injury. A Prince whose character is thus marked by every act which may define a Tyrant, is unfit to be the ruler of a free people.

Nor have We been wanting in attentions to our British brethren. We have warned them from time to time of attempts by their legislature to extend an unwarrantable jurisdiction over us. We have reminded them of the circumstances of our emigration and settlement here. We have appealed to their native justice and magnanimity, and we have conjured them by the ties of our common kindred to disavow these usurpations, which, would inevitably interrupt our connections and correspondence. They too have been deaf to the voice of justice and of consanguinity. We must, therefore, acquiesce in the necessity, which denounces our Separation, and hold them, as we hold the rest of mankind, Enemies in War, in Peace Friends.

We, therefore, the Representatives of the United States of America, in General Congress, Assembled, appealing to the Supreme Judge of the world for the rectitude of our intentions, do, in the Name, and by Authority of the good People of these Colonies, solemnly publish and declare, That these United Colonies are, and of Right ought to be Free and Independent States; that they are Absolved from all Allegiance to the British Crown, and that all political connection between them and the State of Great Britain, is and ought to be totally dissolved; and that as Free and Independent States, they have full Power to levy War, conclude Peace, contract Alliances, establish Commerce, and to do all other Acts and Things which Independent States may of right do. And for the support of this Declaration, with a firm reliance on the protection of divine Providence, we mutually pledge to each other our Lives, our Fortunes and our sacred Honor.

APPENDIX G
Letter to William S. Smith, Paris (1787)

The famous "Tree of Liberty" letter. "[W]hat country can preserve its liberties if their rulers are not warned from time to time that their people preserve the spirit of resistance?" This letter stands as an example of a very good mix of pathos and logos: Jefferson uses very evocative language, but his analysis sounds in solid reason.

DEAR SIR,

I am now to acknoledge the receipt of your favors of October the 4th, 8th, & 26th. In the last you apologise for your letters of introduction to Americans coming here. It is so far from needing apology on your part, that it calls for thanks on mine. I endeavor to shew civilities to all the Americans who come here, & will give me opportunities of doing it: and it is a matter of comfort to know from a good quarter what they are, & how far I may go in my attentions to them. Can you send me Woodmason's bills for the two copying presses for the M. de la Fayette, & the M. de Chastellux? The latter makes one article in a considerable account, of old standing, and which I cannot present for want of this article.—I do not know whether it is to yourself or Mr. Adams I am to give my thanks for the copy of the new constitution. I beg leave through you to place them where due. It will be yet three weeks before I shall receive them from America. There are very good articles in it: & very bad. I do not know which preponderate. What we have lately read in the history of Holland, in the chapter on the Stadtholder, would have sufficed to set me against a chief magistrate eligible for a long duration, if I had ever been disposed towards one: & what we have always read of the elections of Polish kings should have forever excluded the idea of one continuable for life. Wonderful is the effect of impudent & persevering lying. The British ministry have so long hired their gazetteers to repeat and model into every form lies about our being in anarchy, that the world has at length believed them, the English nation has believed them, the ministers themselves have come to believe them, & what is more wonderful, we have believed them ourselves. Yet where does this anarchy exist? Where did it ever exist, except in the single instance of Massachusetts? And can history produce an instance of rebellion so honourably conducted? I say nothing of it's motives. They were founded in ignorance, not wickedness. God forbid we should ever be 20 years without such a rebellion. The people cannot be all, & always, well informed. The part which is wrong will be discontented in proportion to the importance of the facts they misconceive. If they remain quiet under such misconceptions it is a lethargy, the forerunner of death to the public liberty. We have had 13. states independent 11. years. There has been one rebellion. That comes to one rebellion in a century & a half for each state. What country before ever existed a century & half without a rebellion? & what country can preserve it's liberties if their rulers are not warned from time to time that their people preserve the spirit of resistance? Let them take arms. The remedy is to set them right as to facts, pardon & pacify them. What signify a few lives lost in a century or two? The tree of liberty must be refreshed from time to time with the blood of patriots & tyrants. It is natural manure. Our Convention has been too much impressed by the insurrection of Massachusetts: and in the spur of the moment they are setting up a kite to keep the hen-yard in order. I hope in God this article will be rectified before the new constitution is accepted.—You ask me if any thing transpires here on the subject of S. America? Not a word. I know that there are combustible materials there, and that they wait the torch only. But this country probably will join the extinguishers.—The want of facts worth communicating to you has occasioned me to give a little loose to dissertation. We must be contented to amuse, when we cannot inform.

Thomas Jefferson

APPENDIX H
France's Declaration of Rights of Man and of the Citizen (1789)

Thomas Jefferson and his Declaration of Independence *heavily influenced, at least, France's own* Declaration of Rights. *Some believe that Jefferson, who was in France serving as Ambassador before its publication, actually helped to draft the French Declaration.*

Approved by the National Assembly of France, August 26, 1789

The representatives of the French people, organized as a National Assembly, believing that the ignorance, neglect, or contempt of the rights of man are the sole cause of public calamities and of the corruption of governments, have determined to set forth in a solemn declaration the natural, unalienable, and sacred rights of man, in order that this declaration, being constantly before all the members of the Social body, shall remind them continually of their rights and duties; in order that the acts of the legislative power, as well as those of the executive power, may be compared at any moment with the objects and purposes of all political institutions and may thus be more respected, and, lastly, in order that the grievances of the citizens, based hereafter upon simple and incontestable principles, shall tend to the maintenance of the constitution and redound to the happiness of all. Therefore the National Assembly recognizes and proclaims, in the presence and under the auspices of the Supreme Being, the following rights of man and of the citizen:

Articles:

1. Men are born and remain free and equal in rights. Social distinctions may be founded only upon the general good.

2. The aim of all political association is the preservation of the natural and imprescriptible rights of man. These rights are liberty, property, security, and resistance to oppression.

3. The principle of all sovereignty resides essentially in the nation. No body nor individual may exercise any authority which does not proceed directly from the nation.

4. Liberty consists in the freedom to do everything which injures no one else; hence the exercise of the natural rights of each man has no limits except those which assure to the other members of the society the enjoyment of the same rights. These limits can only be determined by law.

5. Law can only prohibit such actions as are hurtful to society. Nothing may be prevented which is not forbidden by law, and no one may be forced to do anything not provided for by law.

6. Law is the expression of the general will. Every citizen has a right to participate personally, or through his representative, in its foundation. It must be the same for all, whether it protects or punishes. All citizens, being equal in the eyes of the law, are equally eligible to all dignities and to all public positions and occupations, according to their abilities, and without distinction except that of their virtues and talents.

7. No person shall be accused, arrested, or imprisoned except in the cases and according to the forms prescribed by law. Any one soliciting, transmitting, executing, or causing to be executed, any arbitrary order, shall be punished. But any citizen summoned or arrested in virtue of the law shall submit without delay, as resistance constitutes an offense.

8. The law shall provide for such punishments only as are strictly and obviously necessary, and no one shall suffer punishment except it be legally inflicted in virtue of a law passed and promulgated before the commission of the offense.

9. As all persons are held innocent until they shall have been declared guilty, if arrest shall be deemed indispensable, all harshness not essential to the securing of the prisoner's person shall be severely repressed by law.

10. No one shall be disquieted on account of his opinions, including his religious views, provided their manifestation does not disturb the public order established by law.

11. The free communication of ideas and opinions is one of the most precious of the rights of man. Every citizen may, accordingly, speak, write, and print with freedom, but shall be responsible for such abuses of this freedom as shall be defined by law.

12. The security of the rights of man and of the citizen requires public military forces. These forces are, therefore, established for the good of all and not for the personal advantage of those to whom they shall be intrusted.

13. A common contribution is essential for the maintenance of the public forces and for the cost of administration. This should be equitably distributed among all the citizens in proportion to their means.

14. All the citizens have a right to decide, either personally or by their representatives, as to the necessity of the public contribution; to grant this freely; to know to what uses it is put; and to fix the proportion, the mode of assessment and of collection and the duration of the taxes.

15. Society has the right to require of every public agent an account of his administration.

16. A society in which the observance of the law is not assured, nor the separation of powers defined, has no constitution at all.

17. Since property is an inviolable and sacred right, no one shall be deprived thereof except where public necessity, legally determined, shall clearly demand it, and then only on condition that the owner shall have been previously and equitably indemnified.

APPENDIX I
Thomas Jefferson's First Inauguration Address (1801)

One of Thomas Jefferson's primary purposes in his first inaugural address was to heal a nation that had gone through its first truly contentious presidential election. Newspapers had been "teeming with every falsehood they c[ould] invent for defamation": Jefferson was labeled an atheist; Adams a monarchist.

Friends and Fellow-Citizens:

CALLED upon to undertake the duties of the first executive office of our country, I avail myself of the presence of that portion of my fellow-citizens which is here assembled to express my grateful thanks for the favor with which they have been pleased to look toward me, to declare a sincere consciousness that the task is above my talents, and that I approach it with those anxious and awful presentiments which the greatness of the charge and the weakness of my powers so justly inspire. A rising nation, spread over a wide and fruitful land, traversing all the seas with the rich productions of their industry, engaged in commerce with nations who feel power and forget right, advancing rapidly to destinies beyond the reach of mortal eye—when I contemplate these transcendent objects, and see the honor, the happiness, and the hopes of this beloved country committed to the issue, and the auspices of this day, I shrink from the contemplation, and humble myself before the magnitude of the undertaking. Utterly, indeed, should I despair did not the presence of many whom I here see remind me that in the other high authorities provided by our Constitution I shall find resources of wisdom, of virtue, and of zeal on which to rely under all difficulties. To you, then, gentlemen, who are charged with the sovereign functions of legislation, and to those associated with you, I look with encouragement for that guidance and support which may enable us to steer with safety the vessel in which we are all embarked amidst the conflicting elements of a troubled world.

During the contest of opinion through which we have passed the animation of discussions and of exertions has sometimes worn an aspect which might impose on strangers unused to think freely and to speak and to write what they think; but this being now decided by the voice of the nation, announced according to the rules of the Constitution, all will, of course, arrange themselves under the will of the law, and unite in common efforts for the common good. All, too, will bear in mind this sacred principle, that though the will of the majority is in all cases to prevail, that will to be rightful must be reasonable; that the minority possess their equal rights, which equal law must protect, and to violate would be oppression. Let us, then, fellow-citizens, unite with one heart and one mind. Let us restore to social intercourse that harmony and affection without which liberty and even life itself are but dreary things. And let us reflect that, having banished from our land that religious intolerance under which mankind so long bled and suffered, we have yet gained little if we countenance a political intolerance as despotic, as wicked, and capable of as bitter and bloody persecutions. During the throes and convulsions of the ancient world, during the agonizing spasms of infuriated man, seeking through blood and slaughter his long-lost liberty, it was not wonderful that the agitation of the billows should reach even this distant and peaceful shore; that this should be more felt and feared by some and less by others, and should divide opinions as to measures of safety. But every difference of opinion is not a difference of principle. We have called by different names brethren of the same principle. We are all Republicans, we are all Federalists. If there be any among us who would wish to dissolve this Union or to change its republican form, let them stand undisturbed as monuments of the safety with which error of opinion may be tolerated where reason is left free to combat it. I know, indeed, that some honest men fear that a republican government can not be strong, that this Government is not strong enough; but would the honest patriot, in the full tide of successful experiment, abandon a government which has so far kept us free and firm on the theoretic and visionary fear that this Government, the world's best hope, may by possibility want energy to preserve itself? I trust not. I believe this, on the contrary, the strongest Government on earth. I believe it the only one where every man, at the call of the law, would fly to the standard of the law, and would meet invasions of the public order as his own personal concern. Sometimes it is said that man can not be trusted with the government of himself. Can he, then, be trusted with the government of others? Or have we found angels in the forms of kings to govern him? Let history answer this question.

Let us, then, with courage and confidence pursue our own Federal and Republican principles, our attachment to union and representative government. Kindly separated by nature and a wide ocean from the exterminating havoc of one quarter of the globe; too high-minded to endure the degradations of the others; possessing a chosen country, with room enough for our descendants to the thousandth and thousandth generation; entertaining a due sense of our equal right to the use of our own faculties, to the acquisitions of our own industry, to honor and confidence from our fellow-citizens, resulting not from birth, but from our actions and their sense of them; enlightened by a benign religion, professed, indeed, and practiced in various forms, yet all of them inculcating honesty, truth, temperance, gratitude, and the love of man; acknowledging and adoring an overruling Providence, which by all its dispensations proves that it delights in the happiness of man here and his greater happiness hereafter—with all these blessings, what more is necessary to make us a happy and a prosperous people? Still one thing more, fellow-citizens— a wise and frugal Government, which shall restrain men from injuring one another, shall leave them otherwise free to regulate their own pursuits of industry and improvement, and shall not take from the mouth of labor the bread it has earned. This is the sum of good government, and this is necessary to close the circle of our felicities.

About to enter, fellow-citizens, on the exercise of duties which comprehend everything dear and valuable to you, it is proper you should understand what I deem the essential principles of our Government, and consequently those which ought to shape its Administration. I will compress them within the narrowest compass they will bear, stating the general principle, but not all its limitations. Equal and exact justice to all men, of whatever state or persuasion, religious or political; peace, commerce, and honest friendship with all nations, entangling alliances with none; the support of the State governments in all their rights, as the most competent administrations for our domestic concerns and the surest bulwarks against antirepublican tendencies; the preservation of the General Government in its whole constitutional vigor, as the sheet anchor of our peace at home and safety abroad; a jealous care of the right of election by the people—a mild and safe corrective of abuses which are lopped by the sword of revolution where peaceable remedies are unprovided; absolute acquiescence in the decisions of the majority, the vital principle of republics, from which is no appeal but to force, the vital principle and immediate parent of despotism; a well disciplined militia, our best reliance in peace and for the first moments of war, till regulars may relieve them; the supremacy of the civil over the military authority; economy in the public expense, that labor may be lightly burthened; the honest payment of our debts and sacred preservation of the public faith; encouragement of agriculture, and of commerce as its handmaid; the diffusion of information and arraignment of all abuses at the bar of the public reason; freedom of religion; freedom of the press, and freedom of person under the protection of the habeas corpus, and trial by juries impartially selected. These principles form the bright constellation which has gone before us and guided our steps through an age of revolution and reformation. The wisdom of our sages and blood of our heroes have been devoted to their attainment. They should be the creed of our political faith, the text of civic instruction, the touchstone by which to try the services of those we trust; and should we wander from them in moments of error or of alarm, let us hasten to retrace our steps and to regain the road which alone leads to peace, liberty, and safety.

I repair, then, fellow-citizens, to the post you have assigned me. With experience enough in subordinate offices to have seen the difficulties of this the greatest of all, I have learnt to expect that it will rarely fall to the lot of imperfect man to retire from this station with the reputation and the favor which bring him into it. Without pretensions to that high confidence you reposed in our first and greatest revolutionary character, whose preeminent services had entitled him to the first place in his country's love and destined for him the fairest page in the volume of faithful history, I ask so much confidence only as may give firmness and effect to the legal administration of your affairs. I shall often go wrong through defect of judgment. When right, I shall often be thought wrong by those whose positions will not command a view of the whole ground. I ask your indulgence for my own errors, which will never be intentional, and your support against the errors of others, who may condemn what they would not if seen in all its parts. The approbation implied by your suffrage is a great consolation to me for the past, and my future solicitude will be to retain the good opinion of those who have bestowed it in advance, to conciliate that of others by doing them all the good in my power, and to be instrumental to the happiness and freedom of all.

Relying, then, on the patronage of your good will, I advance with obedience to the work, ready to retire from it whenever you become sensible how much better choice it is in your power to make. And may that Infinite Power which rules the destinies of the universe lead our councils to what is best, and give them a favorable issue for your peace and prosperity.

APPENDIX J
Letter to Danbury Baptists (1802)

Jefferson often took quips developed in correspondence or earlier works and applied them as more fully developed lines of thought in his later works. The Danbury Baptists exchange is one such example. In this correspondence, Jefferson mentions the need to build a "wall of separation between Church & State."

To messers. Nehemiah Dodge, Ephraim Robbins, & Stephen S. Nelson, a committee of the Danbury Baptist association in the state of Connecticut.

Gentlemen

The affectionate sentiments of esteem and approbation which you are so good as to express towards me, on behalf of the Danbury Baptist association, give me the highest satisfaction. My duties dictate a faithful and zealous pursuit of the interests of my constituents, & in proportion as they are persuaded of my fidelity to those duties, the discharge of them becomes more and more pleasing.

Believing with you that religion is a matter which lies solely between Man & his God, that he owes account to none other for his faith or his worship, that the legitimate powers of government reach actions only, & not opinions, I contemplate with sovereign reverence that act of the whole American people which declared that their legislature should "make no law respecting an establishment of religion, or prohibiting the free exercise thereof," thus building a wall of separation between Church & State. Adhering to this expression of the supreme will of the nation in behalf of the rights of conscience, I shall see

with sincere satisfaction the progress of those sentiments which tend to restore to man all his natural rights, convinced he has no natural right in opposition to his social duties.

I reciprocate your kind prayers for the protection & blessing of the
common father and creator of man, and tender you for yourselves & your
religious association, assurances of my high respect & esteem.

Thomas Jefferson

APPENDIX K
Thomas Jefferson's Second Inauguration Address (1805)

Although still a proponent of a limited role for the federal government, Jefferson needed to persuade the audience of his second inaugural address of the benefits and necessity of his territorial acquisitions and the strengthening of the military during Jefferson's time in office.

Proceeding, fellow citizens, to that qualification which the constitution requires, before my entrance on the charge again conferred upon me, it is my duty to express the deep sense I entertain of this new proof of confidence from my fellow citizens at large, and the zeal with which it inspires me, so to conduct myself as may best satisfy their just expectations.

On taking this station on a former occasion, I declared the principles on which I believed it my duty to administer the affairs of our commonwealth. My conscience tells me that I have, on every occasion, acted up to that declaration, according to its obvious import, and to the understanding of every candid mind.

In the transaction of your foreign affairs, we have endeavored to cultivate the friendship of all nations, and especially of those with which we have the most important relations. We have done them justice on all occasions, favored where favor was lawful, and cherished mutual interests and intercourse on fair and equal terms. We are firmly convinced, and we act on that conviction, that with nations, as with individuals, our interests soundly calculated, will ever be found inseparable from our moral duties; and history bears witness to the fact, that a just nation is taken on its word, when recourse is had to armaments and wars to bridle others.

At home, fellow citizens, you best know whether we have done well or ill. The suppression of unnecessary offices, of useless establishments and expenses, enabled us to discontinue our internal taxes. These covering our land with officers, and opening our doors to their intrusions, had already begun that process of domiciliary vexation which, once entered, is scarcely to be restrained from reaching successively every article of produce and property. If among these taxes some minor ones fell which had not been inconvenient, it was because their amount would not have paid the officers who collected them, and because, if they had any merit, the state authorities might adopt them, instead of others less approved.

The remaining revenue on the consumption of foreign articles, is paid cheerfully by those who can afford to add foreign luxuries to domestic comforts, being collected on our seaboards and frontiers only, and incorporated with the transactions of our mercantile citizens, it may be the pleasure and pride of an American to ask, what farmer, what mechanic, what laborer, ever sees a tax-gatherer of the United States? These contributions enable us to support the current expenses of the government, to fulfil contracts with foreign nations, to extinguish the native right of soil within our limits, to extend those limits, and to apply such a surplus to our public debts, as places at a short day their final redemption, and that redemption once effected, the revenue thereby liberated may, by a just repartition among the states, and a corresponding amendment of the constitution, be applied, _in time of peace_, to rivers, canals, roads, arts, manufactures, education, and other great objects within each state. _In time of war_, if injustice, by ourselves or others, must sometimes produce war, increased as the same revenue will be increased by population and consumption, and aided by other resources reserved for that crisis, it may meet within the year all the expenses of the year, without encroaching on the rights of future generations, by burdening them with the debts of the past. War will then be but a suspension of useful works, and a return to a state of peace, a return to the progress of improvement.

I have said, fellow citizens, that the income reserved had enabled us to extend our limits; but that extension may possibly pay for itself before we are called on, and in the meantime, may keep down the accruing interest; in all events, it will repay the advances we have made. I know that the acquisition of Louisiana has been disapproved by some, from a candid apprehension that the enlargement of our territory would endanger its union. But who can limit the extent to which the federative principle may operate effectively? The larger our association, the less will it be shaken by local passions; and in any view, is it not better that the opposite bank of the Mississippi should be settled by our own brethren and children, than by strangers of another family? With which shall we be most likely to live in harmony and friendly intercourse?

In matters of religion, I have considered that its free exercise is placed by the constitution independent of the powers of the general government. I have therefore undertaken, on no occasion, to prescribe the religious exercises suited to it; but have left them, as the constitution found them, under the direction and discipline of state or church authorities acknowledged by the several religious societies.

The aboriginal inhabitants of these countries I have regarded with the commiseration their history inspires. Endowed with the faculties and the rights of men, breathing an ardent love of liberty and independence, and oc-cupying a country which left them no desire but to be undisturbed, the stream of overflowing population from other regions directed itself on these shores; without power to divert, or habits to contend against, they have been over-whelmed by the current, or driven before it; now reduced within limits too narrow for the hunter's state, humanity enjoins us to teach them agriculture and the domestic arts; to encourage them to that industry which alone can enable them to maintain their place in existence, and to prepare them in time for that state of society, which to bodily comforts adds the improvement of the mind and morals. We have therefore liberally furnished them with the implements of husbandry and household use; we have placed among them instructors in the arts of first necessity; and they are covered with the aegis of the law against aggressors from among ourselves.

But the endeavors to enlighten them on the fate which awaits their present course of life, to induce them to exercise their reason, follow its dictates, and change their pursuits with the change of circumstances, have powerful obstacles to encounter; they are combated by the habits of their bodies, preju-dice of their minds, ignorance, pride, and the influence of interested and crafty individuals among them, who feel themselves something in the present order of things, and fear to become nothing in any other. These persons inculcate a sanctimonious reverence for the customs of their ancestors; that whatsoever they did, must be done through all time; that reason is a false guide, and to advance under its counsel, in their physical, moral, or political condition, is perilous innovation; that their duty is to remain as their Creator made them, ignorance being safety, and knowledge full of danger; in short, my friends, among them is seen the action and counteraction of good sense and bigotry; they, too, have their anti-philosophers, who find an interest in keeping things in their present state, who dread reformation, and exert all their faculties to maintain the ascendency of habit over the duty of improving our reason, and obeying its mandates.

In giving these outlines, I do not mean, fellow citizens, to arrogate to myself the merit of the measures; that is due, in the first place, to the reflecting character of our citizens at large, who, by the weight of public opinion, influence and strengthen the public measures; it is due to the sound discretion with which they select from among themselves those to whom they confide the legislative duties; it is due to the zeal and wisdom of the characters thus selected, who lay the foundations of public happiness in wholesome laws, the execution of which alone remains for others; and it is due to the able and faithful auxiliaries, whose patriotism has associated with me in the executive functions.

During this course of administration, and in order to disturb it, the artillery of the press has been levelled against us, charged with whatsoever its licentiousness could devise or dare. These abuses of an institution so important to freedom and science, are deeply to be regretted, inasmuch as they tend to lessen its usefulness, and to sap its safety; they might, indeed, have been corrected by the wholesome punishments reserved and provided by the laws of the several States against falsehood and defamation; but public duties more urgent press on the time of public servants, and the offenders have therefore been left to find their punishment in the public indignation.

Nor was it uninteresting to the world, that an experiment should be fairly and fully made, whether freedom of discussion, unaided by power, is not sufficient for the propagation and protection of truth—whether a government, conducting itself in the true spirit of its constitution, with zeal and purity, and doing no act which it would be unwilling the whole world should witness, can be written down by falsehood and defamation. The experiment has been tried;

you have witnessed the scene; our fellow citizens have looked on, cool and collected; they saw the latent source from which these outrages proceeded; they gathered around their public functionaries, and when the constitution called them to the decision by suffrage, they pronounced their verdict, honorable to those who had served them, and consolatory to the friend of man, who believes he may be intrusted with his own affairs.

No inference is here intended, that the laws, provided by the State against false and defamatory publications, should not be enforced; he who has time, renders a service to public morals and public tranquillity, in reforming these abuses by the salutary coercions of the law; but the experiment is noted, to prove that, since truth and reason have maintained their ground against false opinions in league with false facts, the press, confined to truth, needs no other legal restraint; the public judgment will correct false reasonings and opinions, on a full hearing of all parties; and no other definite line can be drawn between the inestimable liberty of the press and its demoralizing licentiousness. If there be still improprieties which this rule would not restrain, its supplement must be sought in the censorship of public opinion.

Contemplating the union of sentiment now manifested so generally, as auguring harmony and happiness to our future course, I offer to our country sincere congratulations. With those, too, not yet rallied to the same point, the disposition to do so is gaining strength; facts are piercing through the veil drawn over them; and our doubting brethren will at length see, that the mass of their fellow citizens, with whom they cannot yet resolve to act, as to principles and measures, think as they think, and desire what they desire; that our wish, as well as theirs, is, that the public efforts may be directed honestly to the public good, that peace be cultivated, civil and religious liberty unassailed, law and order preserved; equality of rights maintained, and that state of property, equal or unequal, which results to every man from his own industry, or that of his fathers. When satisfied of these views, it is not in human nature that they should not approve and support them; in the meantime, let us cherish them with patient affection; let us do them justice, and more than justice, in all competitions of interest; and we need not doubt that truth, reason, and their own interests, will at length prevail, will gather them into the fold of their country, and will complete their entire union of opinion, which gives to a nation the blessing of harmony, and the benefit of all its strength.

I shall now enter on the duties to which my fellow citizens have again called me, and shall proceed in the spirit of those principles which they have approved. I fear not that any motives of interest may lead me astray; I am sensible of no passion which could seduce me knowingly from the path of justice; but the weakness of human nature, and the limits of my own understanding, will produce errors of judgment sometimes injurious to your interests. I shall need, therefore, all the indulgence I have heretofore experienced—the want of it will certainly not lessen with increasing years. I shall need, too, the favor of that Being in whose hands we are, who led our forefathers, as Israel of old, from their native land, and planted them in a country flowing with all the necessaries and comforts of life; who has covered our infancy with his providence, and our riper years with his wisdom and power; and to whose goodness I ask you to join with me in supplications, that he will so enlighten the minds of your servants, guide their councils, and prosper their measures, that whatsoever they do, shall result in your good, and shall secure to you the peace, friendship, and approbation of all nations.

APPENDIX L
Excerpt from Letter to Samuel Kercheval (1816)

Jefferson's letter to Samuel Kercheval offers us some of Jefferson's reflections on the experiment in democracy from the distance of four decades after the Declaration of Independence *truly sparked that experiment.*

SIR,

I duly received your favor of June the 13th, with the copy of the letters on the calling a convention, on which you are pleased to ask my opinion. I have not been in the habit of mysterious reserve on any subject, nor of buttoning up my opinions within my own doublet. On the contrary, while in public service especially, I thought the public entitled to frankness, and intimately to know whom they employed. But I am now retired: I resign myself, as a passenger, with confidence to those at present at the helm, and ask but for rest, peace and good will. The question you propose, on equal representation, has become a party one, in which I wish to take no public share. Yet, if it be asked for your own satisfaction only, and not to be quoted before the public, I have no motive to withhold it, and the less from you, as it coincides with your own. At the birth of our republic, I committed that opinion to the world, in the draught of a constitution annexed to the "Notes on Virginia," in which a provision was inserted for a representation permanently equal. The infancy of the subject at that moment, and our inexperience of self-government, occasioned gross departures in that draught from genuine republican canons. In truth, the abuses of monarchy had so much filled all the space of political contemplation, that we imagined everything republican which was not monarchy. We had not yet penetrated to the mother principle, that "governments are republican only in proportion as they embody the will of their people, and execute it." Hence, our first constitutions had really no leading principles in them. But experience and reflection have but more and more confirmed me in the particular importance of the equal representation then proposed. On that point, then, I am entirely in sentiment with your letters; and only lament that a copy-right of your pamphlet prevents their appearance in the newspapers, where alone they would be generally read, and produce general effect. The present vacancy too, of other matter, would give them place in every paper, and bring the question home to every man's conscience.

But inequality of representation in both Houses of our legislature, is not the only republican heresy in this first essay of our revolutionary patriots at forming a constitution. For let it be agreed that a government is republican in proportion as every member composing it has his equal voice in the direction of its concerns (not indeed in person, which would be impracticable beyond the limits of a city, or small township, but) by representatives chosen by himself, and responsible to him at short periods, and let us bring to the test of this canon every branch of our constitution.

In the legislature, the House of Representatives is chosen by less than half the people, and not at all in proportion to those who do choose. The Senate are still more disproportionate, and for long terms of irresponsibility. In the Executive, the Governor is entirely independent of the choice of the people, and of their control; his Council equally so, and at best but a fifth wheel to a wagon. In the Judiciary, the judges of the highest courts are dependent on none but themselves. In England, where judges were named and removable at the will of an hereditary executive, from which branch most misrule was feared, and has flowed, it was a great point gained, by fixing them for life, to make them independent of that executive. But in a government founded on the public will, this principle operates in an opposite direction, and against that will. There, too, they were still removable on a concurrence of the executive and legislative branches. But we have made them independent of the nation itself. They are irremovable, but by their own body, for any depravities of conduct, and even by their own body for the imbecilities of dotage. The justices of the inferior courts are self-chosen, are for life, and perpetuate their own body in succession forever, so that a faction once possessing themselves of the bench of a county, can never be broken up, but hold their county in chains, forever indissoluble. Yet these justices are the real executive as well as judiciary, in all our minor and most ordinary concerns. They tax us at will; fill the office of sheriff, the most important of all the executive officers of the county; name nearly all our military leaders, which leaders, once named, are removable but by themselves. The juries, our judges of all fact, and of law when they choose it, are not selected by the people, nor amenable to them. They are chosen by an officer named by the court and executive. Chosen, did I say? Picked up by the sheriff from the loungings of the court yard, after everything respectable has retired from it. Where then is our republicanism to be found? Not in our constitution certainly, but merely in the spirit of our people. That would oblige even a despot to govern us republicanly. Owing to this spirit, and to nothing in the form of our constitution, all things have gone well. But this fact, so triumphantly misquoted by the enemies of reformation, is not the fruit of our constitution, but has prevailed in spite of it. Our functionaries have done well, because generally honest men. If any were not so, they feared to show it.

. . .

Thomas Jefferson

APPENDIX M
The Gettysburg Address
(1863)

Nearly one hundred years after the Declaration of Independence *declared that "all men are created equal,"* Lincoln's Emancipation Proclamation *and* Gettysburg Address *finally gave America the proper reading of those words. As Jefferson wrote in the face of allegations of treason and the very real threat that he would "hang together" with his fellow founding fathers, Lincoln wrote the* Gettysburg Address *in the face of a Civil War and declared that the principles for which the war was being fought were worth fighting even to the last full measure of devotion—and that nothing short of complete victory would suffice.*

Fourscore and seven years ago our fathers brought forth on this continent a new nation, conceived in liberty and dedicated to the proposition that all men are created equal. Now we are engaged in a great civil war, testing whether that nation or any nation so conceived and so dedicated can long endure. We are met on a great battlefield of that war. We have come to dedicate a portion of that field as a final resting-place for those who here gave their lives that that nation might live. It is altogether fitting and proper that we should do this. But in a larger sense, we cannot dedicate, we cannot consecrate, we cannot hallow this ground. The brave men, living and dead who struggled here have consecrated it far above our poor power to add or detract. The world will little note nor long remember what we say here, but it can never forget what they did here. It is for us the living rather to be dedicated here to the unfinished work which they who fought here have thus far so nobly advanced.

It is rather for us to be here dedicated to the great task remaining before us—that from these honored dead we take increased devotion to that cause for which they gave the last full measure of devotion—that we here highly resolve that these dead shall not have died in vain, that this nation under God shall have a new birth of freedom, and that government of the people, by the people, for the people shall not perish from the earth.

ABOUT THE AUTHOR

Arthur Rizer is an Associate Professor of Law at College of Law, West Virginia University (WVU). Before joining the faculty at WVU Law, Rizer worked at the U.S. Department of Justice (DOJ) for nine years as a trial attorney. His most recent assignment at DOJ was as a prosecutor in the Criminal Division working on narcotics and national security cases, primarily focused on international drug cartels and narco-terrorists. His other postings at DOJ included national security litigator with Federal Program's Guantanamo Bay Litigation Team; prosecutor in the U.S. Attorney's Office for the Southern District of California; and civil litigator with the Office of Immigration Litigation.

Rizer started his legal career as a federal judicial law clerk in the U.S. District Court for the Middle District of Pennsylvania. He has also taught at Georgetown University Law Center as an Adjunct Professor of Law and currently holds an appointment as a Visiting Professor of Law. Before law school, Rizer served as a Military Police and Armor officer in the reserve and active U.S. Army. He retired as a Lieutenant Colonel from the West Virginia National Guard. In the military, Rizer was deployed to Fallujah, Iraq, where he helped train the Iraqi Army to fight the insurgency and was awarded the Bronze Star and Purple Heart Medals. Also before law school, Rizer worked as a civilian police officer in Washington State.

Rizer earned LLM, with distinction, from Law Center, Georgetown University and his JD, *magna cum laude*, from School of Law, Gonzaga University. He is also a graduate of the U.S. Marine Corps' Command Staff College. He is currently a D.Phil candidate in Criminology at the University of Oxford, Faculty of Law.

RECOMMENDED READS

For anyone who wants to learn to write, speak, and live more persuasively, the best reads are the biographies of persuaders, the histories of the times in which they wrote or spoke, and their written texts or transcribed speeches. This type of complete immersion will give a reader a complete picture of just how a given persuader was able to rise to such a status that we want to read more about them and emulate their methods.

So, if there is a business, political, or social leader out there whose persuasive style you wish to emulate, find as much information about them, about the context in which they persuade, and about what they have written or said as you can.

If there is not a particular persuader you wish to emulate, below are some recommended reads to give you a broader foundation in practical persuasive tactics, generally, and more material on Thomas Jefferson to get you even further toward becoming the most persuasive you that you can be:

Maria Keckler, *Bridge Builders: How Superb Communicators Get What They Want in Business and in Life* (New York: Morgan James Publishing, 2015). This book serves as a good example of the power of storytelling in effective communication.

Peter Frederick, *Persuasive Writing: How to Harness the Power of Words* (Harlow, UK: Pearson, 2012). This book focuses on efficient persuasive writing toward a practical end, be it getting a point across in an e-mail or trying to close a deal.

Jon Meacham, *Thomas Jefferson: The Art of Power* (New York: Random House, 2013). A great, engaging biography written by the Pulitzer Prize-winning author of such other biographies as *American Lion: Andrew Jackson in the White House* and *Franklin and Winston: A Portrait of Friendship*.

Joseph Ellis, *American Sphinx* (New York: Vintage Books, 1996). This autobiography of our third president focuses primarily on the contradictions that marked Jefferson's life and writings, contradictions so important to study in order to avoid in our own lives and writing.

NOTES

1. Provided in full in Appendix F at page 233.
2. Provided in full in Appendix H at page 239.
3. Christopher Hitchens, *Thomas Jefferson: Author of America* (New York: Harper-Collins, 2005), 2 ("Many tales of the last words of famous men are apocryphal, or are pious fabrications, but these seem tolerably well authenticated.").
4. *Id.*
5. *Id.*
6. Edward Dumbauld, *Thomas Jefferson and the Law*, at xi (1978).
7. Available at http://shop.americanbar.org/eBus/Store/ProductDetails .aspx?productId=137292594.
8. Thomas Jefferson, *Autobiography of Thomas Jefferson, 1743–1790, Together with a Summary of the Chief Events in Jefferson's Life* (New York: G. P. Putnam's Sons, 1914) (1821), 5.
9. *Id.*
10. *Id.* at 4.
11. *Id.* at 5–6.
12. Gaye Wilson, Monticello Research Report, December 1999, http://www .monticello.org/site/research-and-collections/jeffersons-formal-education.
13. *Id.*
14. D. T. Konig, *Thomas Jefferson and the Practice of Law*, Encyclopedia Virginia (December 20, 2012), http://www.EncyclopediaVirginia.org/Jefferson_ Thomas_and_the_Practice_of_Law.
15. Frank L. Dewey, *Thomas Jefferson, Lawyer* (Charlottesville: University Press of Virginia, 1986), 14.
16. Konig, *supra* note 14.
17. Dewey, *supra* note 15, at 14.
18. Konig, *supra* note 14.
19. *Id.*
20. Jefferson, *supra* note 8, at 6.
21. Konig, *supra* note 14.
22. *Id.*
23. *Id.*
24. Dewey, *supra* note 15, at 18–19.
25. *Id.* at 18.
26. Konig, *supra* note 14.

27. *Id.*
28. *Id.*
29. Dewey, *supra* note 15, at 26.
30. *Id.*
31. *Id.* at 27.
32. *Id.*
33. *Id.*
34. Konig, *supra* note 14.
35. Dewey, *supra* note 15, at 28.
36. Konig, *supra* note 14.
37. Dewey, *supra* note 15, at 22.
38. *Id.* at 23.
39. *Id.*
40. Konig, *supra* note 14.
41. *Id.*
42. *Id.*
43. *Id.*
44. Annette Gordon-Reed, *The Hemmingses of Monticello: An American Family* (New York: Norton, 2008), 99–100.
45. *Id.* at 100.
46. Konig, *supra* note 14.
47. *Id.*
48. Gordon-Reed, *supra* note 44, at 100.
49. *Id.*
50. *Id.*
51. Konig, *supra* note 14.
52. *Id.*
53. *Id.*; Dewey, *supra* note 15, at 24 ("Arbitration was particularly well suited to complex issues that might baffle lay judges. A competent arbitrator could be selected, and the arguments could be made to him in writing, giving him the opportunity to analyze the case before rendering his opinion.").
54. Dumbauld, supra note 6, at 49.
55. Jefferson, *supra* note 8, at 70.
56. *Bolling v. Bolling*, http://lawlibrary.wm.edu/wythepedia/index.php/ Bolling_v._Bolling.
57. *Id.*
58. *Id.*
59. Dewey, 107.
60. *Id.*
61. *Id.*
62. *Id.* at 108–09.
63. *Id.* at 110–11.
64. *Id.* at 111–12.
65. *Id.* at 112.
66. *Id.*

67. *Id.* at 113.
68. William Shakespeare, *The Second Part of King Henry the Sixth*, act 2, sc. 2.
69. Daniel Kornstein, *Kill All the Lawyers? Shakespeare's Legal Appeal* (Princeton, NJ: Princeton University Press, 1994), 29.
70. William Shakespeare, *The Second Part of King Henry the Sixth*, act 2, sc. 2.
71. See *Id.* 30.
72. Norman Gross, *America's Lawyer-Presidents* (Evanston, Illinois: Northwestern University Press, 2004), xiii.
73. *Id.* at ix.
74. *Id.* at ix.
75. Andrew Burstein and Nancy Isenberg, *Madison and Jefferson*, at xvi (2010).
76. *Id.*
77. Michael Kranish, *Flight from Monticello: Thomas Jefferson at War* (New York: Oxford University Press, 2010), 30.
78. *Id.* at 31.
79. *Id.*
80. *Id.*
81. *Id.*
82. *Id.* at 32.
83. *Id.*
84. *Id.*
85. Konig, supra note 14.
86. *Id.*
87. *Id.*
88. *Id.*
89. *Id.*
90. *Id.*
91. *Id.*
92. *Id.*
93. *Id.*
94. *Id.*
95. *Id.*
96. *Id.*
97. *Id.*
98. *Id.*
99. *Id.*
100. David G. Post, *"Words Fitly Spoken": Thomas Jefferson, Slavery, and Sally Hemings* (Philadelphia: Temple Law School), accessed October 19, 2015, http://www.temple.edu/lawschool/dpost/slavery.PDF.
101. Konig, *supra* note 14.
102. *Id.*
103. *Id.*
104. *Id.*
105. Kranish, *supra* note 77, at 28.
106. Hitchens, supra note 3, at 16.

107. HBO Mini-Series, *John Adams*.
108. Hitchens, *supra* note 3, at 17.
109. *Id.*
110. *Id.*
111. It should be noted that while the revelation was slowing igniting, Jefferson continued his law practice while he sat in the General Assembly. In 1773, he became the Albemarle County surveyor—a profession of note: George Washington and Abraham Lincoln were also surveyors.
112. Hitchens, *supra* note 95, at 17.
113. *Id.* at 18.
114. *Id.* at 22.
115. *Id.* at 31.
116. *Id.* at 40.
117. *Id.* at 40.
118. *Id.* at 67.
119. Gordon Lloyd, *The Constitutional Convention*, http://teachingamericanhistory .org/convention/correspondence/.
120. Hitchens, *supra* note 95, at 76.
121. *Id.*
122. *Id.* at 76.
123. *Id.*
124. *Id.* at 77.
125. *Id.* at 80.
126. *Id.* at 84.
127. *Id.* at 87.
128. *Id.* at 90.
129. *Id.* at 94.
130. *Id.*
131. *Id.* at 95.
132. *Id.*
133. *Id.* at 99.
134. *Id.*
135. *Id.* at 105.
136. *Id.* at 105–106.
137. *Id.* at 106.
138. *Id.*
139. *Id.* at 108.
140. *Id.* at 112.
141. *Id.*
142. *Id.* at 118.
143. *Id.* at 126.
144. *Id.* at 127. The Barbary pirates acquired their name from both their original Berber population, but also "because of the handy euphony of the word with barbarism." *Id.*
145. *Id.*

146. *Id.*
147. *Id.* at 128.
148. *Id.*
149. *Id.* at 129.
150. *Id.* at 133.
151. *Id.*
152. *Id.* at 134.
153. *Id.* at 135.
154. *Id.* at 136.
155. *Id.*
156. *Id.* at 152.
157. *Id.*
158. *Id.*
159. *Id.*
160. *Id.*
161. *Id.* at 163.
162. *Id.* at 171–172.
163. *Id.* at 172.
164. *Id.* at 179.
165. *Id.* at 181.
166. *Id.* at 167–168 (citing Henry Adams, a great-grandson of John Adams).
167. *Id.* at 168.
168. *Id.* at 77.
169. *Id.* at 24.
170. *Id.* at 25.
171. Burstein and Isenberg, supra note 75, at 76.
172. *Id.* at *xxi.*
173. *Id.*
174. Hitchens, *supra* note 3, at 18.
175. *Id.* at 18.
176. *Id.* at 18–19.
177. *Id.* at 19.
178. Stephen Ambrose, Undaunted Courage: Meriwether Lewis, Thomas Jefferson, and the Opening of the West (New York: Simon and Schuster, 1997), 76.
179. *Id.* at 64.
180. Joyce Appleby, *Thomas Jefferson* (New York: Times Books, 2003), 37.
181. *Id.* at 46.
182. *Id.* at 47.
183. *Id.* at 40.
184. *Id.*
185. *Id.*
186. Ambrose, *supra* note 178, at 72.
187. *Id.*
188. *Id.*
189. Burstein and Isenberg, *supra* note 75, at 9.

190. Ambrose, *supra* note 178, at 56.
191. Hitchens, *supra* note 3, at 51.
192. The Presidents—The Good and the Bad, *LA Times*, http://www.latimes .com/opinion/la-oe-catania18-2009jan18-story.html#page=1 (accessed October 23, 2015).
193. Appleby, *supra* note 180, at 44.
194. Hitchens, *supra* note 3, at 44.
195. *Id.* at 44–45.
196. Appleby, *supra* note 180, at 3.
197. *Id.* at 3.
198. *Id.* at 51.
199. *Id.*
200. *Id.* at 52, 58.
201. *Id.* at 68.
202. Burstein and Isenberg, *supra* note 75, at xviii.
203. *Id.*
204. Hitchens, *supra* note 3, at 40.
205. *Id.*
206. Ambrose, *supra* note 178, at 56.
207. Hitchens, *supra* note 3, at 14.
208. *Id.* at 26.
209. *Id.*
210. *Id.*
211. *Id.*
212. *Id.*
213. Christopher Hitchens, *Thomas Jefferson: Author of America* (New York: Harper-Collins, 2005), 155.
214. *Id.* 155.
215. *Id.*
216. Stephen Ambrose, *Undaunted Courage: Meriwether Lewis, Thomas Jefferson, and the Opening of the West* (New York: Simon and Schuster, 1997), 36.
217. *Id.*
218. *Id.* at 56.
219. *Id.*
220. Gordon-Reed, supra note 44, at 99–100.
221. *Id.* at 100.
222. *Id.* at 100–01.
223. *Id.* at 101.
224. Hitchens, *supra* note 3, at 151.
225. Ambrose, *supra* note 178, at 349.
226. *Id.*
227. *Id.*
228. *Id.*
229. *Id.*
230. *Id.*

231. Appleby, supra note 180, at 77.
232. *Id.*
233. Hitchens, *supra* note 3, at 27–28.
234. *Id.* at 34.
235. *Id.* at 100.
236. *Id.* at 135.
237. *Id.* at 59.
238. *Id.* at 60.
239. *Id.* at 61.
240. *Id.*
241. *Id.* at 59.
242. *Id.* at 64.
243. *Id.* at 62; Gordon-Reed, *supra* note 44, at 100.
244. Hitchens, *supra* note 3, at 65.
245. *Id.* at 34.
246. Ambrose, *supra* note 178, at 35.
247. Hitchens, *supra* note 3, at 48.
248. *Id.* at 49.
249. Burstein and Isenberg, supra note 75, at 24–25.
250. *Id.* at 23.
251. Dewey, supra note 15, at 35.
252. *Id.* at 35.
253. *Id.*
254. *Id.* at 37.
255. *Id.* at 40.
256. *Id.* at 80.
257. Jon Meacham, *Thomas Jefferson: The Art of Power* (New York: Random House, 2012), 40–41.
258. *Id.* at 41.
259. *Id.* at 42.
260. *Id.*
261. *Id.*
262. Hitchens, *supra* note 3, at 63.
263. Margherita Marchione, ed., *Philip Mazzei: Selected Writings and Correspondence* (Prato, Italy: Cassa di Risparmi e Depositi, 1985), vol. 1, xxi.
264. *Id.* at vol. 2, 181.
265. *Id.*
266. Hitchens, *supra* note 3, at 186.
267. *Id.* at 155.
268. Burstein and Isenberg, *supra* note 75, at xvii.
269. *Id.* at xix.
270. *Id.* at 16.
271. *Id.* at 19–20.
272. Appleby, *supra* note 180, at 45.
273. Hitchens, *supra* note 3, at 68.

274. *Id.* at 69.

275. To identify a narcissist today, you need only observe them. Jefferson existed at a time before paparazzi and reporters were there to record his every public (and private) utterance. So we have less material. The psychoanalyst Heinz Kohut coined the term "narcissistic rage," which seems to describe Jefferson. Narcissistic rage is a continuum disorder (it has a broad range, from minor to severe) and some of its manifestations include instances of aloofness, constant anger or irritation with someone, and strong reaction to perceived slights or threats. While those are reactions most humans have from time to time, the level Jefferson manifested could easily be analyzed as narcissistic rage by a modern psychiatrist. Did this condition help Jefferson or hinder him? Probably both, at various times and in various circumstances, but the net effect would seem to be negative.

276. Appleby, *supra* note 180, at 4.

277. President Abraham Lincoln, Gettysburg Address (November 19, 1863).

278. Gerry Wills, *Lincoln at Gettysburg: The Words That Remade America* (New York: Simon & Schuster, 2006), 38.

279. President Abraham Lincoln, Speech at Independence Hall, Philadelphia (February 22, 1861).

280. *Id.*

281. *Id.*

282. Meacham, supra note 257, at 100.

283. *Id.*

284. *Id.* at 100–01.

285. Letter from John Adams to Timothy Pickering (August 6, 1822).

286. Meacham, *supra* note 257, at 101.

287. Letter from John Adams to Timothy Pickering (August 6, 1822).

288. *Id.*

289. Meacham, *supra* note 257, at 102.

290. Letter from John Adams to Timothy Pickering (August 6, 1822).

291. *Id.*

292. Meacham, *supra* note 257, at 103.

293. *Id.*

294. Letter from Thomas Jefferson to Henry Lee (May 8, 1825).

295. Meacham, *supra* note 257, at 103.

296. Letter from Thomas Jefferson to Henry Lee (May 8, 1825).

297. Meacham, *supra* note 257, at 106.

298. John D. Rampage and John C. Bean, *Writing Arguments: A Rhetoric with Readings*, 4th ed. (Boston: Allyn & Bacon, 1998), 81–82.

299. *Id.* at 81–82.

300. *Id.* at 82.

301. Joseph C. Morton, *The American Revolution* (Westport, CT: Greenwood Press, 2003), 143.

302. Dumbauld, supra note 6, at 18.

303. Letter from Thomas Jefferson to John W. Campbell (September 3, 1809).

304. Dumbauld, *supra* note 6, at 18.
305. Andrew Burstein and Nancy Isenberg, *Madison and Jefferson*, at 30 (2010).
306. *Id.* at 30.
307. *Id.*
308. *Id.*
309. *Id.*
310. *Id.* at 30–31.
311. Dumbauld, *supra* note 6, at 19.
312. *Id.* at 20.
313. John Ragosta, *Virginia Statute for Establishing Religious Freedom (1786)*, Ency-clopediaVirginia, http://www.EncyclopediaVirginia.org/Virginia_Statute_ for_Establishing_Religious_Freedom_1786 (last modified July 2, 2014).
314. Edwin Scott Gaustad, *Sworn on the Alter of God: A Religious Biography of Thomas Jefferson* (Grand Rapids, MI: Eerdmans, 1996), 69.
315. This provides us a lesson from Jefferson that simply would not get to see but for his personal letters. Humor can be used very effectively to accentuate a position by showing just how ridiculous an opponent's position actually is. So when you can, **be funny enough** to get your audience to smirk. Actual laughter may detract from your more serious points. But witty remarks, especially those aimed at your opponent's points, will be appreciated and remembered by the audience. While Jefferson did not have a reputation for being a jokester, per se, he was known to have a quick wit and the ability to use that wit to persuade an audience toward his position. This lesson illustrates how **humor can make a convoluted point crystal clear and put things into perspective**. But to be perfectly honest, I'm not even sure the stiffish Jefferson was even trying to be funny.
316. Josh Horwitx, *Thomas Jefferson and "The Blood of Tyrants"*, Huffington Post (October 17, 2009), http://www.huffingtonpost.com/josh-horwitz/thomas-jefferson-and-the_b_273800.html.
317. Horwitx, *supra* note 316.
318. Horwitx, *supra* note 316.

INDEX